Sue & Tai-chan

D1231270

4

Konami Kanata

Contents

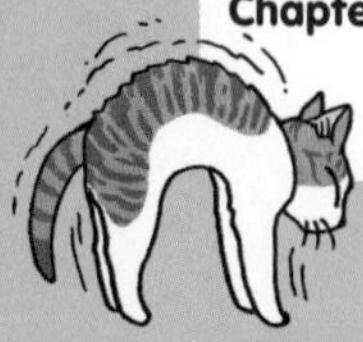

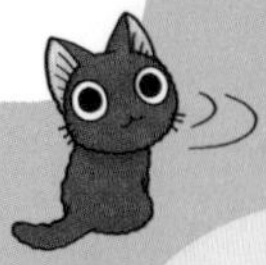

CHAPTER 52 Hurricane Cat

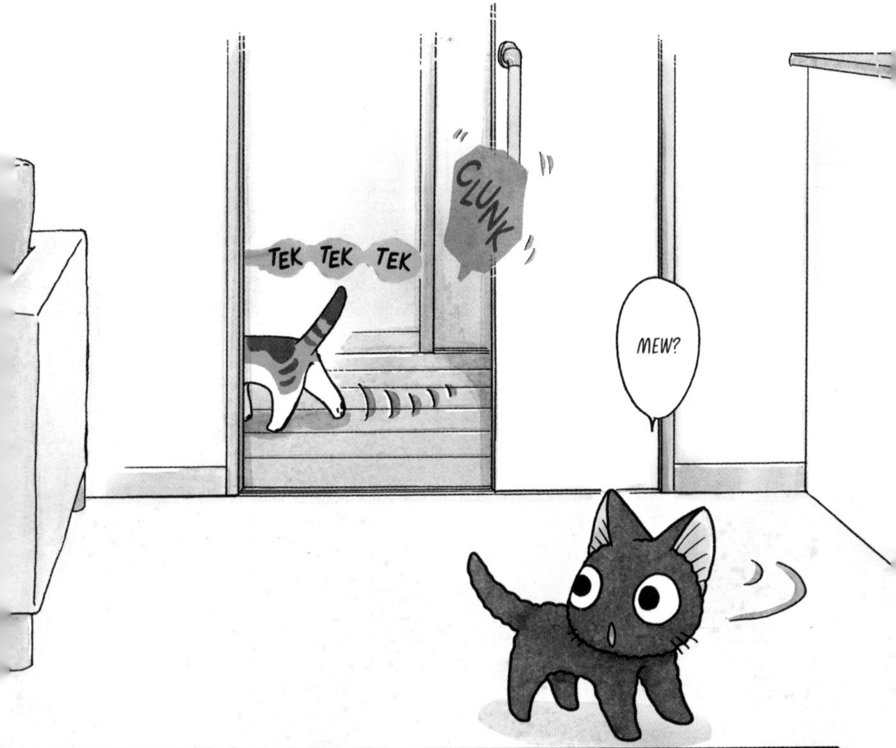
CLUNK
TEK TEK TEK
MEW?

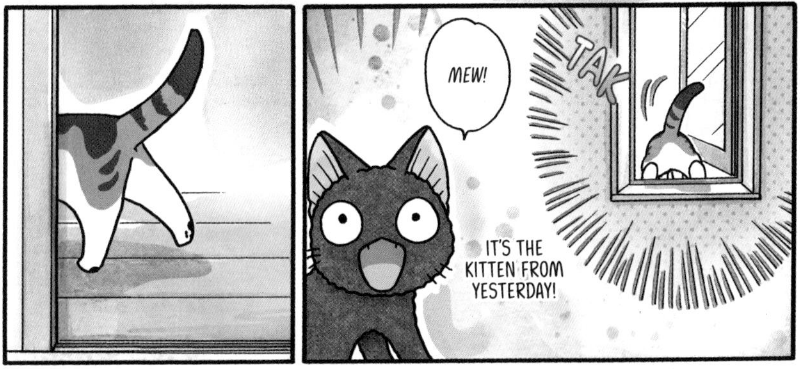
TAK
MEW!
IT'S THE KITTEN FROM YESTERDAY!

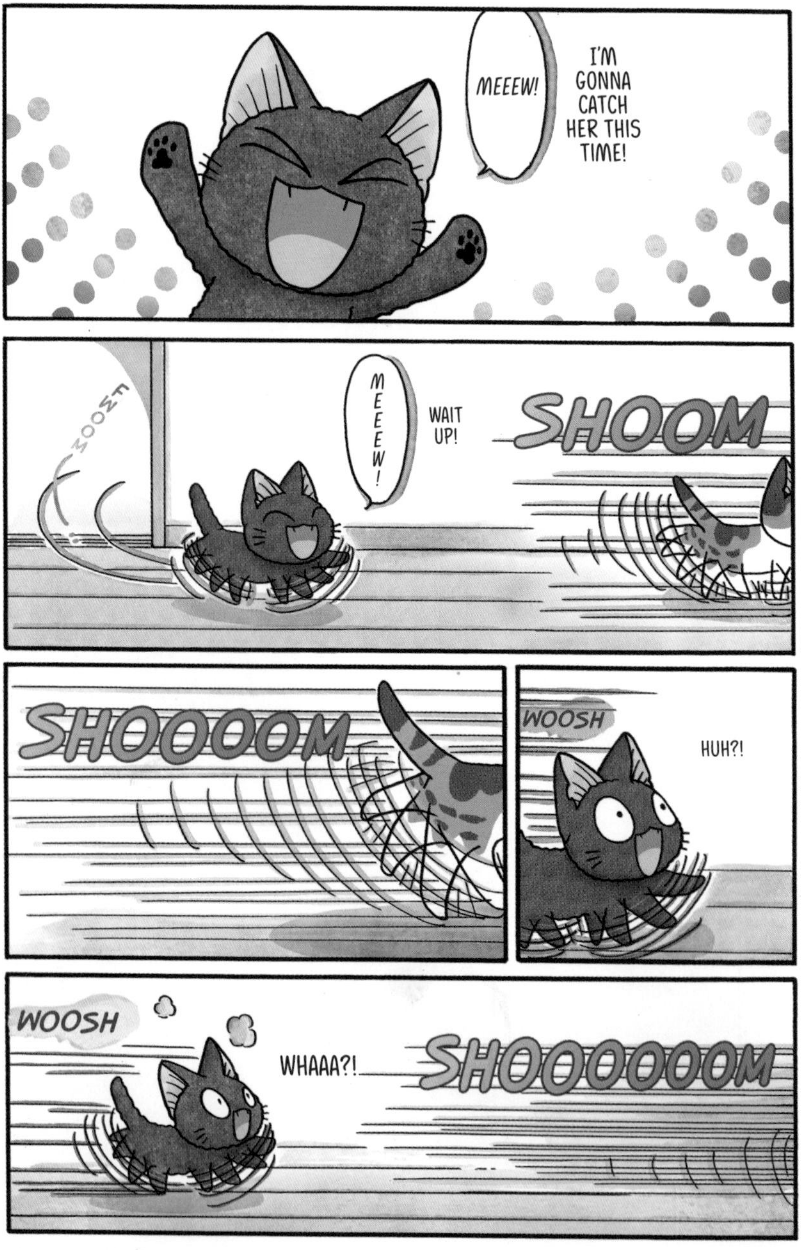
I'M GONNA CATCH HER THIS TIME!
MEEEW!
SHOOM
WAIT UP!
MEEEW!
FWOOSH
HUH?!
WOOSH
SHOOOOM
SHOOOOOOM
WHAAA?!
WOOSH

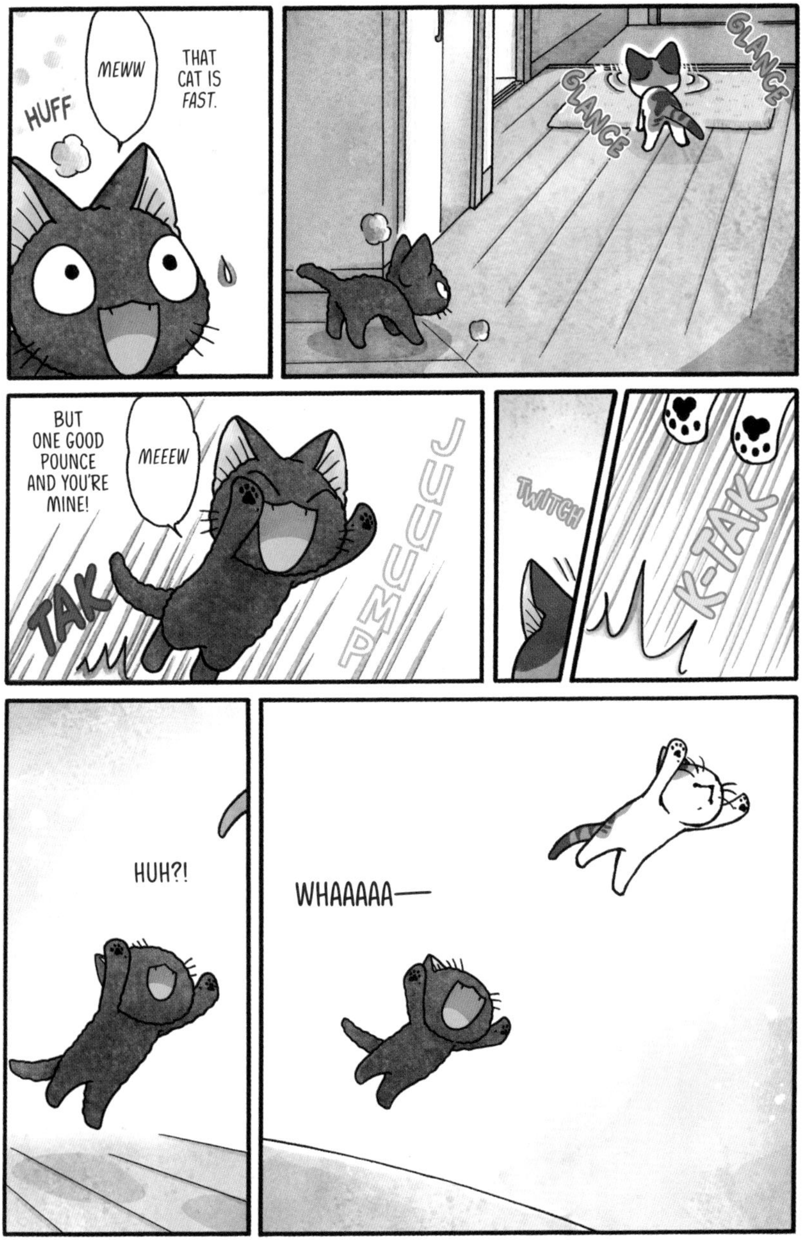
HUFF
MEWW
THAT CAT IS FAST.
GLANCE
GLANCE
BUT ONE GOOD POUNCE AND YOU'RE MINE!
MEEEW
TAK
JUUUMP
TWITCH
K-TAK
HUH?!
WHAAAAA—

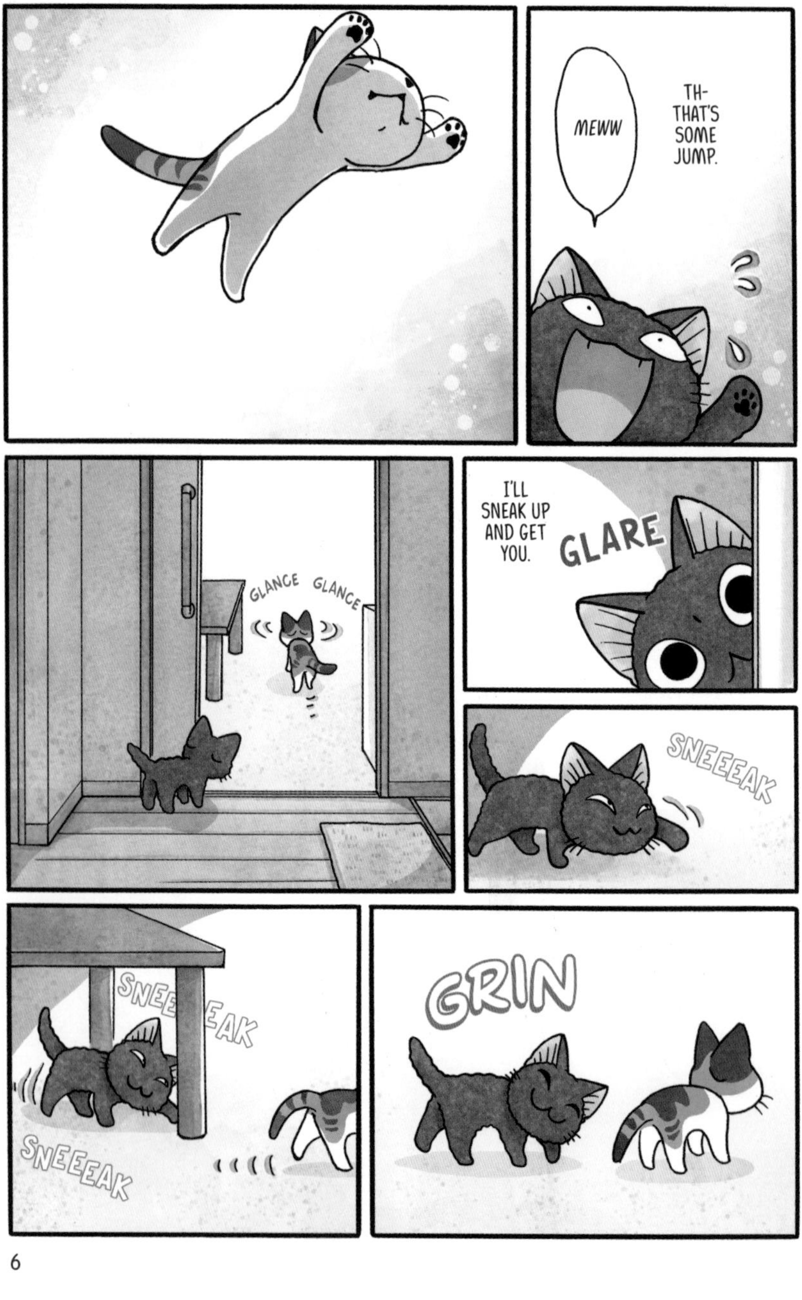
MEWW
TH- THAT'S SOME JUMP.
GLANCE GLANCE
I'LL SNEAK UP AND GET YOU.
GLARE
SNEEEAK
SNEEEAK
SNEEEAK
GRIN

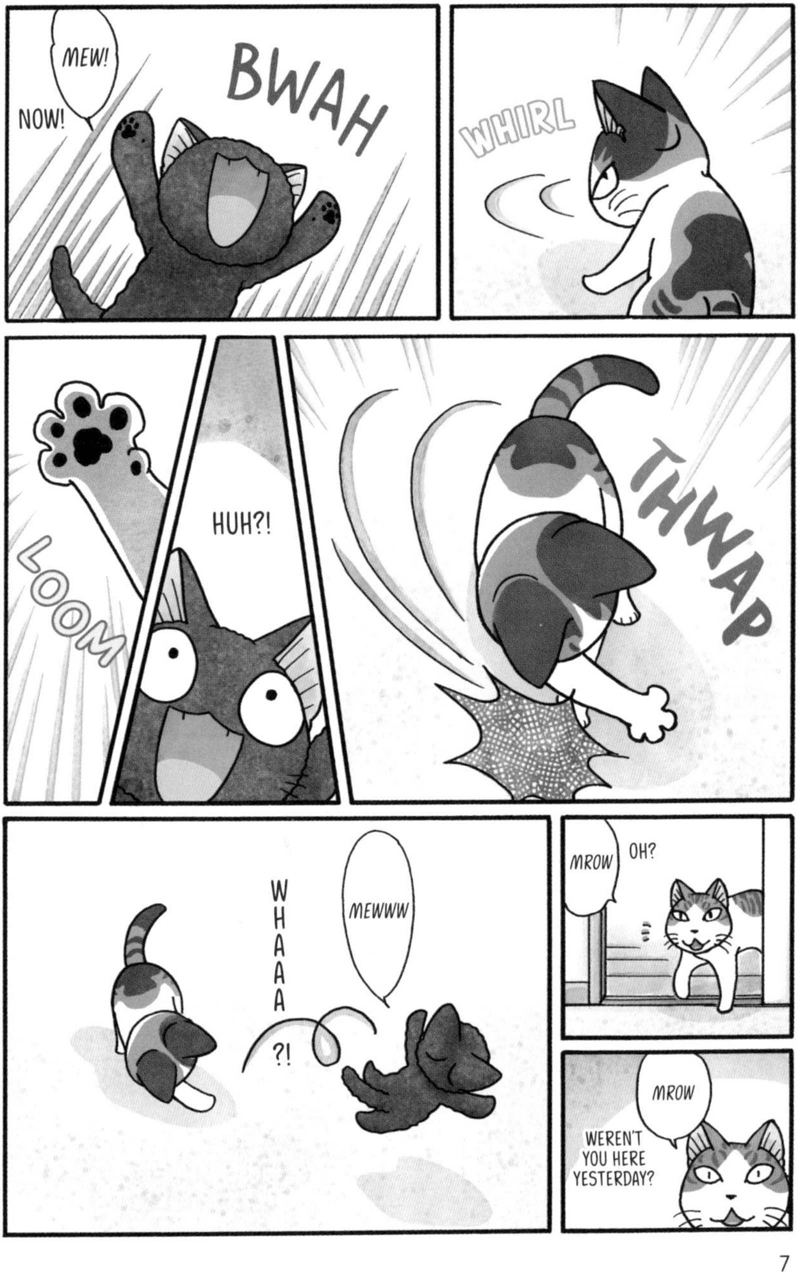
NOW!
MEW!
BWAH
WHIRL
LOOM
HUH?!
THWAP
WHAAAA ?!
MEWWW
MROW
OH?
MROW
WEREN'T YOU HERE YESTERDAY?

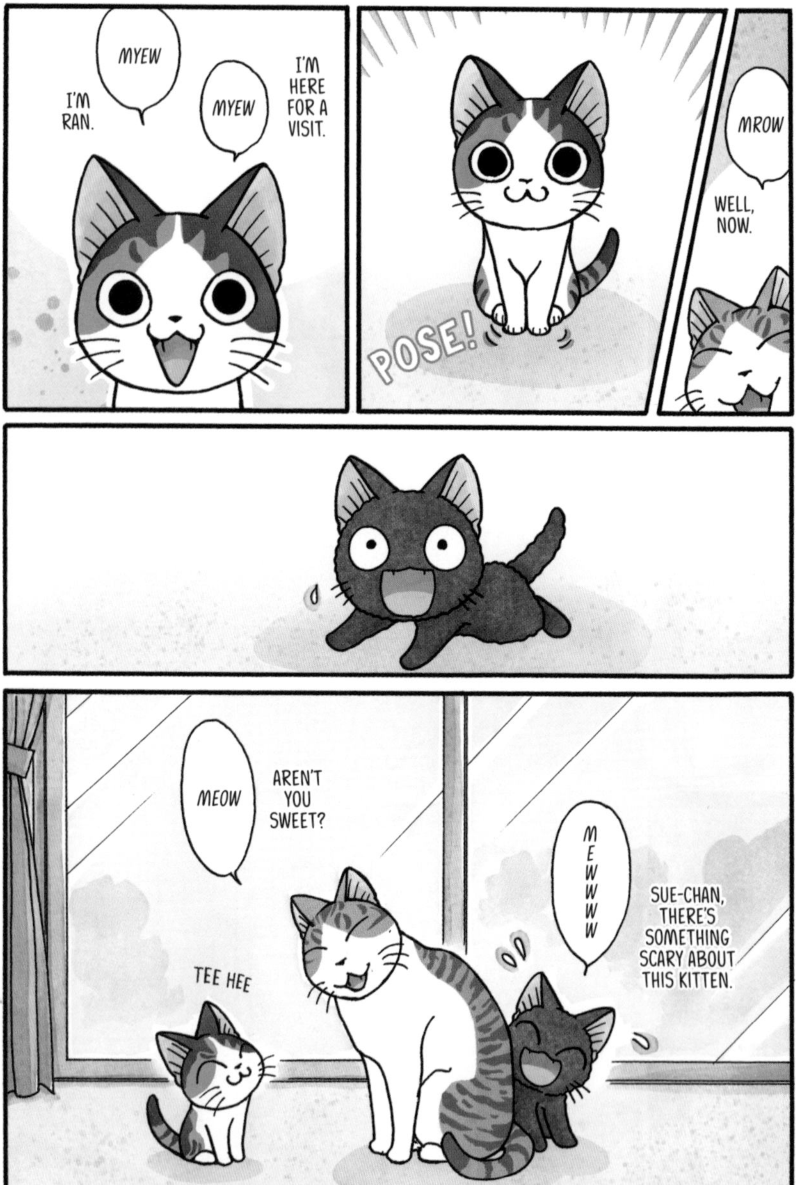
MROW
WELL, NOW.
POSE!
MYEW
I'M RAN.
MYEW
I'M HERE FOR A VISIT.
MEWWWW
SUE-CHAN, THERE'S SOMETHING SCARY ABOUT THIS KITTEN.
MEOW
AREN'T YOU SWEET?
TEE HEE

CHAPTER 53 I'm (Not) a Scaredy Cat!

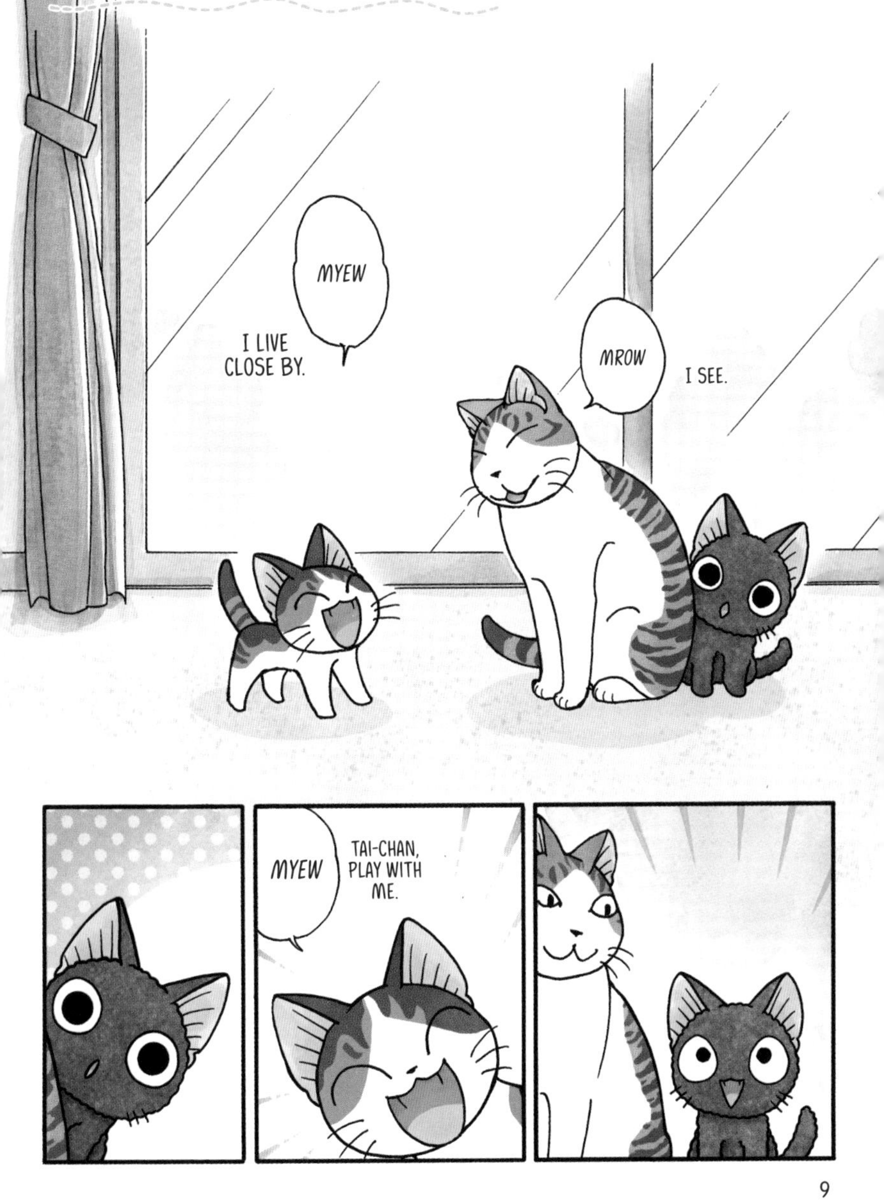
MYEW
I LIVE CLOSE BY.
MROW
I SEE.
MYEW
TAI-CHAN, PLAY WITH ME.

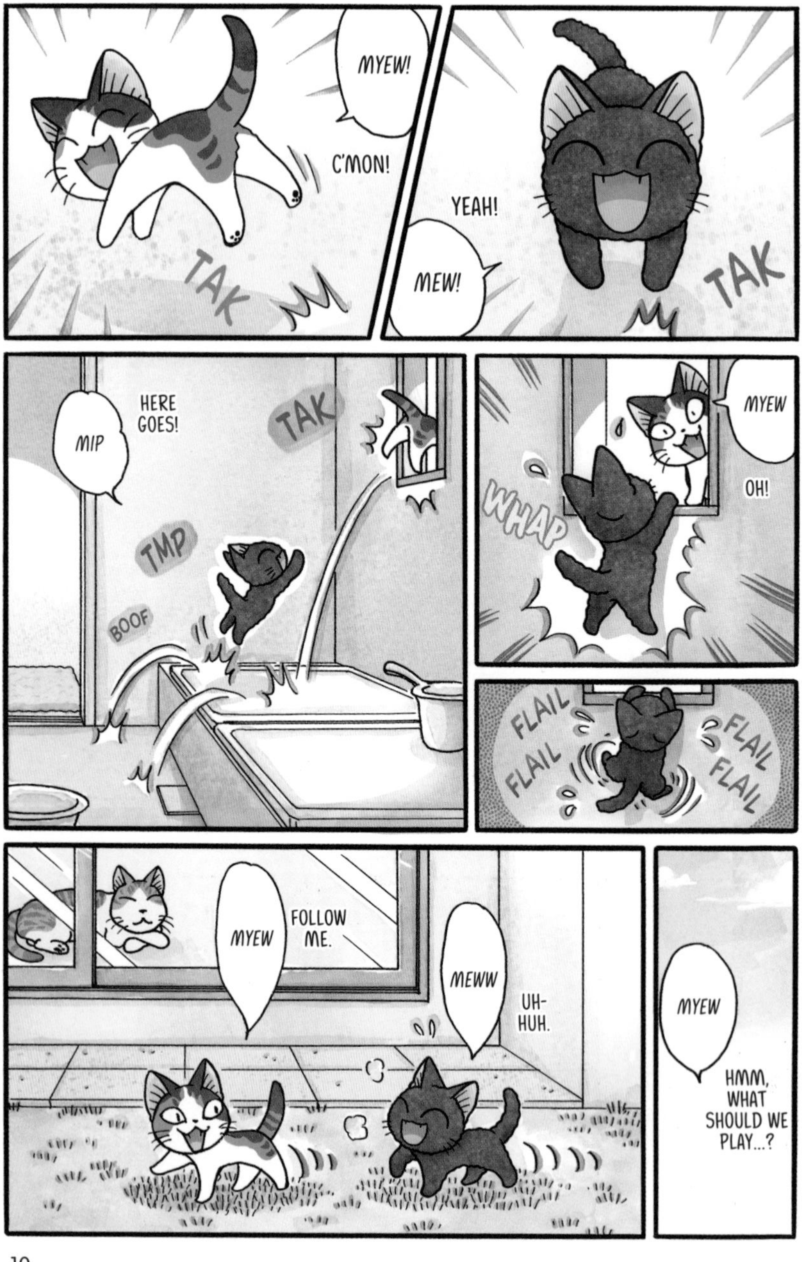
MYEW!
C'MON!
TAK
YEAH!
MEW!
TAK
MIP
HERE GOES!
TAK
TMP
BOOF
MYEW
OH!
WHAP
FLAIL
FLAIL
FLAIL
FLAIL
MYEW
FOLLOW ME.
MEWW
UH-HUH.
MYEW
HMM, WHAT SHOULD WE PLAY...?

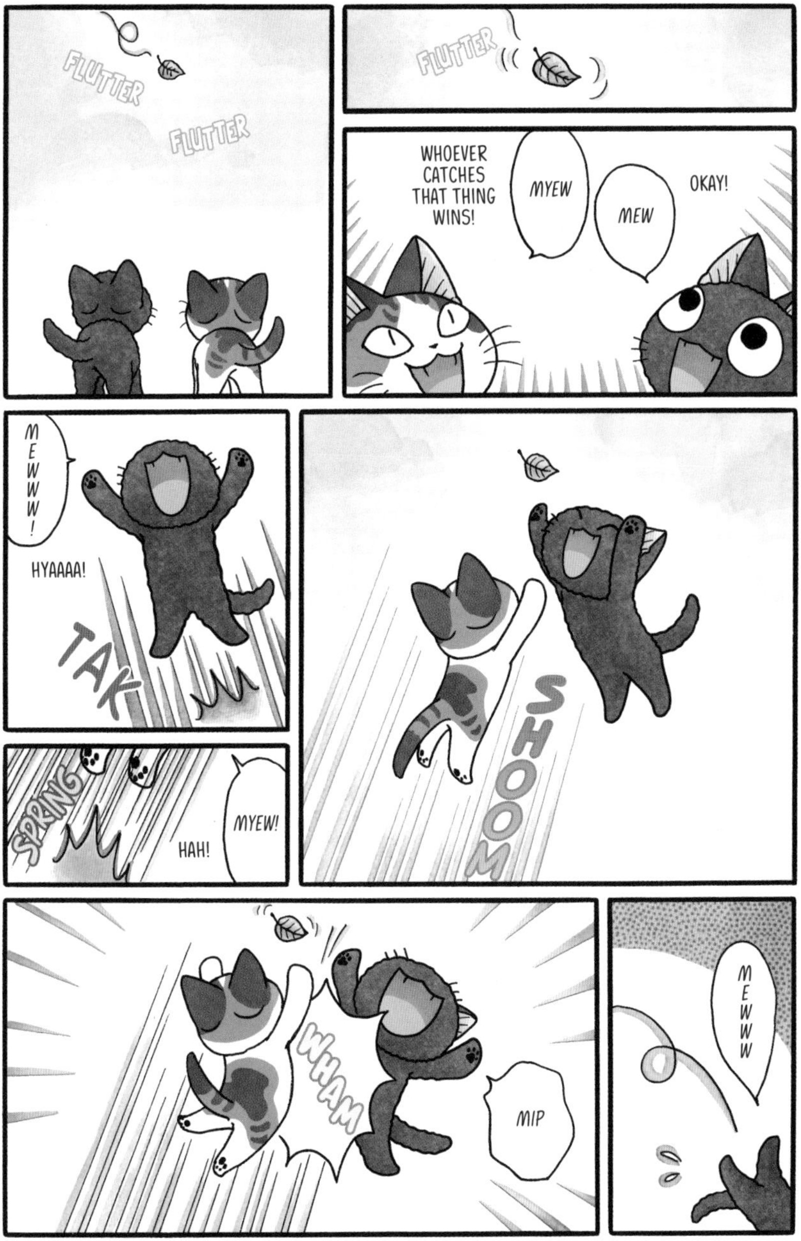
FLUTTER
FLUTTER
FLUTTER
WHOEVER CATCHES THAT THING WINS!
MYEW
MEW
OKAY!
MEWWW!
HYAAAA!
TAK
SPRING
HAH!
MYEW!
SHOOOM
WHAM
MIP
MEWWW

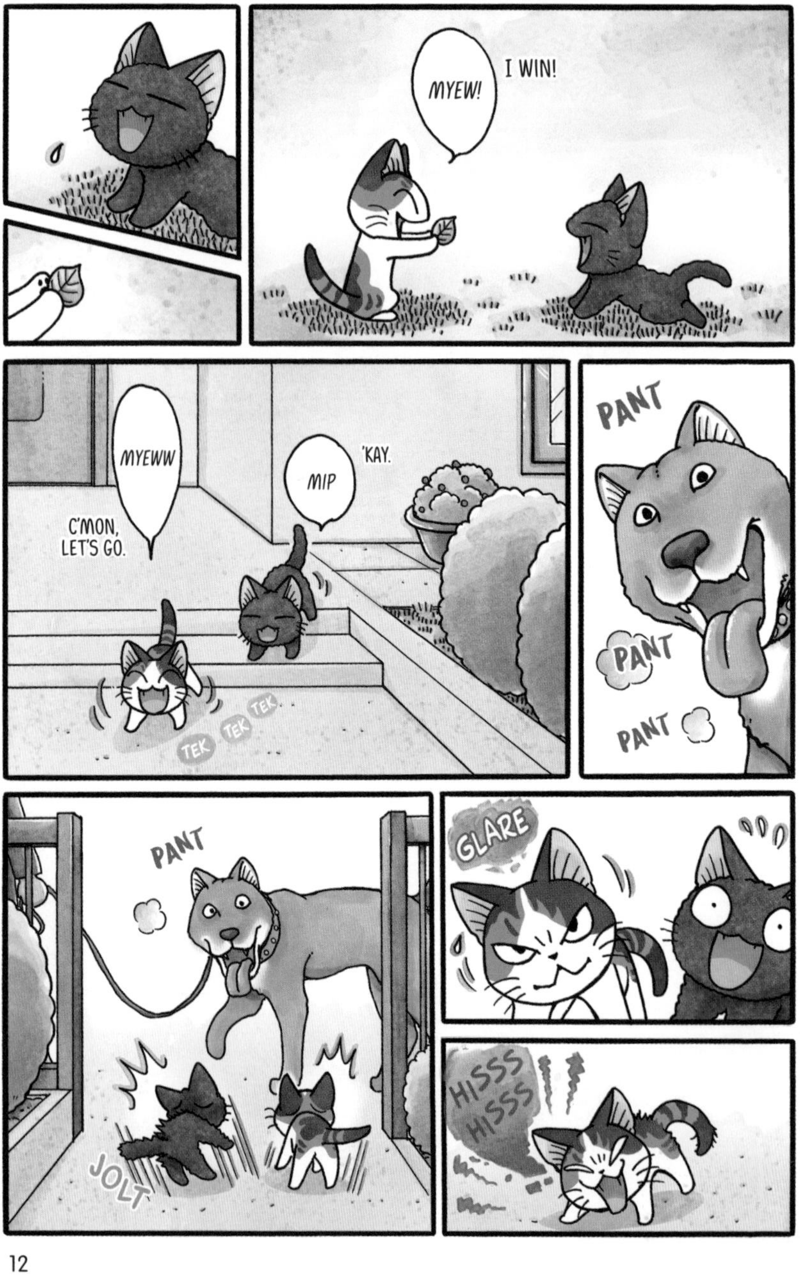
MYEW!
I WIN!
PANT
PANT
PANT
MYEWW
C'MON, LET'S GO.
MIP
'KAY.
TEK TEK TEK
GLARE
HISSS HISSS
PANT
JOLT

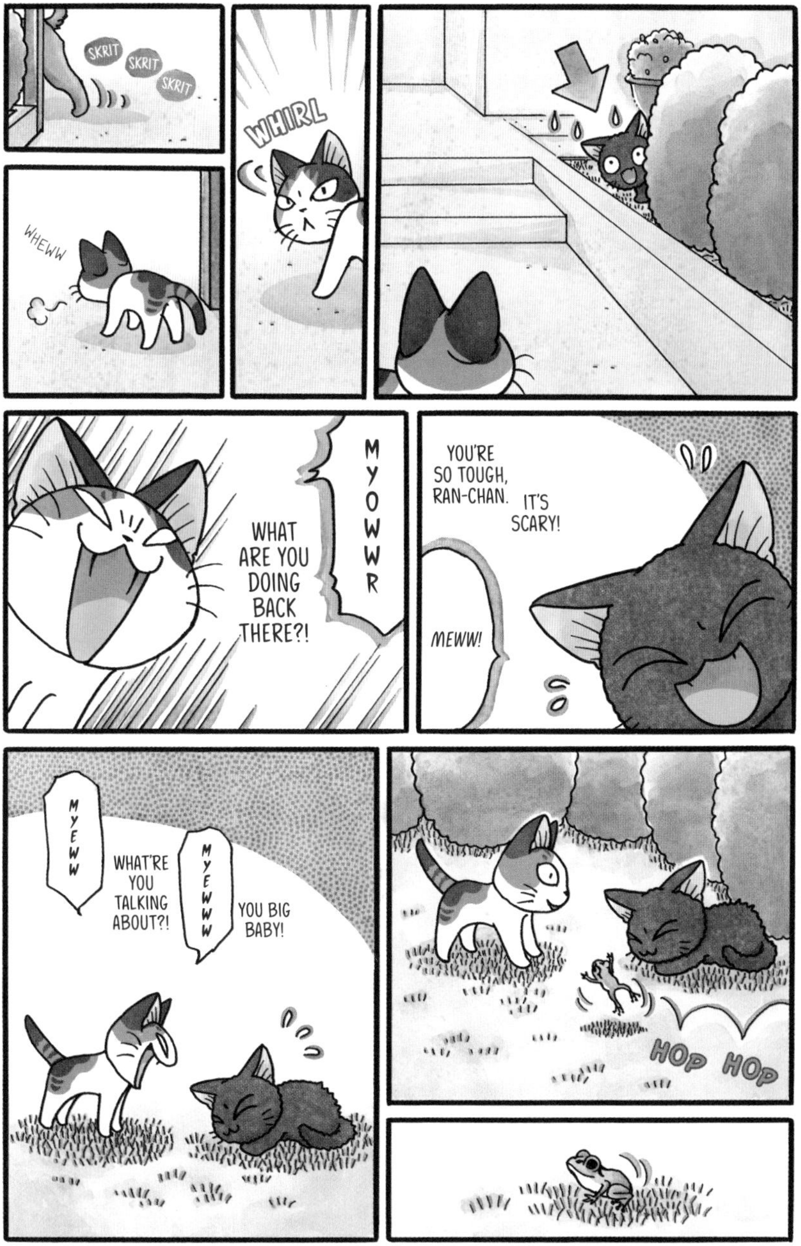
SKRIT SKRIT SKRIT
WHEWW
WHIRL
MYOWWR
WHAT ARE YOU DOING BACK THERE?!
YOU'RE SO TOUGH, RAN-CHAN.
IT'S SCARY!
MEWW!
MYEWW
WHAT'RE YOU TALKING ABOUT?!
MYEWWW
YOU BIG BABY!
HOP HOP

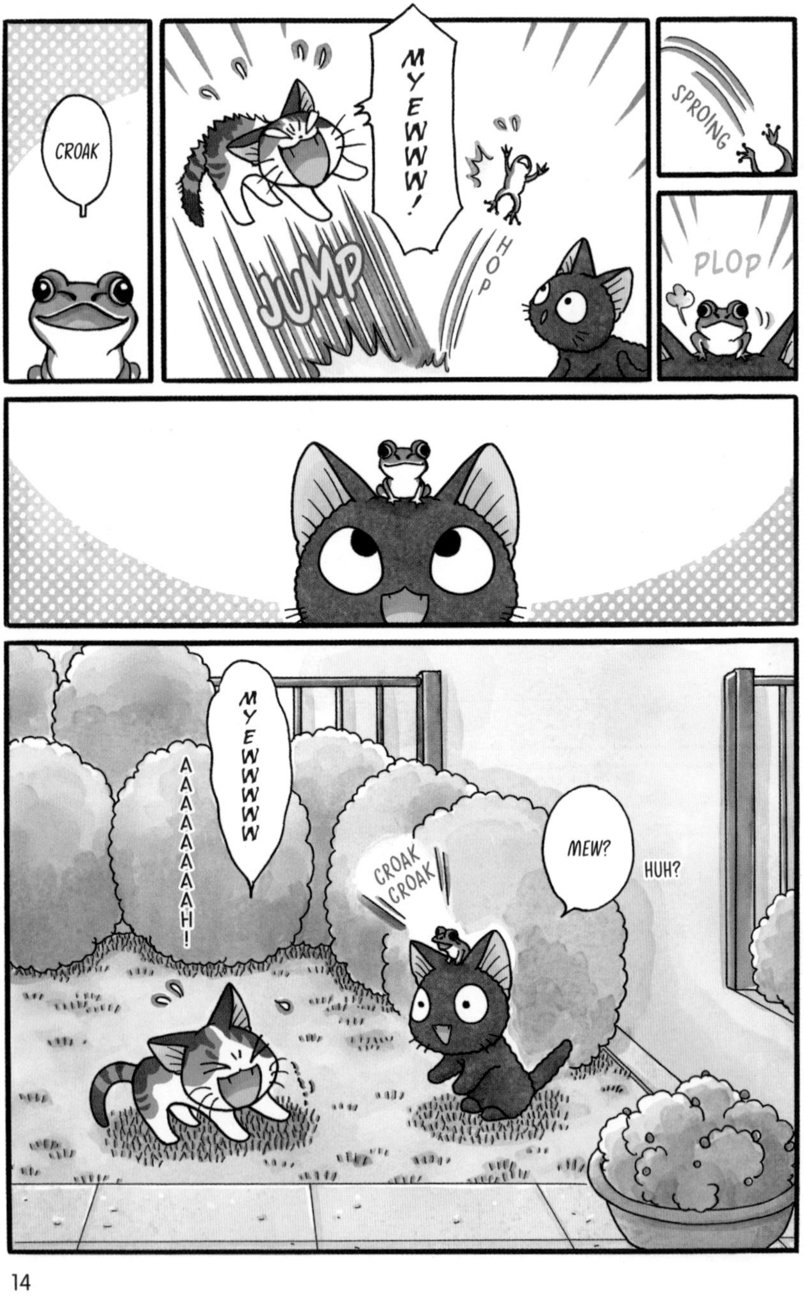
CROAK
MYEWWWW!
JUMP
HOP
SPROING
PLOP
MYEWWWWWW
AAAAAAAAAH!
CROAK CROAK
MEW?
HUH?

CHAPTER 54 A Burst of Kitty Power ☆

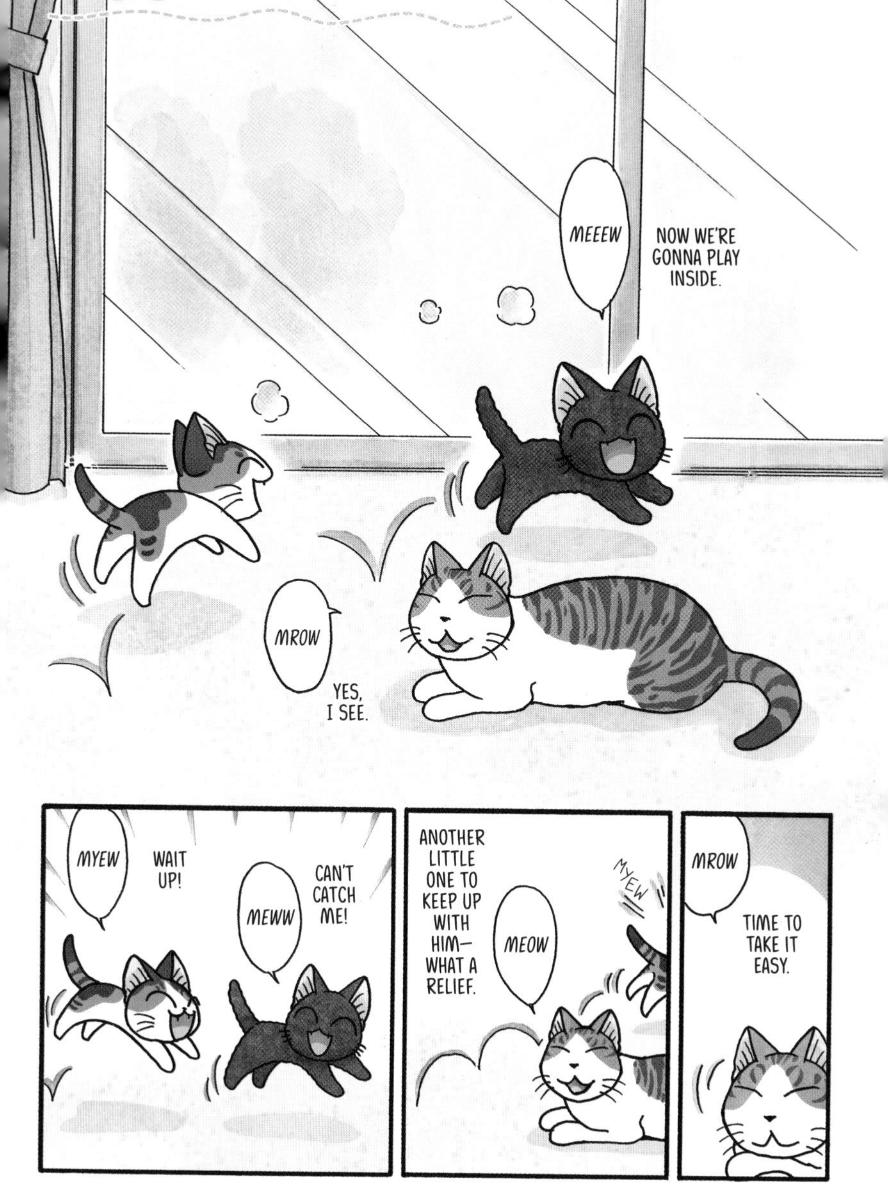
MEEEW
NOW WE'RE GONNA PLAY INSIDE.
MROW
YES, I SEE.
MYEW
WAIT UP!
MEWW
CAN'T CATCH ME!
ANOTHER LITTLE ONE TO KEEP UP WITH HIM— WHAT A RELIEF.
MYEW
MEOW
MROW
TIME TO TAKE IT EASY.

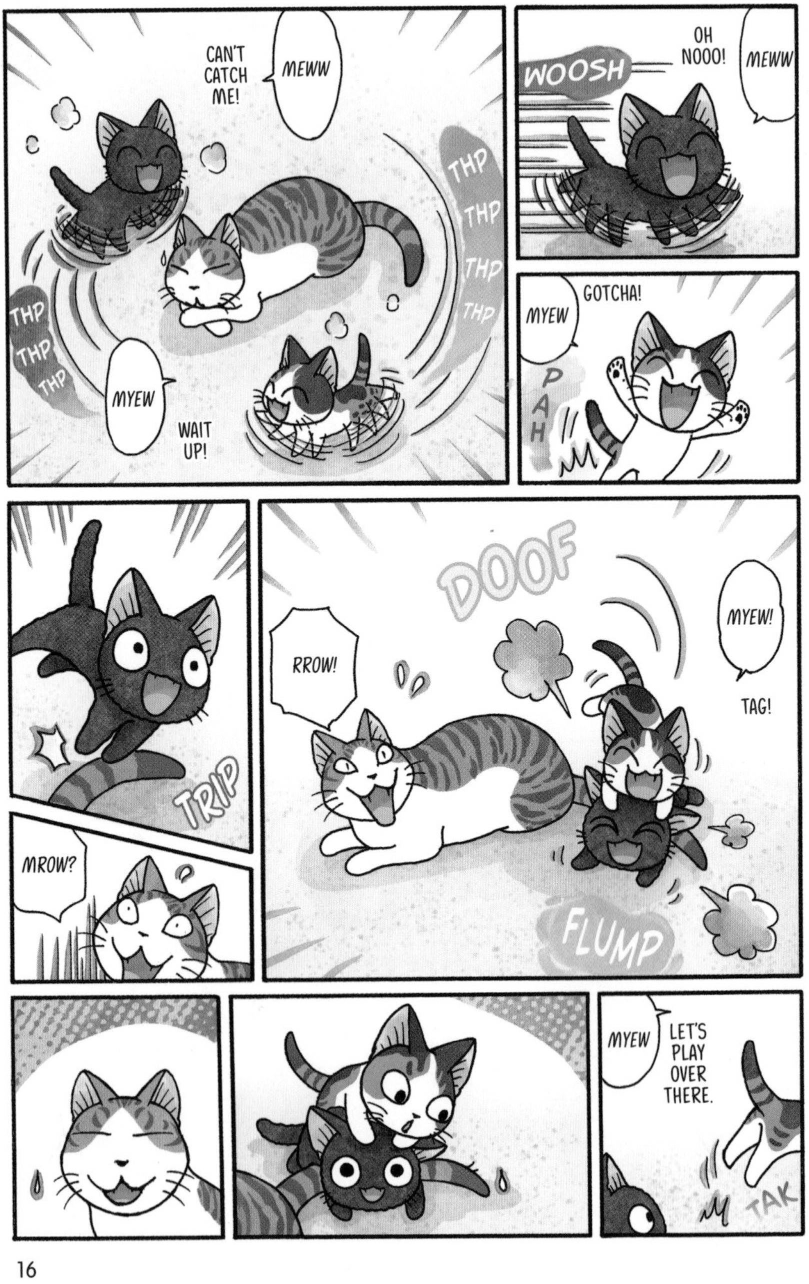
MEWW
CAN'T CATCH ME!
THP THP THP THP
THP THP THP
MYEW
WAIT UP!
WOOSH
MEWW
OH NOOO!
MYEW
GOTCHA!
PAH
TRIP
MROW?
DOOF
RROW!
MYEW!
TAG!
FLUMP
MYEW
LET'S PLAY OVER THERE.
TAK

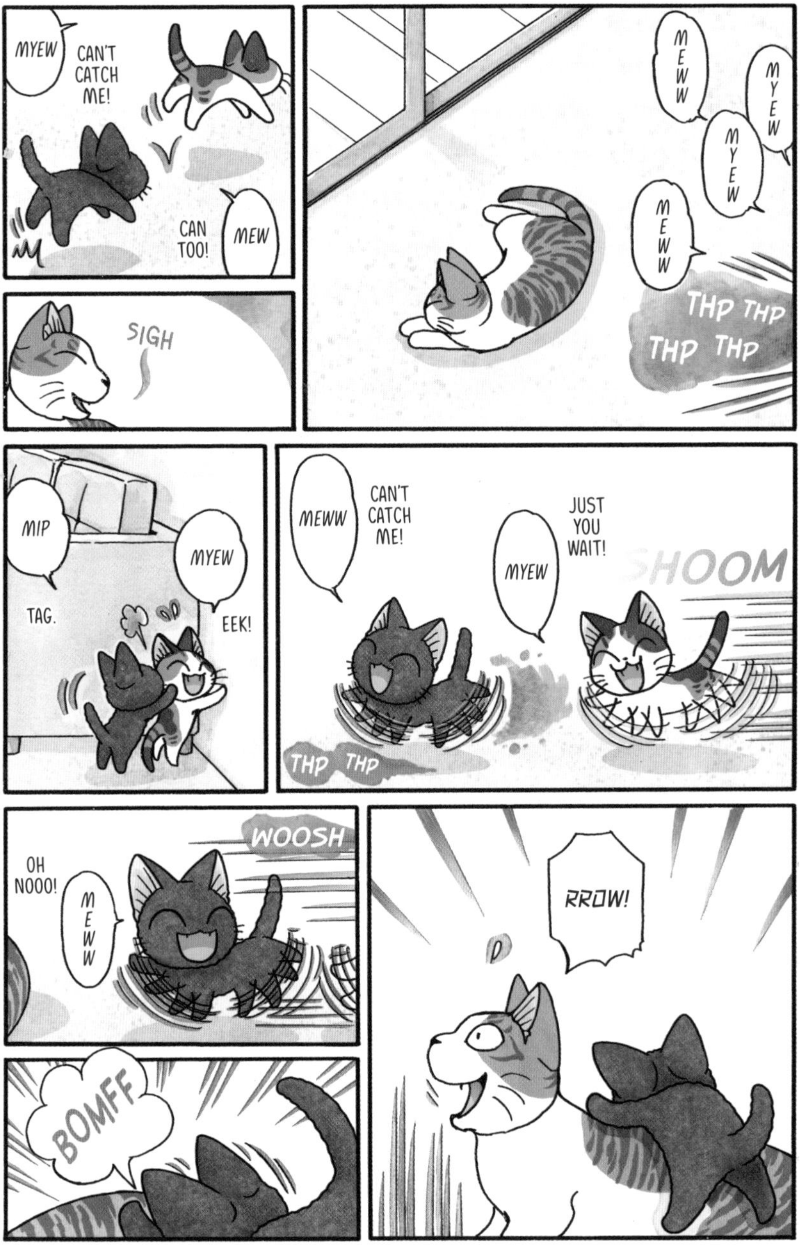
MYEW
CAN'T CATCH ME!
CAN TOO!
MEW
SIGH
MEWW
MYEW
MYEW
MEWW
THP THP THP THP
MIP
TAG.
MYEW
EEK!
MEWW
CAN'T CATCH ME!
MYEW
JUST YOU WAIT!
SHOOM
THP THP
WOOSH
OH NOOO!
MEWW
BOMFF
RROW!

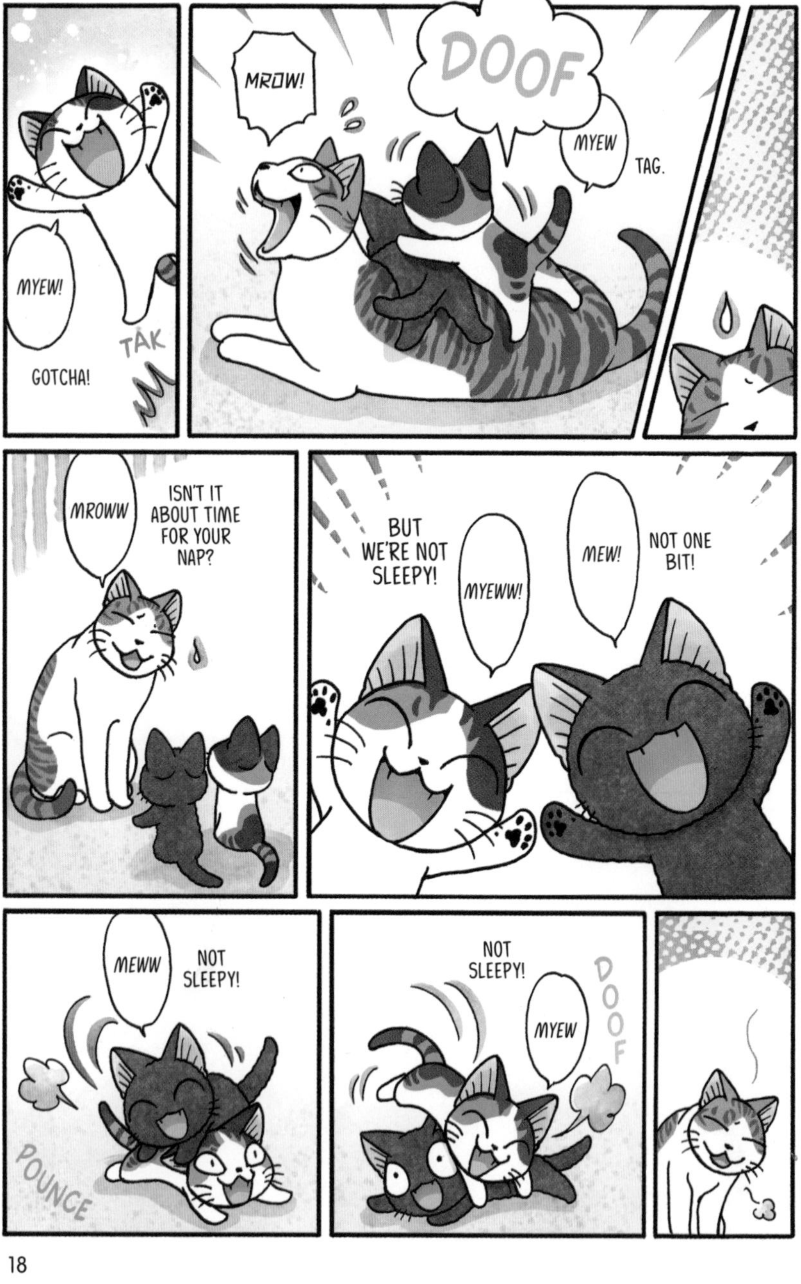
MYEW!
GOTCHA!
TAK
MROW!
DOOF
MYEW
TAG.
MROWW
ISN'T IT ABOUT TIME FOR YOUR NAP?
BUT WE'RE NOT SLEEPY!
MYEWW!
MEW!
NOT ONE BIT!
MEWW
NOT SLEEPY!
POUNCE
NOT SLEEPY!
MYEW
DOOF

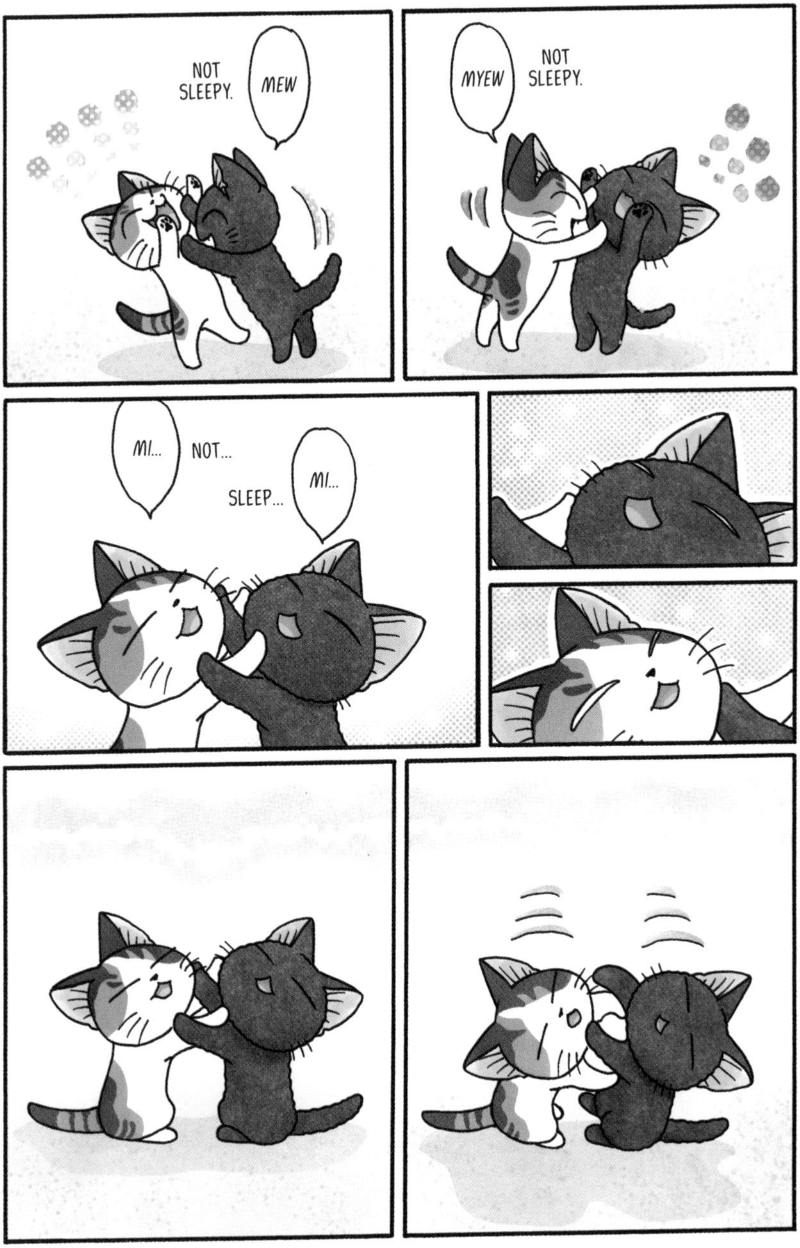
NOT SLEEPY.
MYEW
MEW
NOT SLEEPY.
MI...
NOT...
SLEEP...
MI...

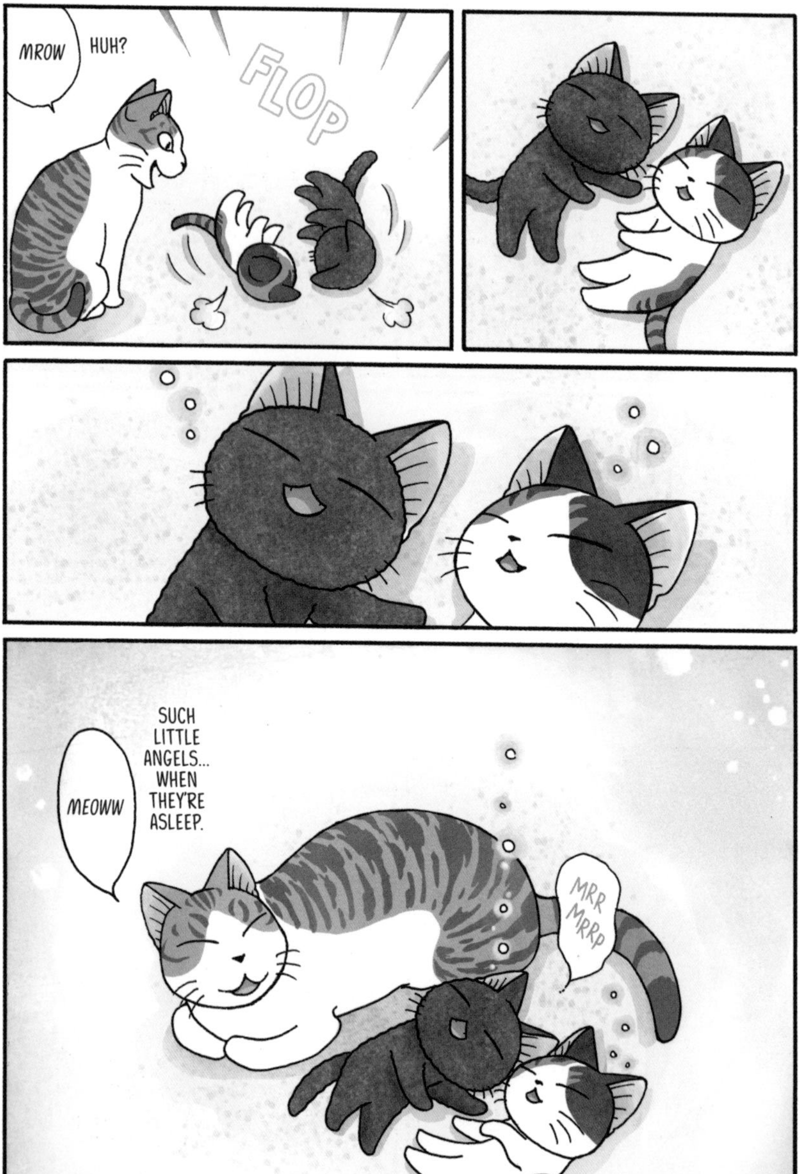
MROW
HUH?
FLOP
MEOWW
SUCH LITTLE ANGELS... WHEN THEY'RE ASLEEP.
MRR MRRP

Sue & Tai-chan

CHAPTER 55 The Cool Spot Search Party

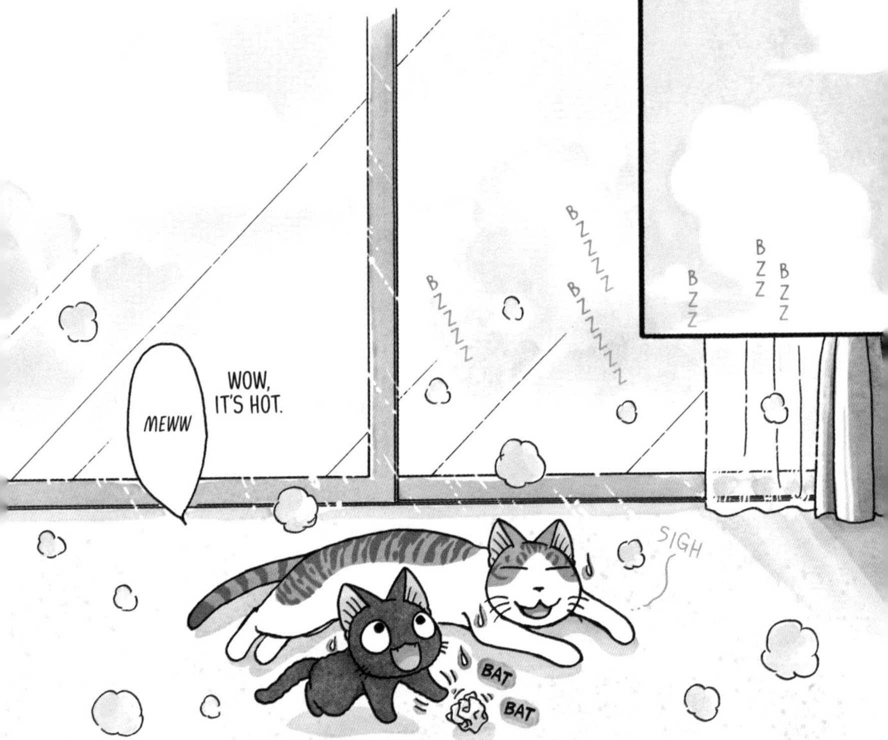
BZZ
BZZ
BZZ
BZZZZZ
BZZZZZ
BZZZZZZZ
MEWW
WOW, IT'S HOT.
SIGH
BAT
BAT

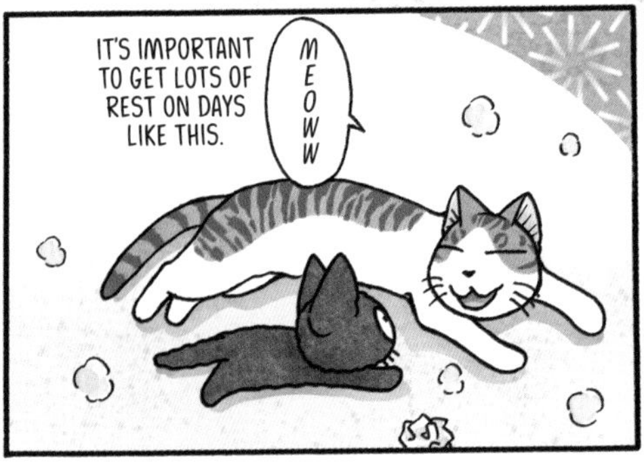
IT'S IMPORTANT TO GET LOTS OF REST ON DAYS LIKE THIS.
MEOWW

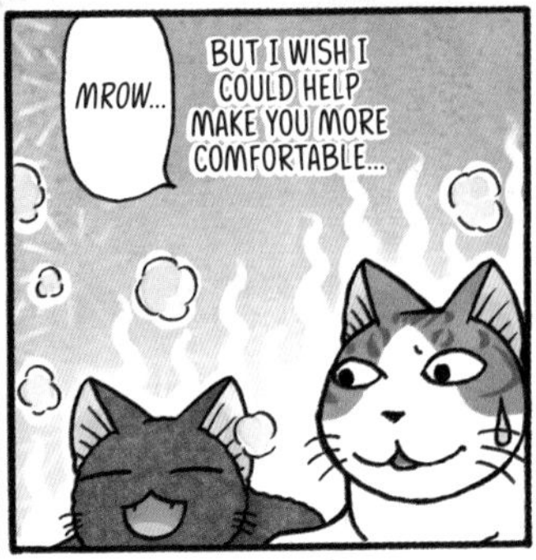
MROW...
BUT I WISH I COULD HELP MAKE YOU MORE COMFORTABLE...

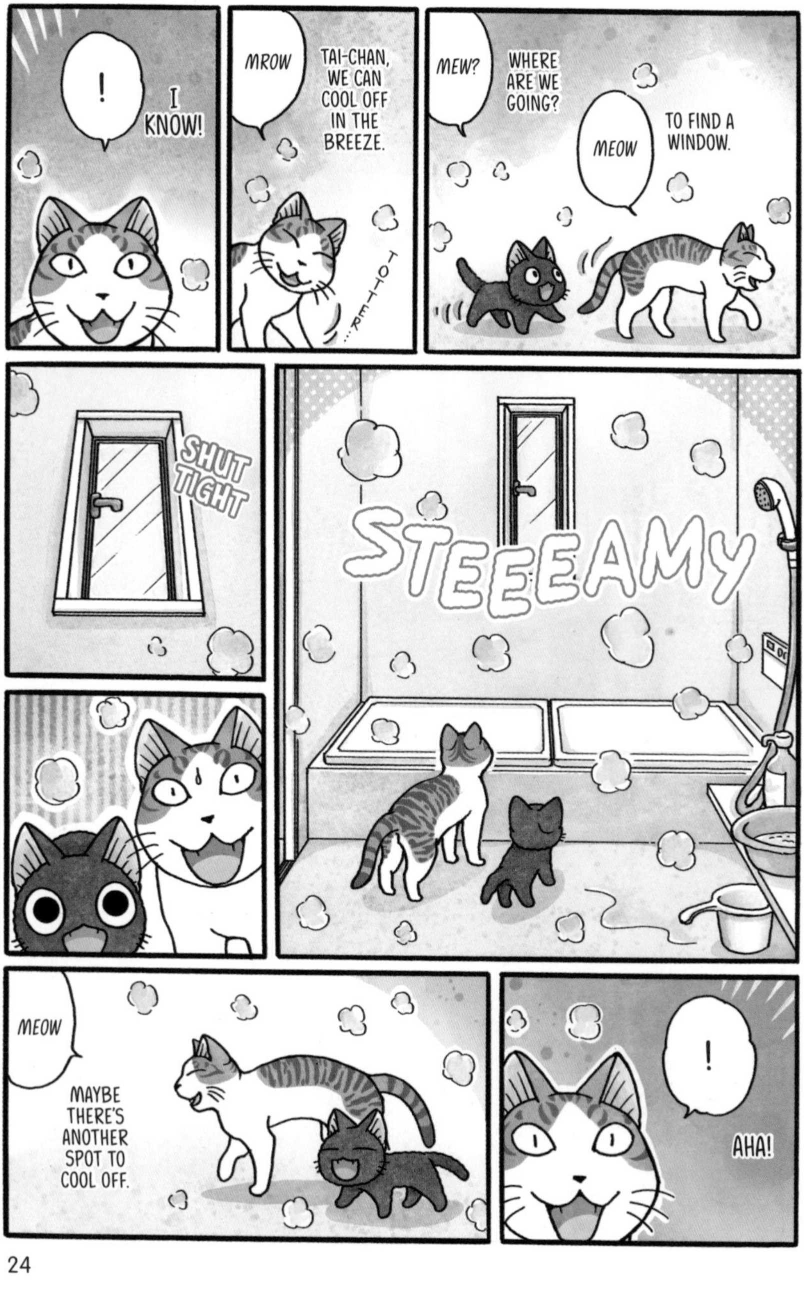
!
I KNOW!
MROW
TAI-CHAN, WE CAN COOL OFF IN THE BREEZE.
TOTTER...
MEW?
WHERE ARE WE GOING?
MEOW
TO FIND A WINDOW.
SHUT TIGHT
STEEEAMY
MEOW
MAYBE THERE'S ANOTHER SPOT TO COOL OFF.
!
AHA!

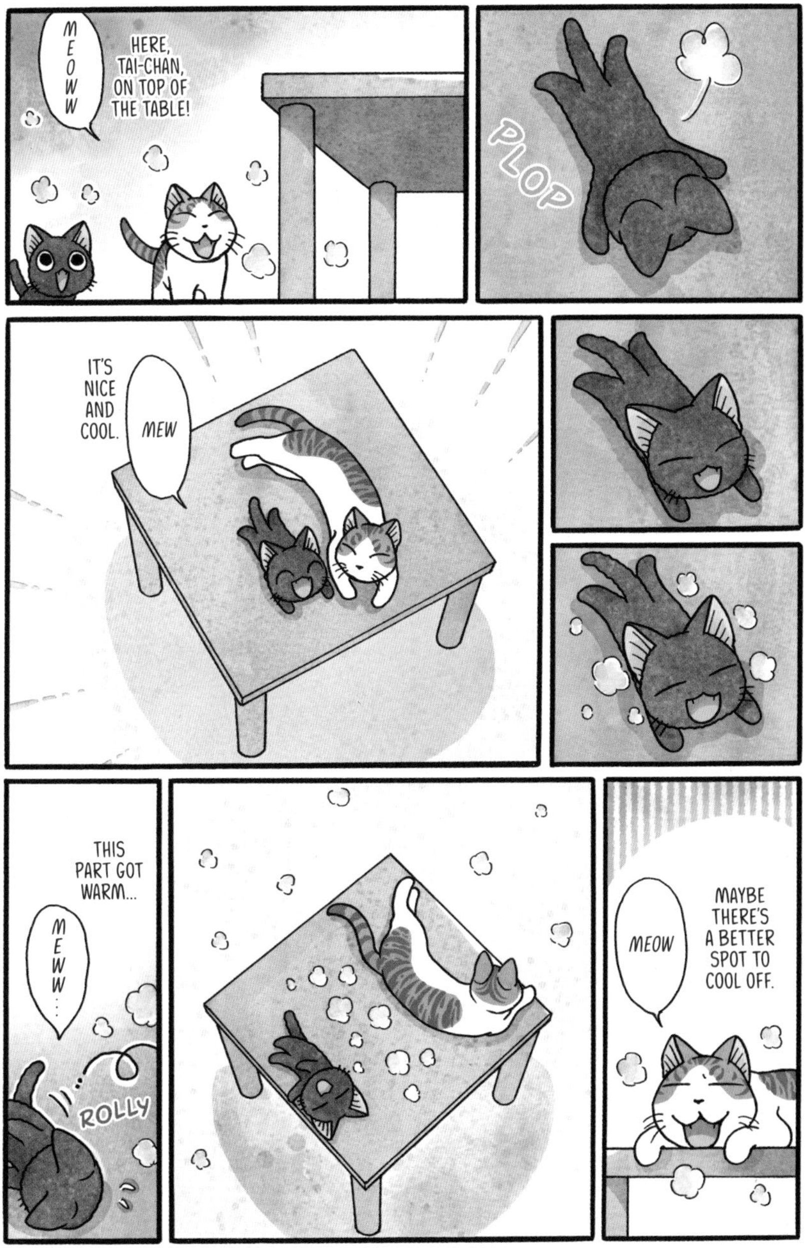
MEOWW
HERE, TAI-CHAN, ON TOP OF THE TABLE!
PLOP
IT'S NICE AND COOL.
MEW
THIS PART GOT WARM...
MEWW...
ROLLY
MEOW
MAYBE THERE'S A BETTER SPOT TO COOL OFF.

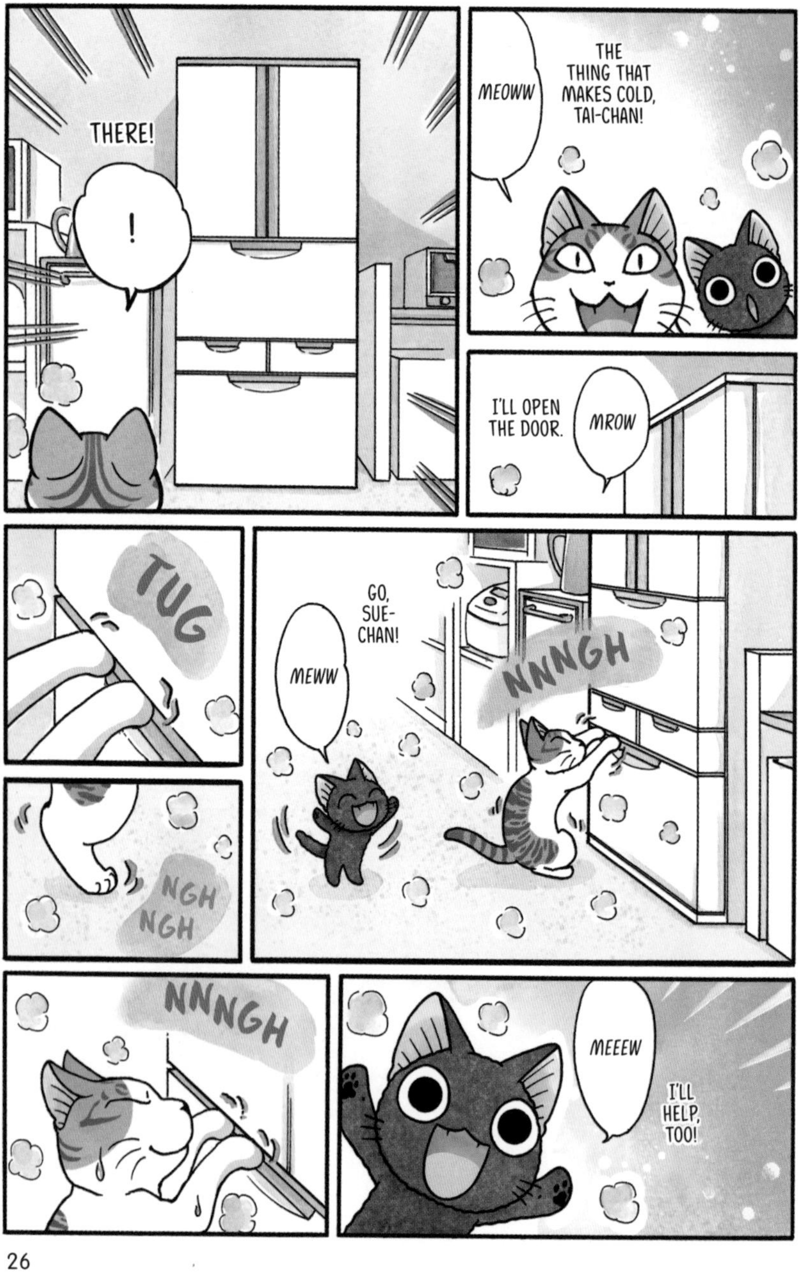
THE THING THAT MAKES COLD, TAI-CHAN!
MEOWW
MROW
I'LL OPEN THE DOOR.
THERE!
!
GO, SUE-CHAN!
MEWW
NNNGH
TUG
NGH NGH
MEEEW
I'LL HELP, TOO!
NNNGH

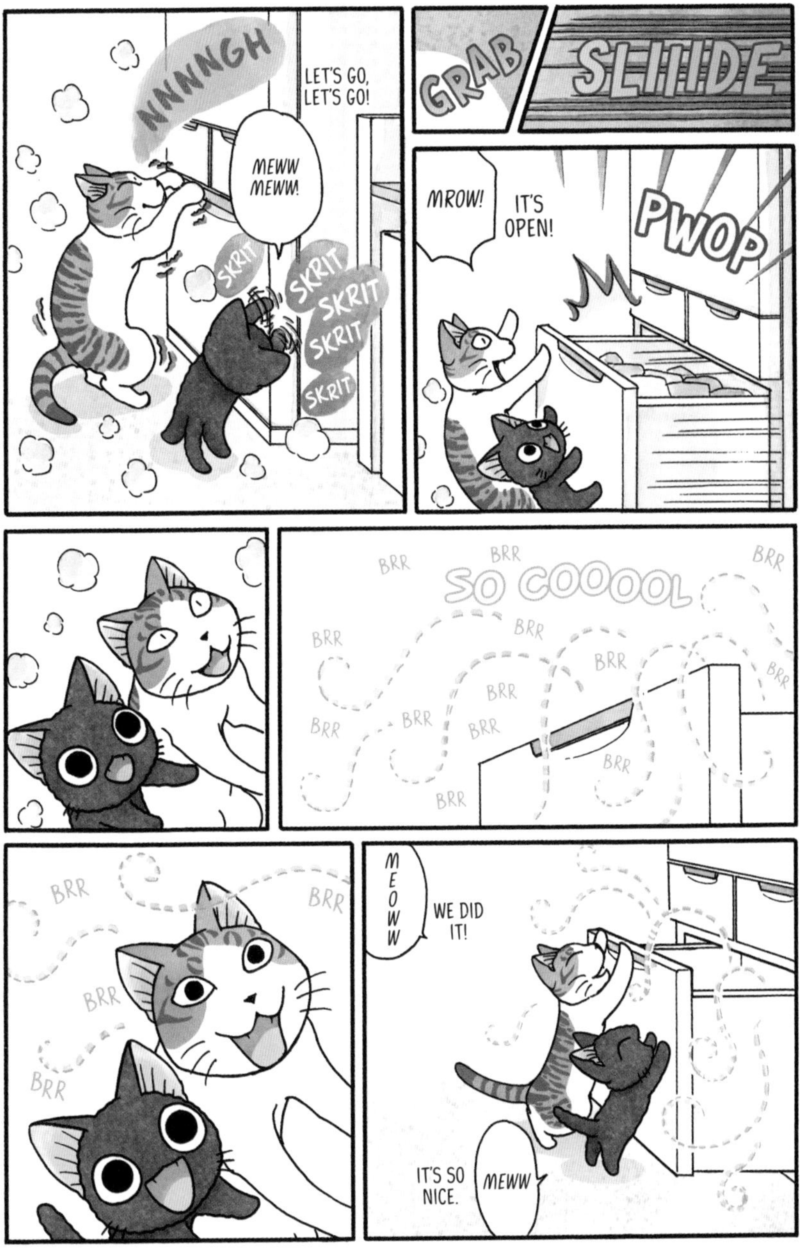
NNNNGH
LET'S GO, LET'S GO!
MEWW MEWW!
SKRIT
SKRIT
SKRIT
SKRIT
SKRIT
GRAB
SLIIIDE
MROW!
IT'S OPEN!
PWOP
BRR
BRR
SO COOOOL
BRR
BRR
BRR
BRR
BRR
BRR
BRR
BRR
BRR
BRR
BRR
BRR
BRR
BRR
BRR
MEOWW
WE DID IT!
IT'S SO NICE.
MEWW

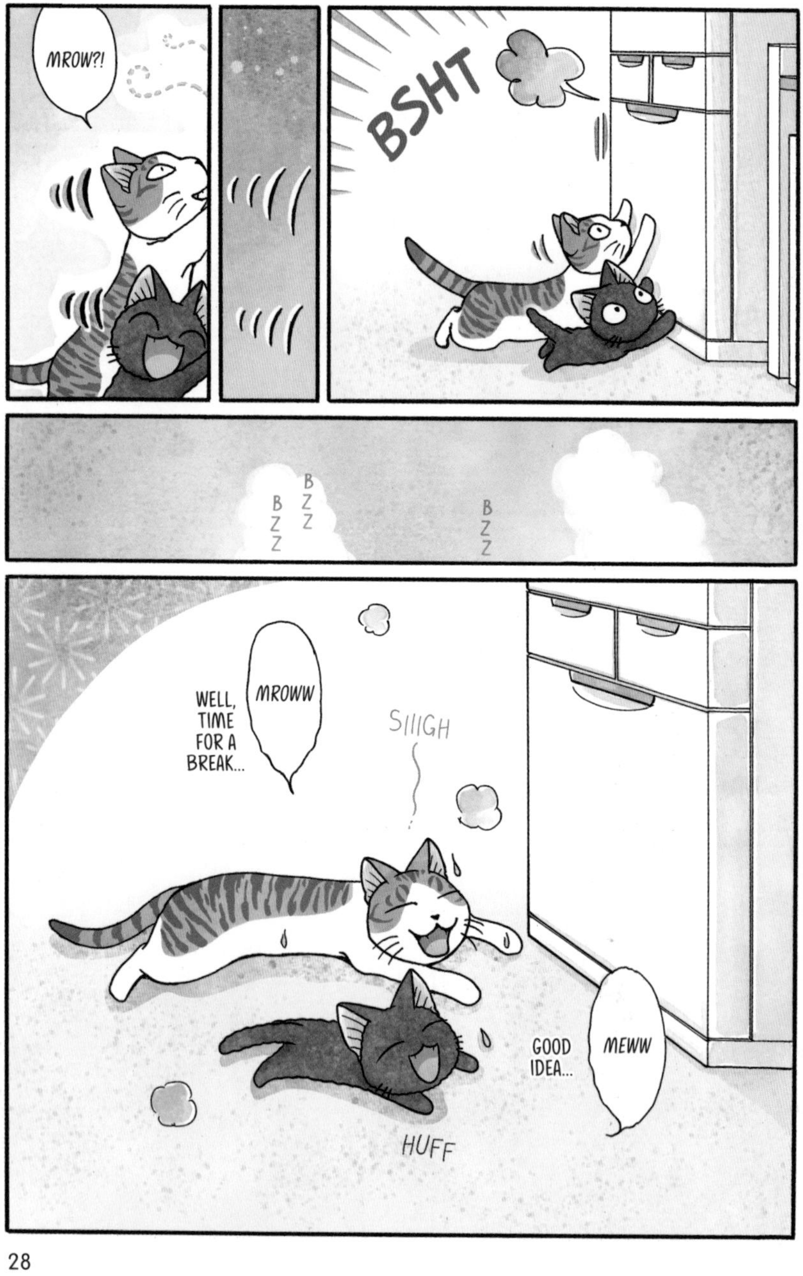
BSHT
MROW?!
B Z Z
B Z Z
B Z Z
SIIIGH
MROWW
WELL, TIME FOR A BREAK...
MEWW
GOOD IDEA...
HUFF

CHAPTER 56 A Grown-Up's Patience

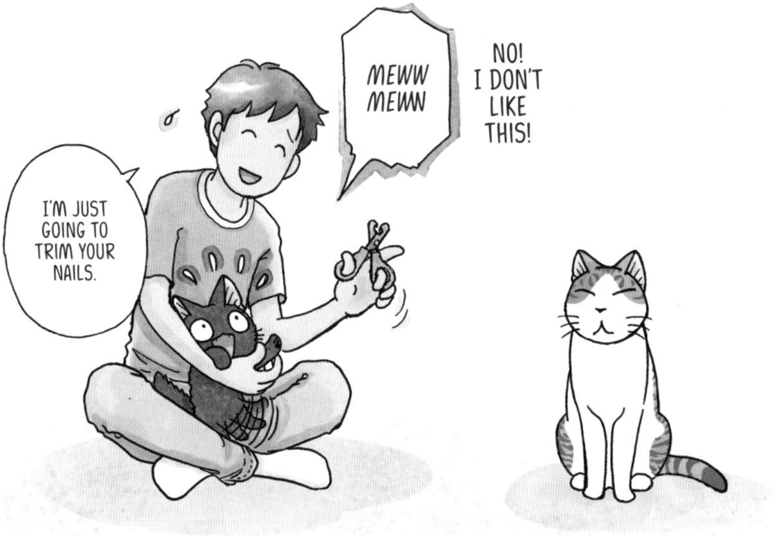
I'M JUST GOING TO TRIM YOUR NAILS.
MEWW MEWW
NO! I DON'T LIKE THIS!

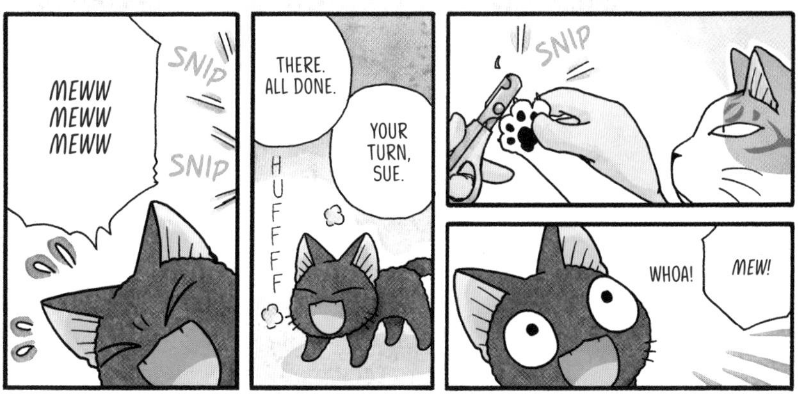
MEWW MEWW MEWW
SNIP
SNIP
THERE. ALL DONE.
YOUR TURN, SUE.
HUFFFF
SNIP
WHOA!
MEW!

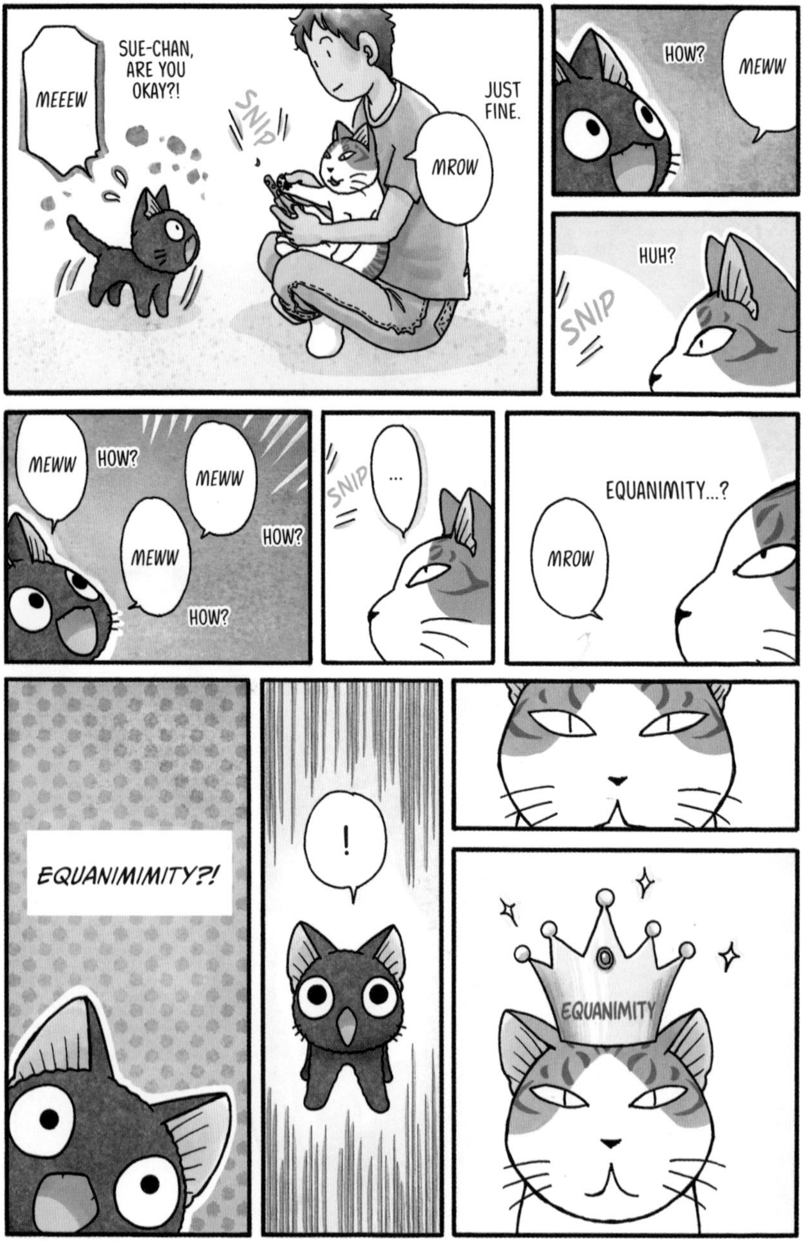
MEEEW
SUE-CHAN, ARE YOU OKAY?!
SNIP
MROW
JUST FINE.
MEWW
HOW?
SNIP
HUH?
MEWW
HOW?
MEWW
HOW?
MEWW
HOW?
SNIP
...
MROW
EQUANIMITY...?
EQUANIMIMITY?!
!
EQUANIMITY

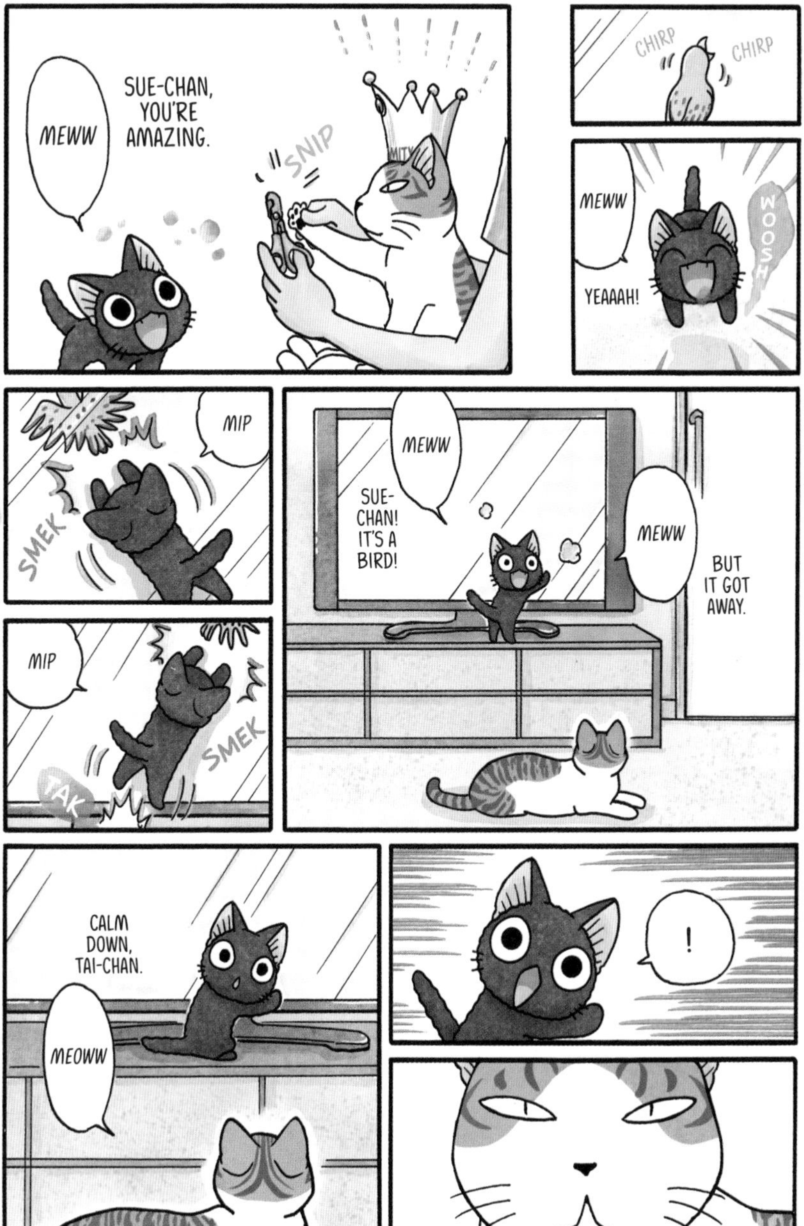
MEWW
SUE-CHAN, YOU'RE AMAZING.
SNIP
MITY
CHIRP
CHIRP
MEWW
YEAAAH!
WOOSH
MIP
SMEK
MIP
SMEK
TAK
MEWW
SUE-CHAN! IT'S A BIRD!
MEWW
BUT IT GOT AWAY.
CALM DOWN, TAI-CHAN.
MEOWW
!

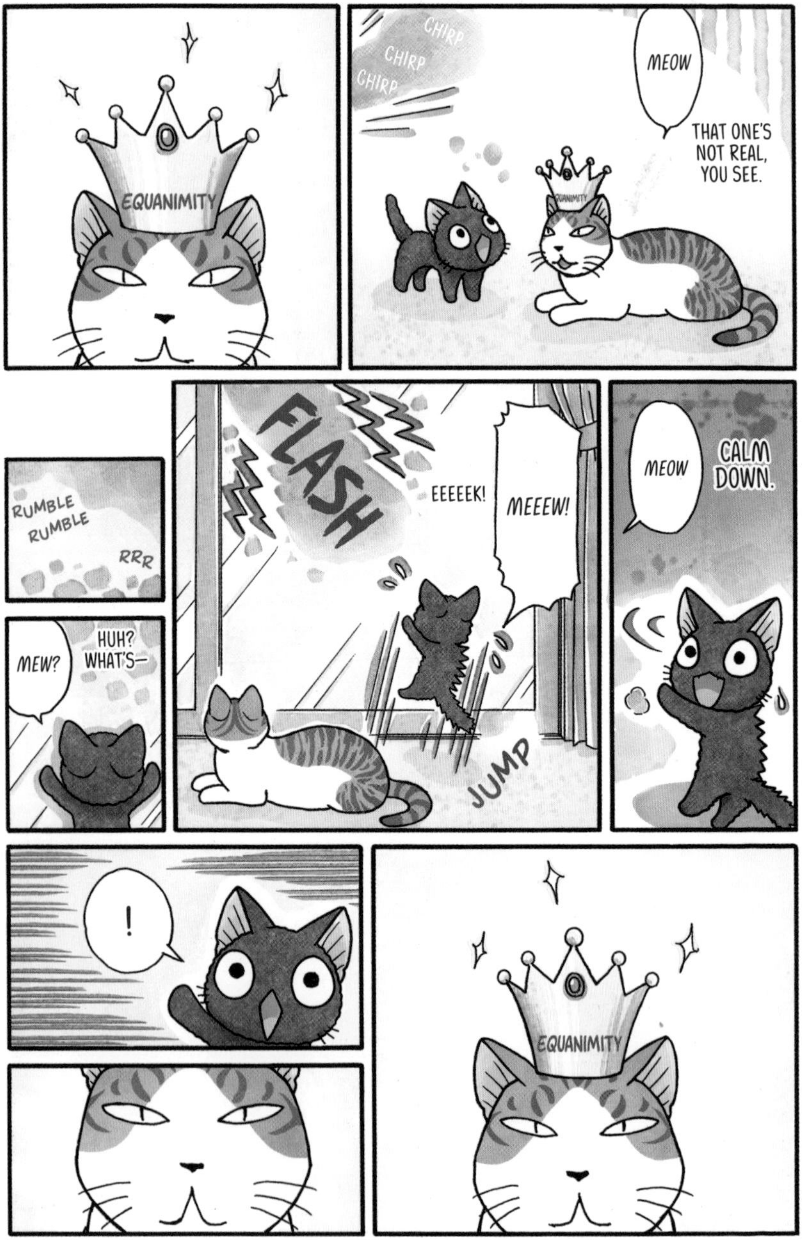
EQUANIMITY
CHIRP
CHIRP
CHIRP
MEOW
THAT ONE'S NOT REAL, YOU SEE.
EQUANIMITY
RUMBLE
RUMBLE
RRR
MEW?
HUH? WHAT'S—
FLASH
EEEEEK!
MEEEW!
JUMP
MEOW
CALM DOWN.
!
EQUANIMITY

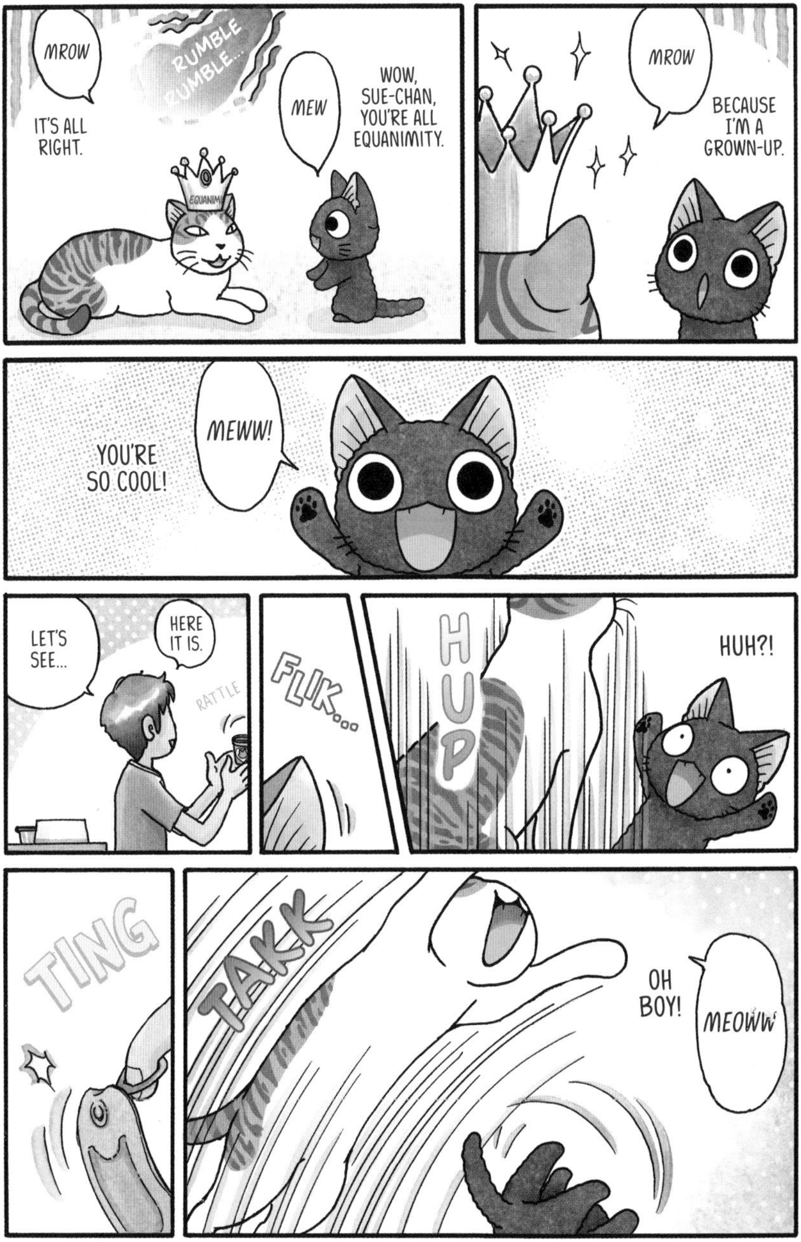
MROW
IT'S ALL RIGHT.
RUMBLE RUMBLE...
MEW
WOW, SUE-CHAN, YOU'RE ALL EQUANIMITY.
EQUANIMI
MROW
BECAUSE I'M A GROWN-UP.
MEWW!
YOU'RE SO COOL!
LET'S SEE...
HERE IT IS.
RATTLE
FLIK...
HUP
HUH?!
TING
TAKK
OH BOY!
MEOWW

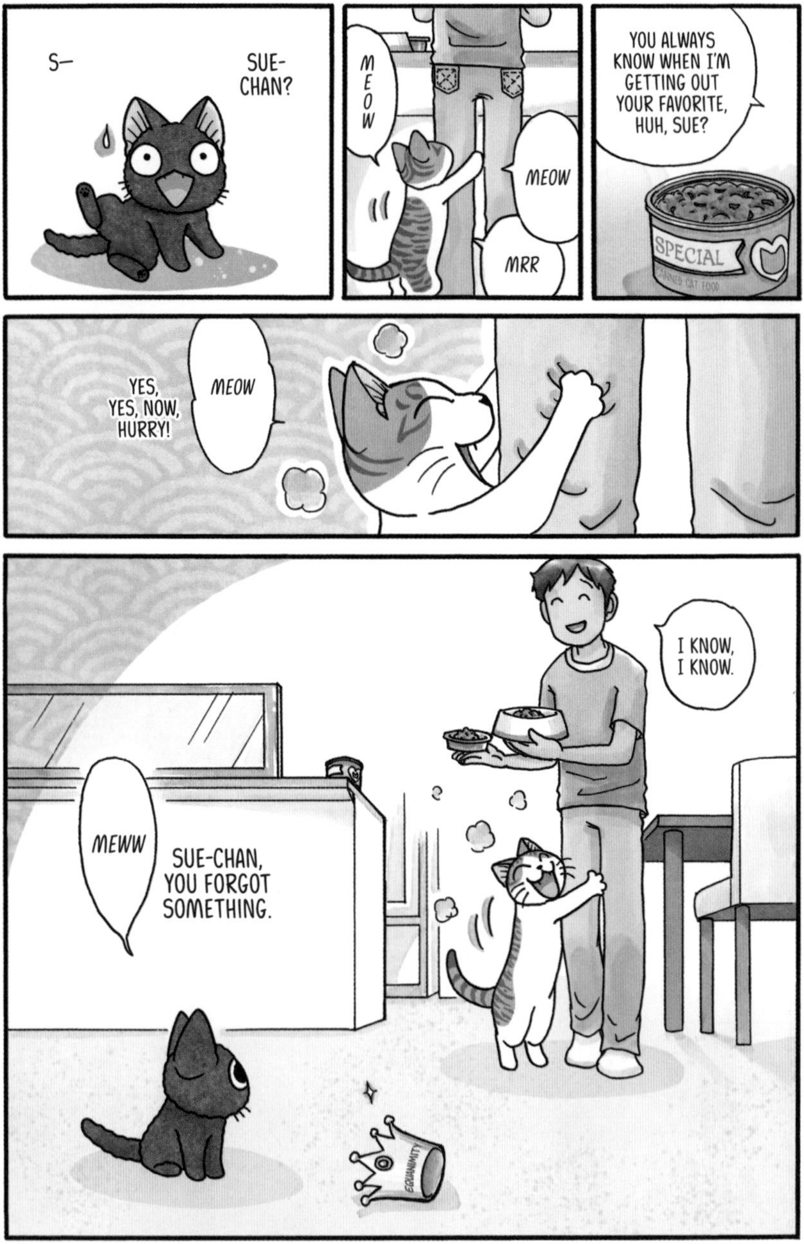
YOU ALWAYS KNOW WHEN I'M GETTING OUT YOUR FAVORITE, HUH, SUE?
SPECIAL
CANNED CAT FOOD
MEOW
MEOW
MRR
S—
SUE-CHAN?
MEOW
YES, YES, NOW, HURRY!
I KNOW, I KNOW.
MEWW
SUE-CHAN, YOU FORGOT SOMETHING.
EQUANIMITY

CHAPTER 57 Tai's Sneak Attack

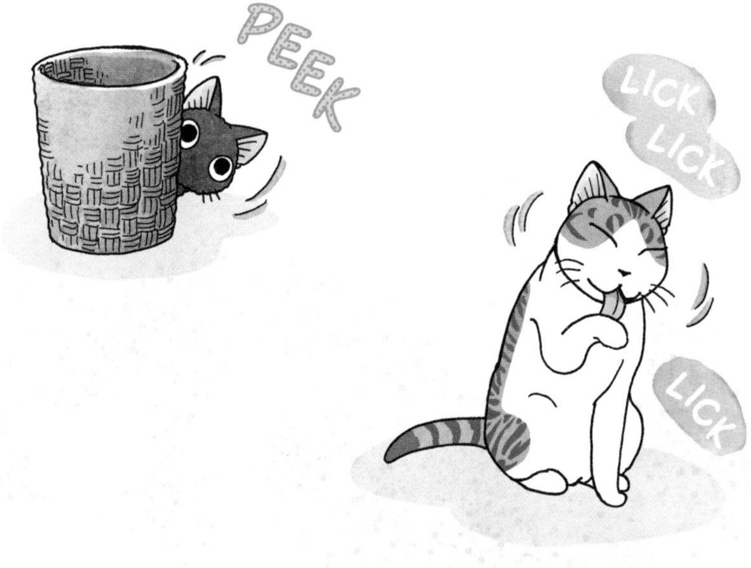
PEEK
LICK LICK
LICK

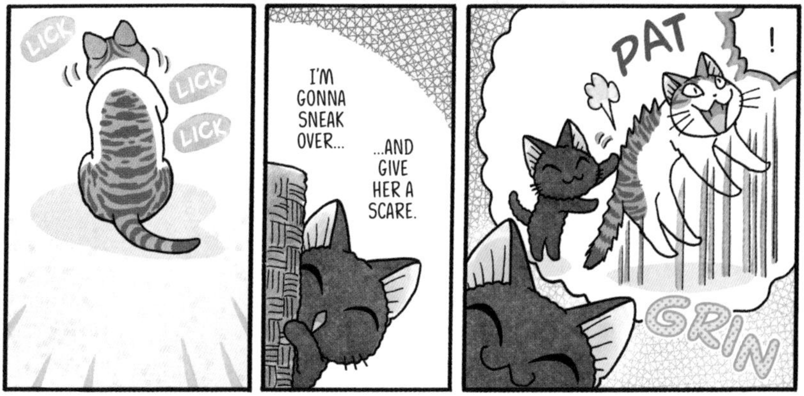
LICK
LICK
LICK
I'M GONNA SNEAK OVER...
...AND GIVE HER A SCARE.
PAT
!
GRIN

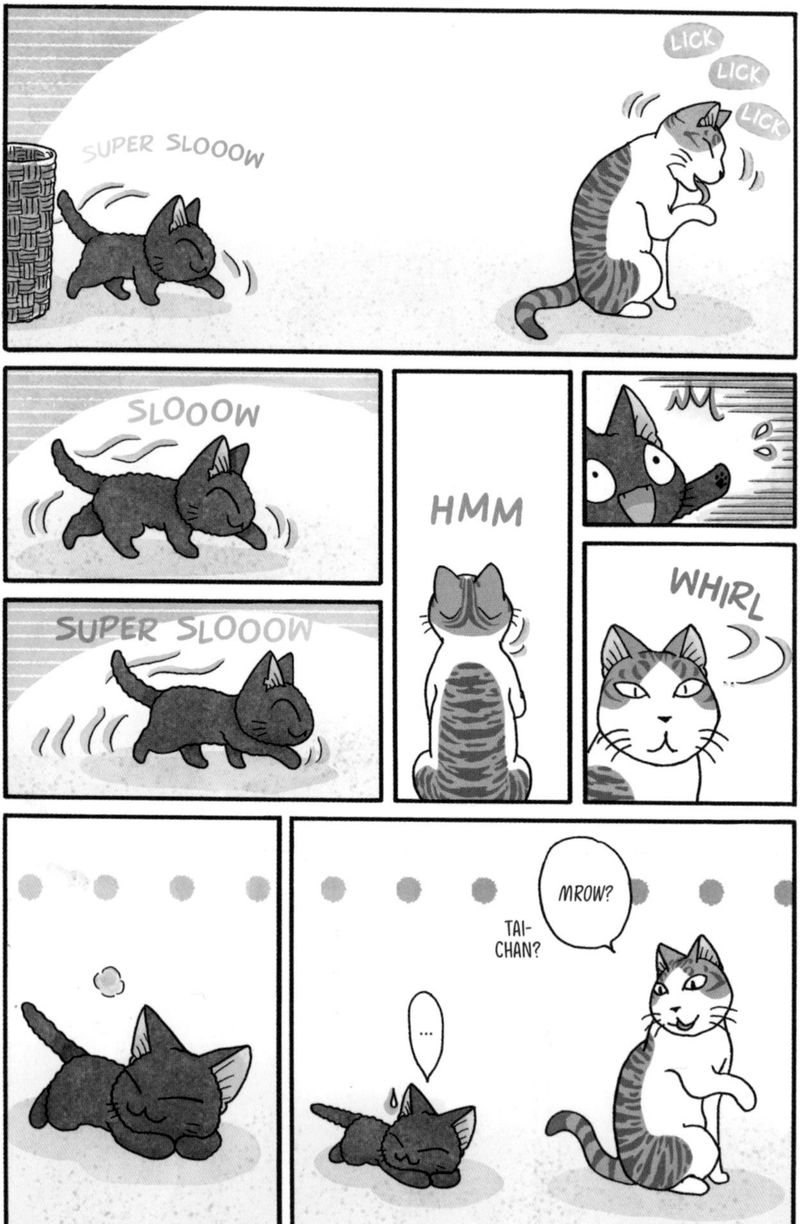
SUPER SLOOOW
LICK
LICK
LICK
SLOOOW
SUPER SLOOOW
HMM
WHIRL
...
TAI-CHAN?
MROW?

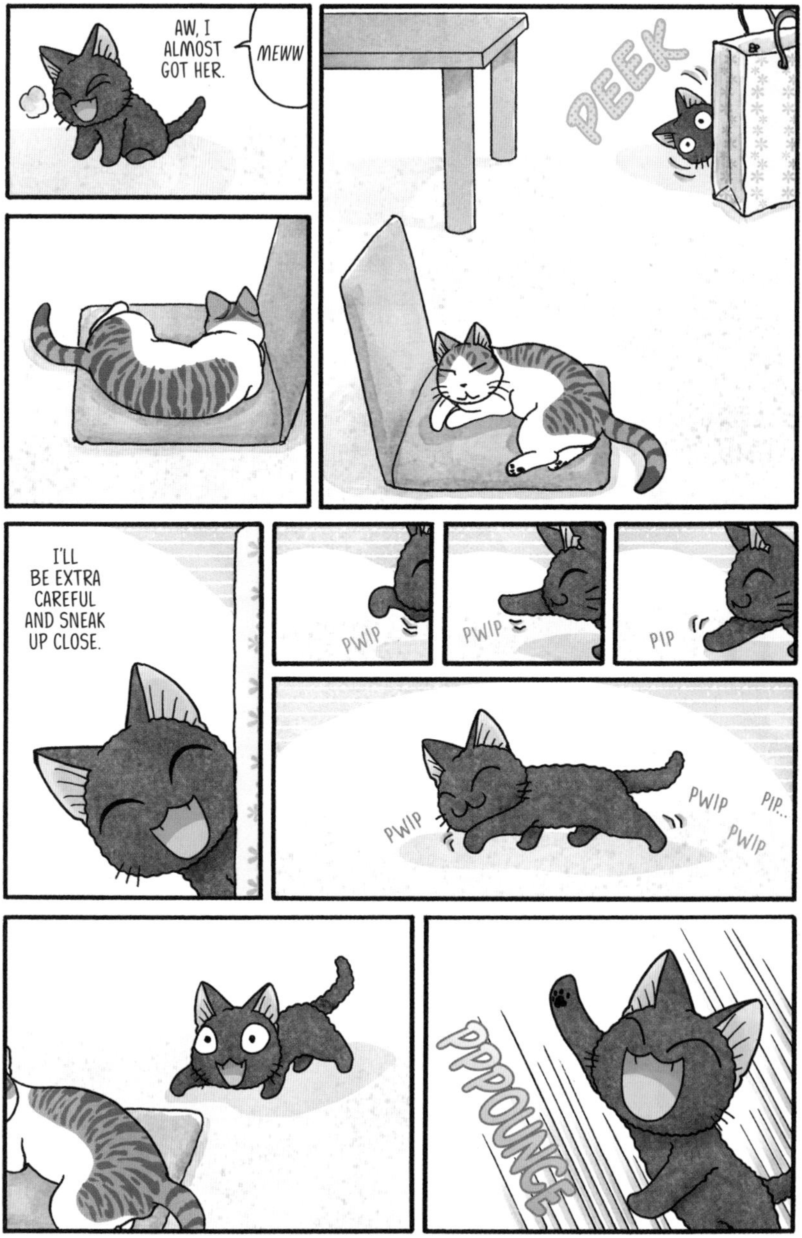
AW, I ALMOST GOT HER.
MEWW
PEEK
I'LL BE EXTRA CAREFUL AND SNEAK UP CLOSE.
PWIP
PWIP
PIP
PWIP
PWIP
PIP...
PWIP
PPPOUNCE

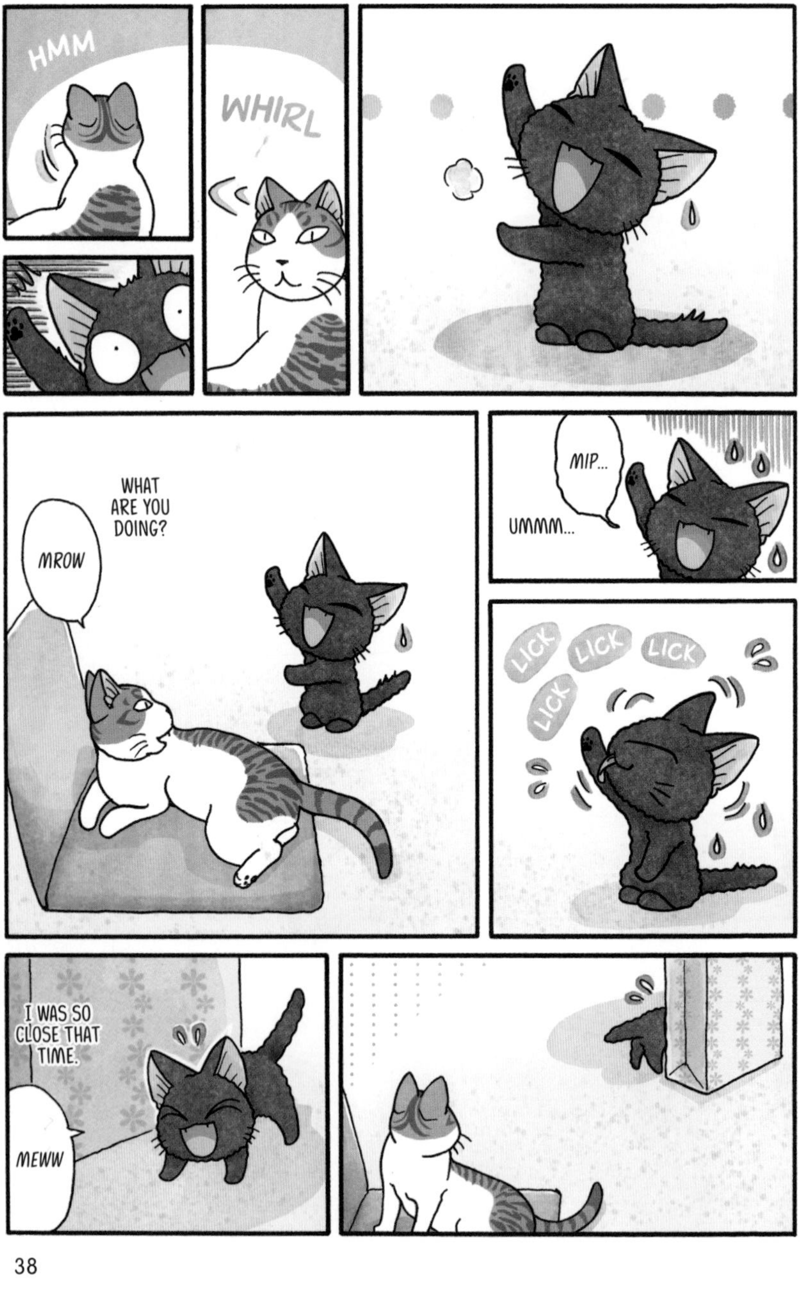
HMM
WHIRL
MROW
WHAT ARE YOU DOING?
MIP...
UMMM...
LICK LICK LICK LICK
I WAS SO CLOSE THAT TIME.
MEWW

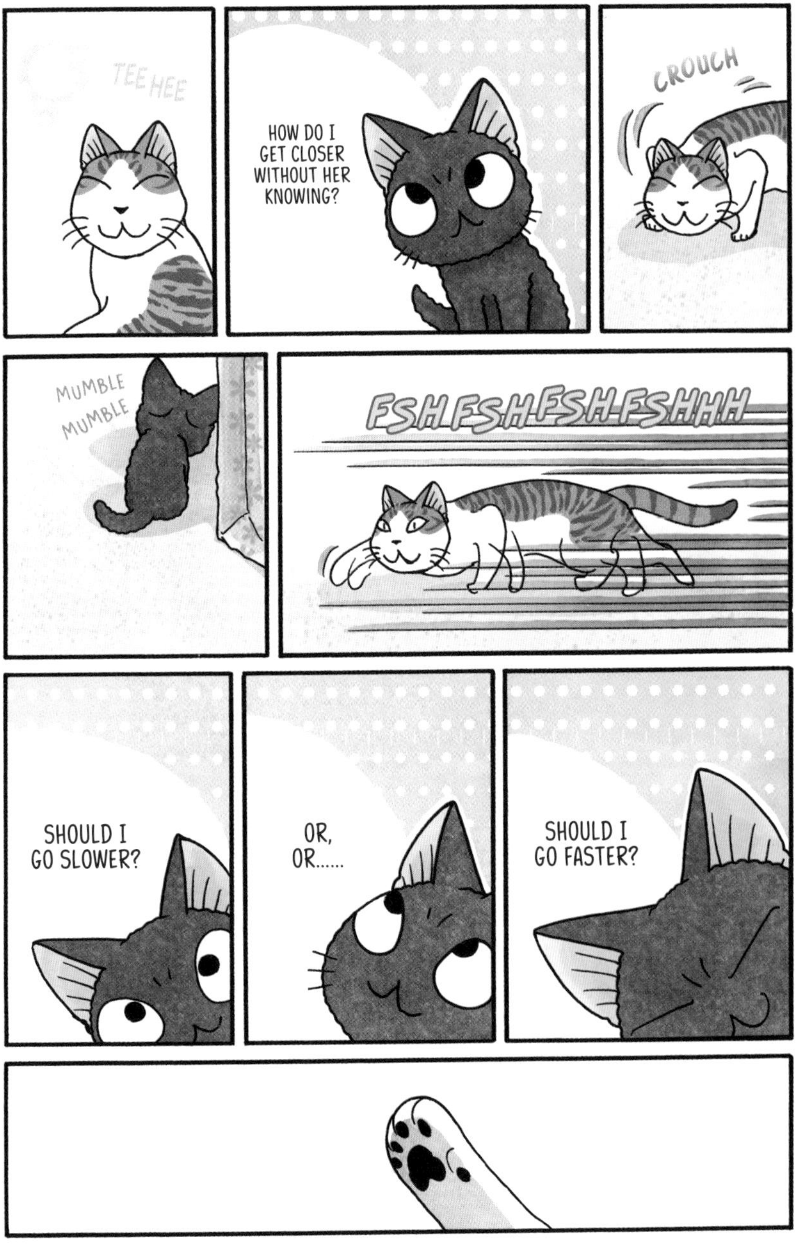
TEE HEE
HOW DO I GET CLOSER WITHOUT HER KNOWING?
CROUCH
MUMBLE MUMBLE
FSHFSHFSHFSHHH
SHOULD I GO SLOWER?
OR, OR......
SHOULD I GO FASTER?

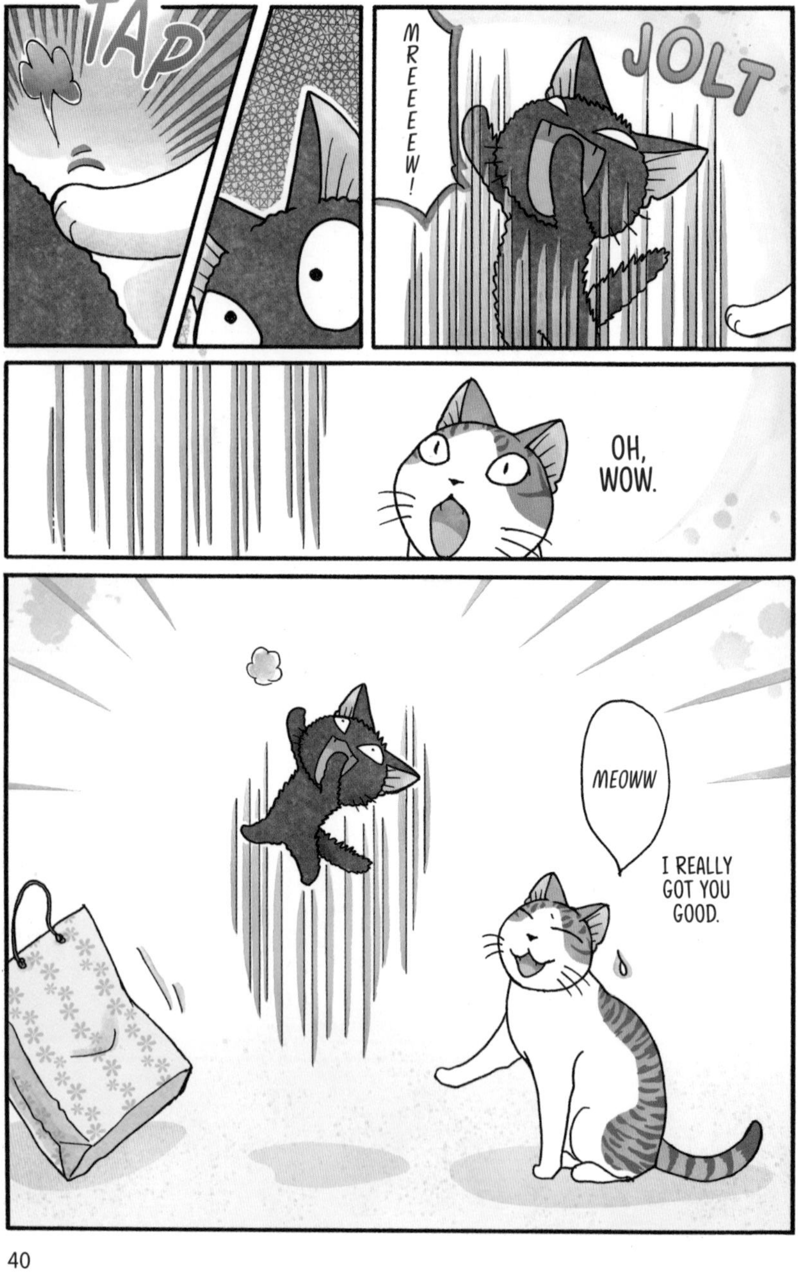
JOLT
MREEEEEW!
TAP
OH, WOW.
I REALLY GOT YOU GOOD.
MEOWW

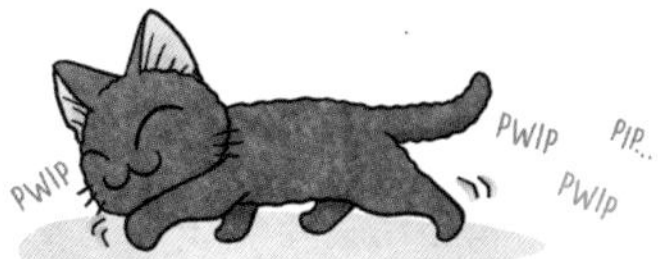
PWIP
PWIP
PIP...
PWIP

Sue & Tai-chan

CHAPTER 58 Sue Trying Her Best

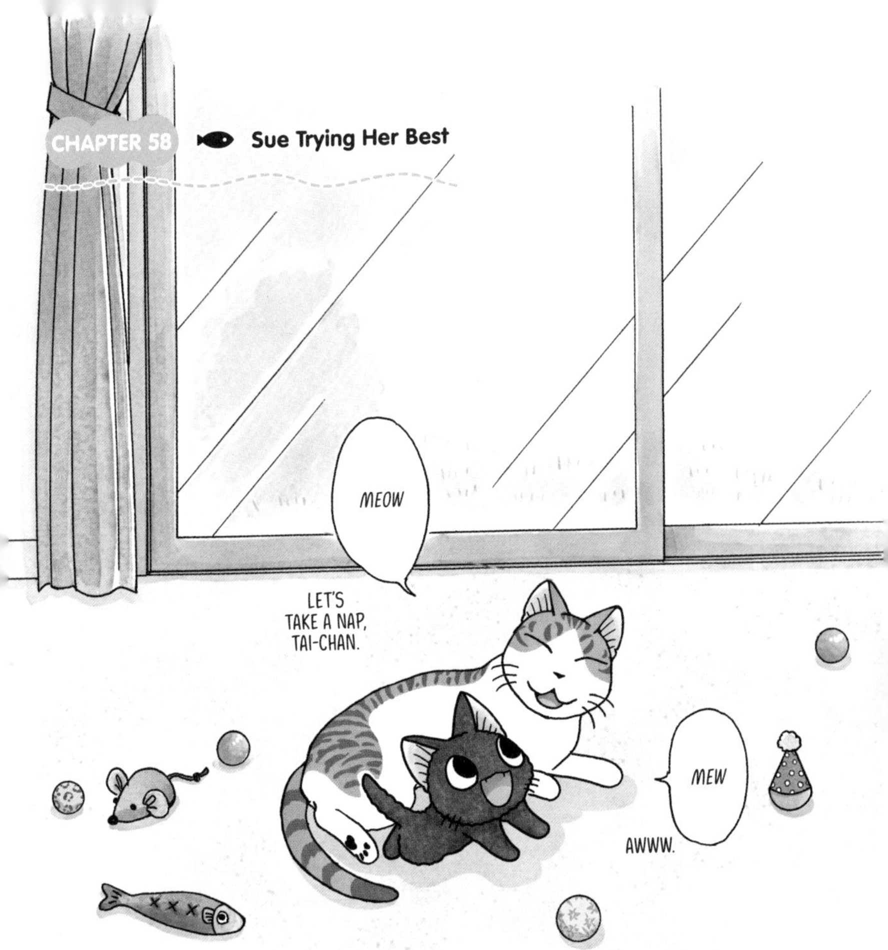
MEOW
LET'S TAKE A NAP, TAI-CHAN.
MEW
AWWW.

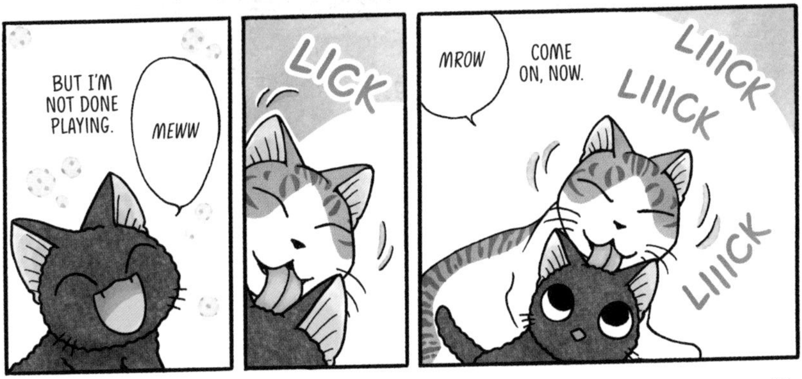
BUT I'M NOT DONE PLAYING.
MEWW
LICK
MROW
COME ON, NOW.
LIIICK
LIIICK
LIIICK

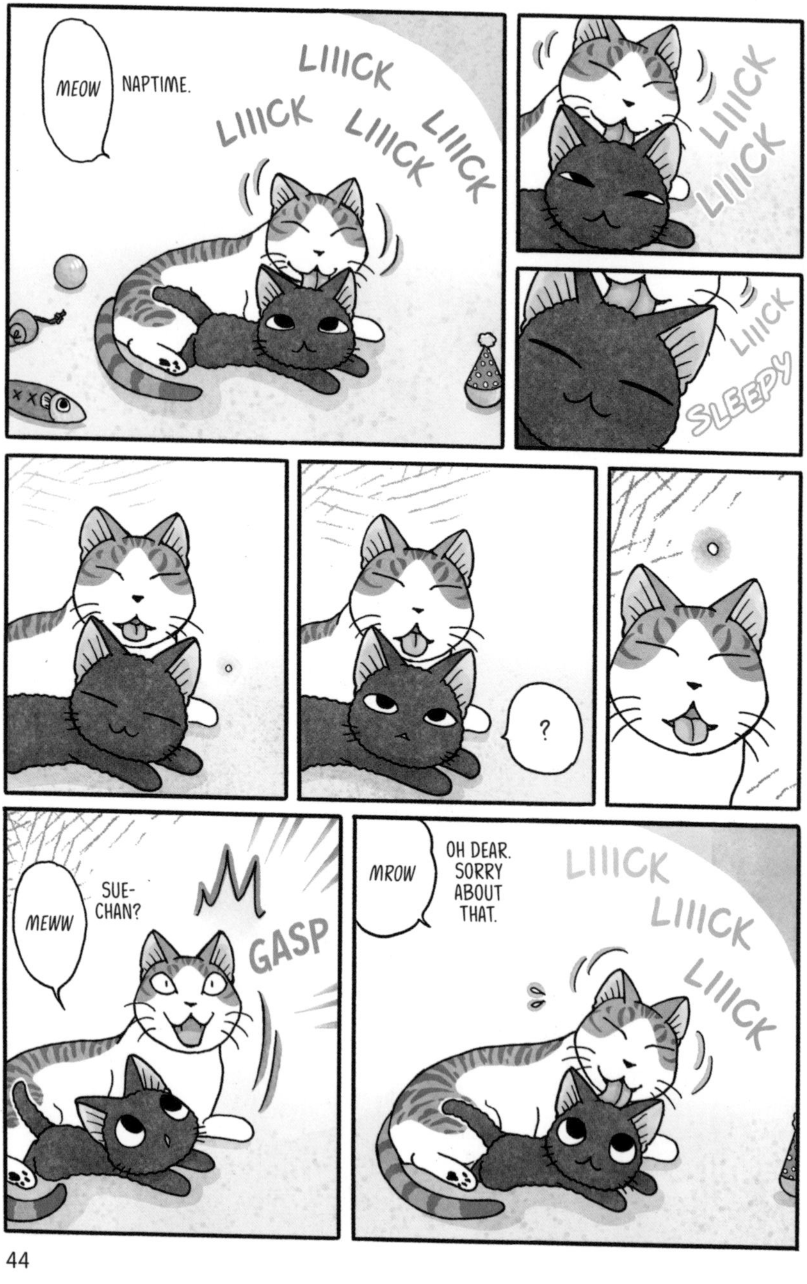
MEOW
NAPTIME.
LIIICK
LIIICK
LIIICK
LIIICK
LIIICK
LIIICK
LIIICK
SLEEPY
?
MEWW
SUE-CHAN?
GASP
MROW
OH DEAR. SORRY ABOUT THAT.
LIIICK
LIIICK
LIIICK

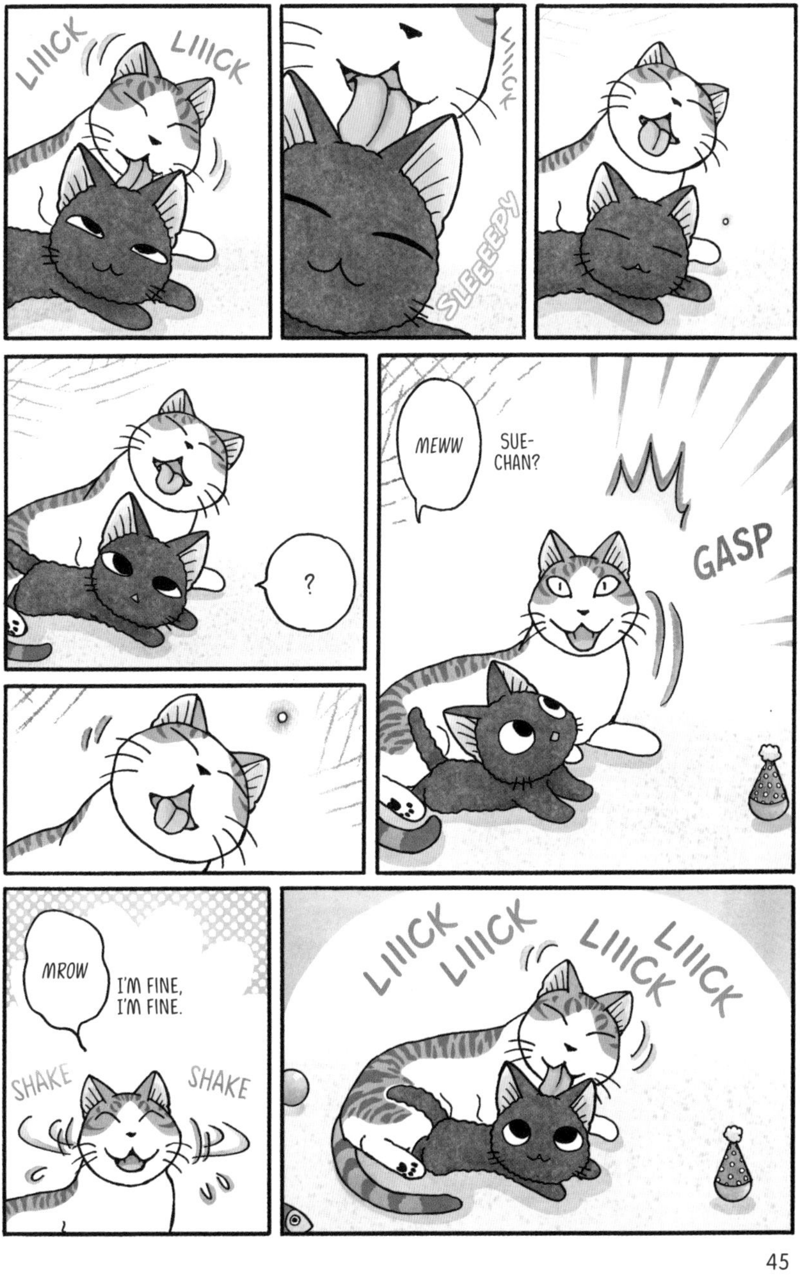
LIIICK
LIIICK
LIIICK
SLEEEEPY
?
MEWW
SUE-CHAN?
GASP
MROW
I'M FINE, I'M FINE.
SHAKE
SHAKE
LIIICK
LIIICK
LIIICK
LIIICK

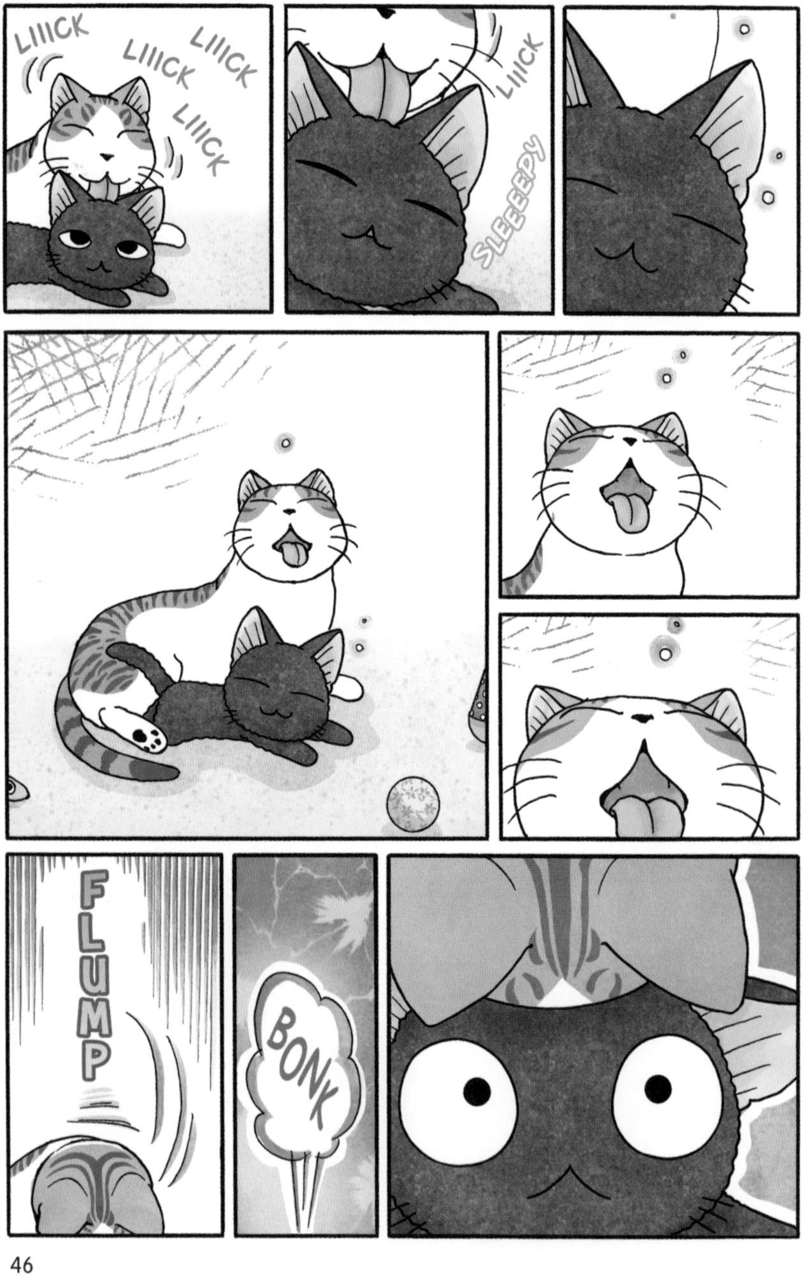
LIIICK
SLEEEEPY
LIIICK
LIIICK
LIIICK
LIIICK
BONK
FLUMP

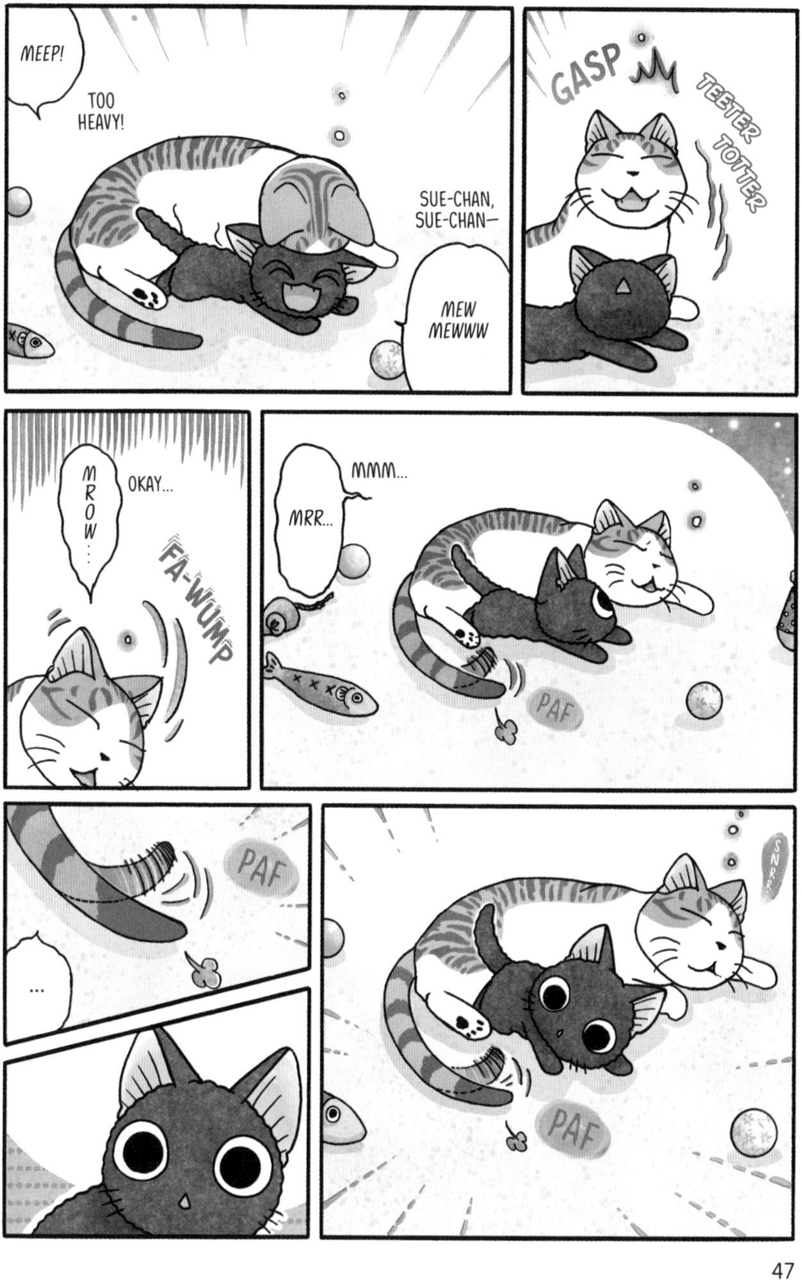
MEEP!
TOO HEAVY!
SUE-CHAN, SUE-CHAN—
MEW MEWWW
GASP
TEETER TOTTER
MROW...
OKAY...
FA-WUMP
MRR...
MMM...
PAF
PAF
...
SNRR
PAF

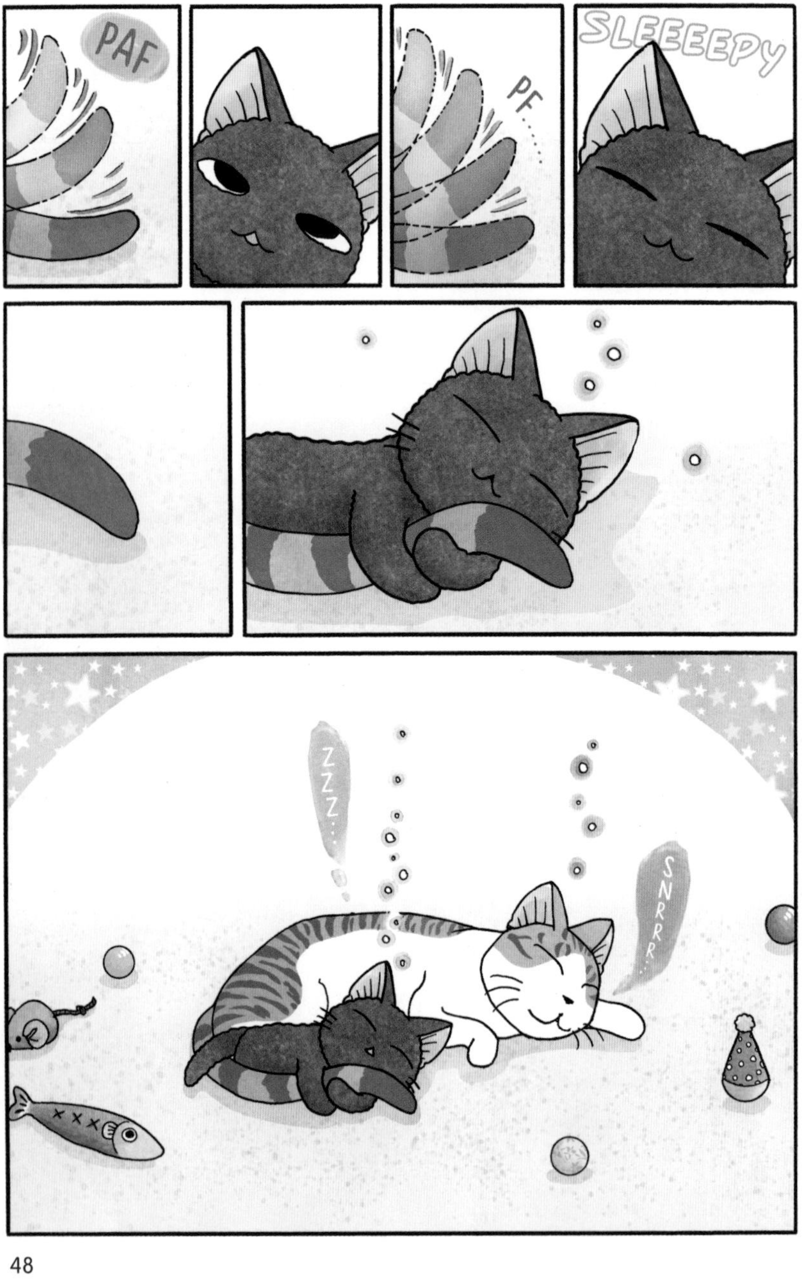
SLEEEEPy
PF...
PAF
SNRRR...
ZZZ...

CHAPTER 59 Happy Santa!

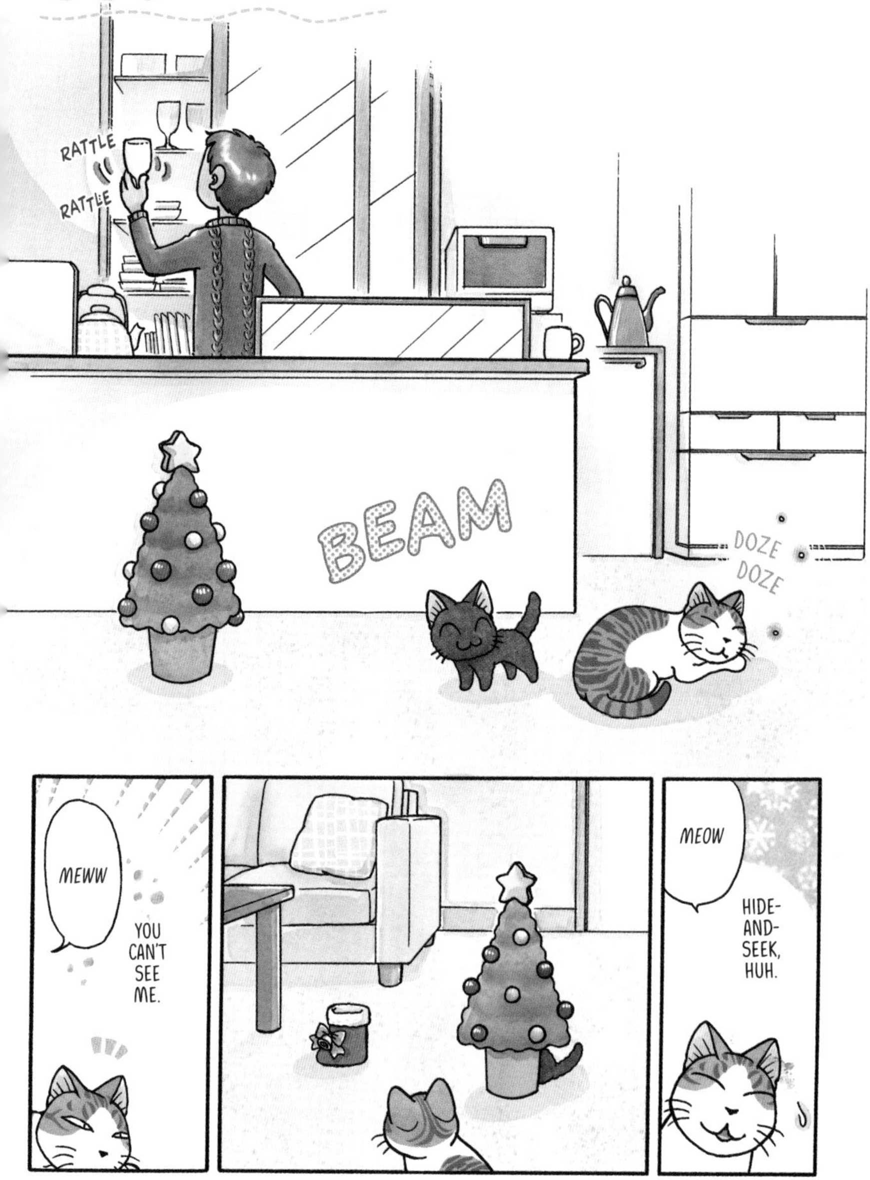
RATTLE
RATTLE
BEAM
DOZE
DOZE
MEWW
YOU CAN'T SEE ME.
MEOW
HIDE-AND-SEEK, HUH.

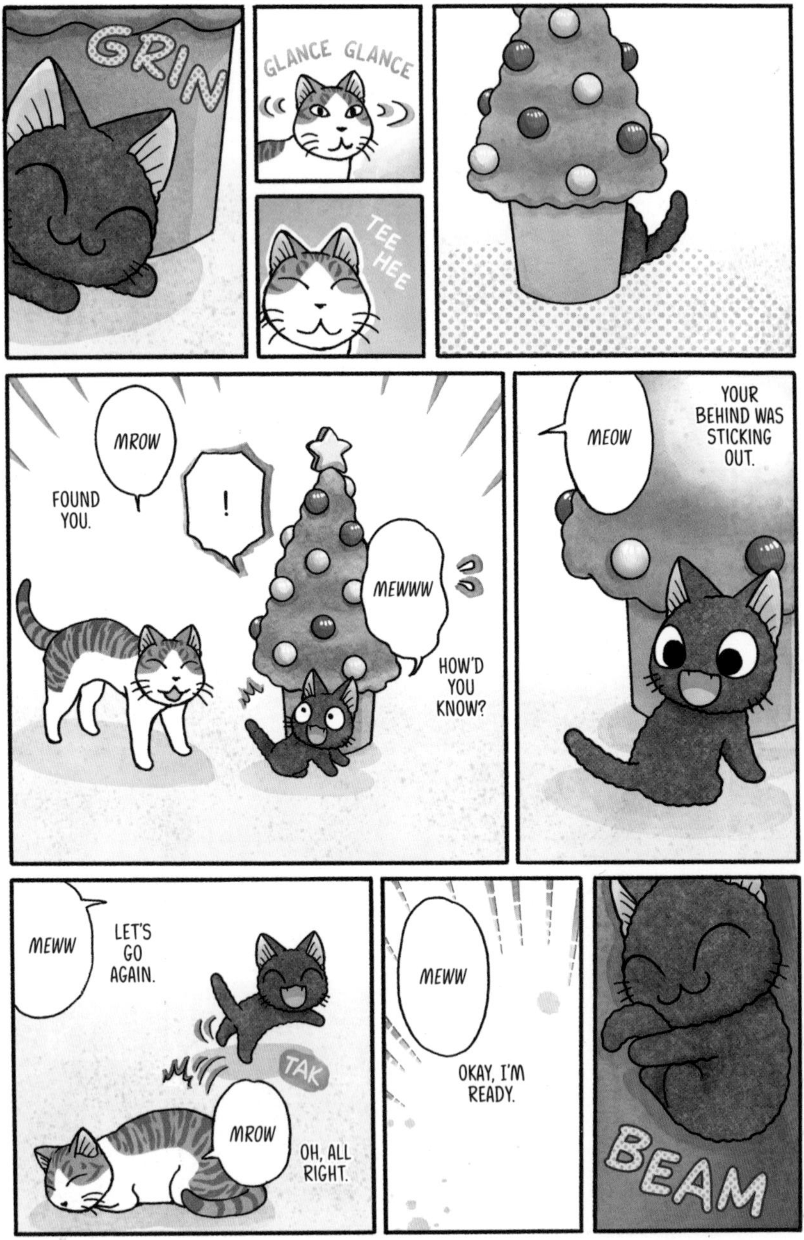
GRIN
GLANCE GLANCE
TEE HEE
MROW
FOUND YOU.
!
MEWWW
HOW'D YOU KNOW?
MEOW
YOUR BEHIND WAS STICKING OUT.
MEWW
LET'S GO AGAIN.
TAK
MROW
OH, ALL RIGHT.
MEWW
OKAY, I'M READY.
BEAM

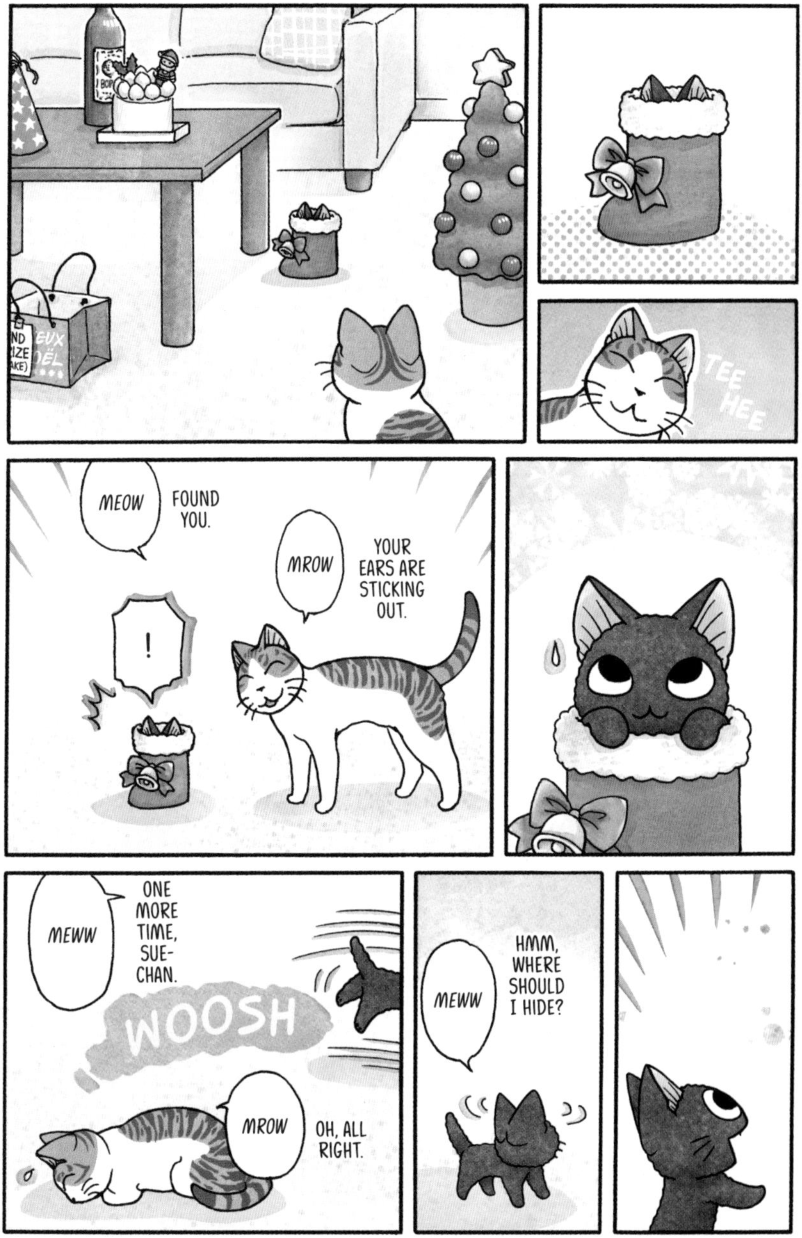
TEE HEE
MEOW
FOUND YOU.
MROW
YOUR EARS ARE STICKING OUT.
!
MEWW
ONE MORE TIME, SUE-CHAN.
WOOSH
MROW
OH, ALL RIGHT.
MEWW
HMM, WHERE SHOULD I HIDE?

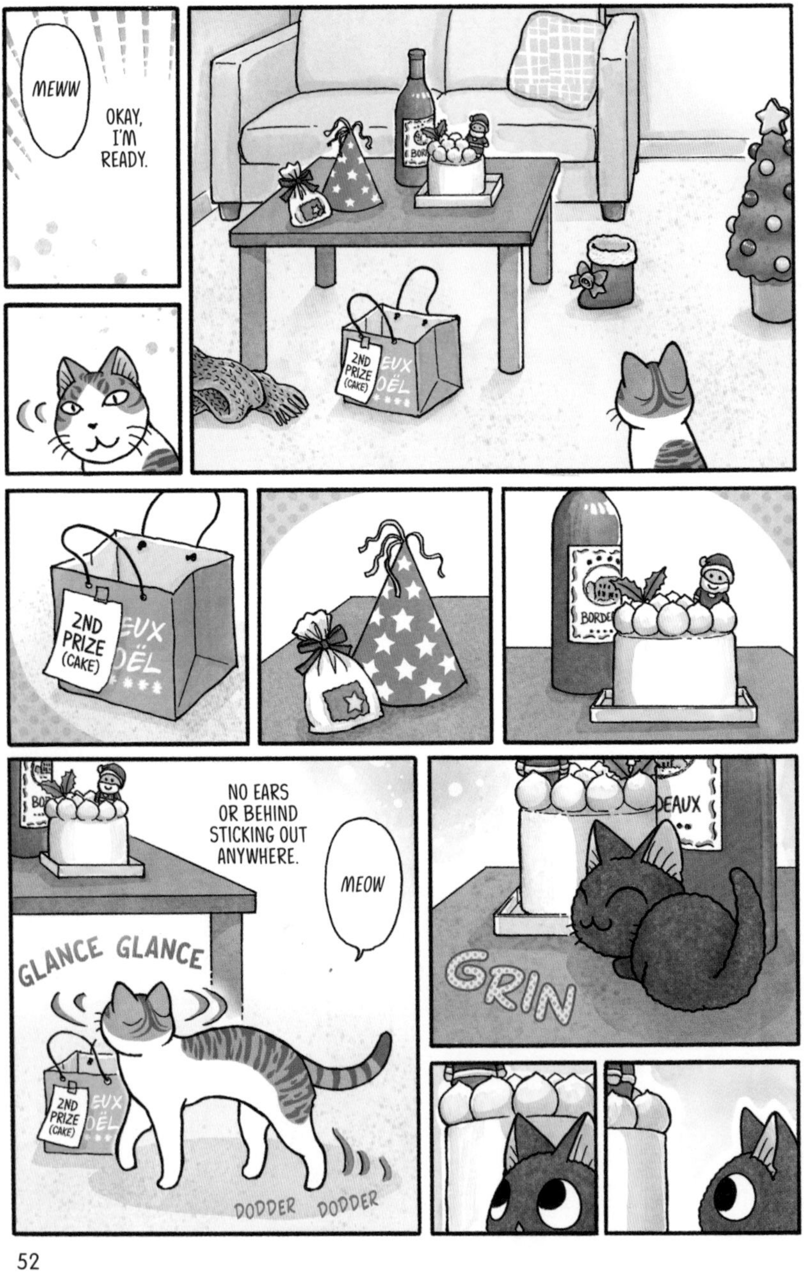
MEWW
OKAY, I'M READY.
2ND PRIZE (CAKE)
NO EARS OR BEHIND STICKING OUT ANYWHERE.
MEOW
GLANCE GLANCE
DODDER DODDER
GRIN

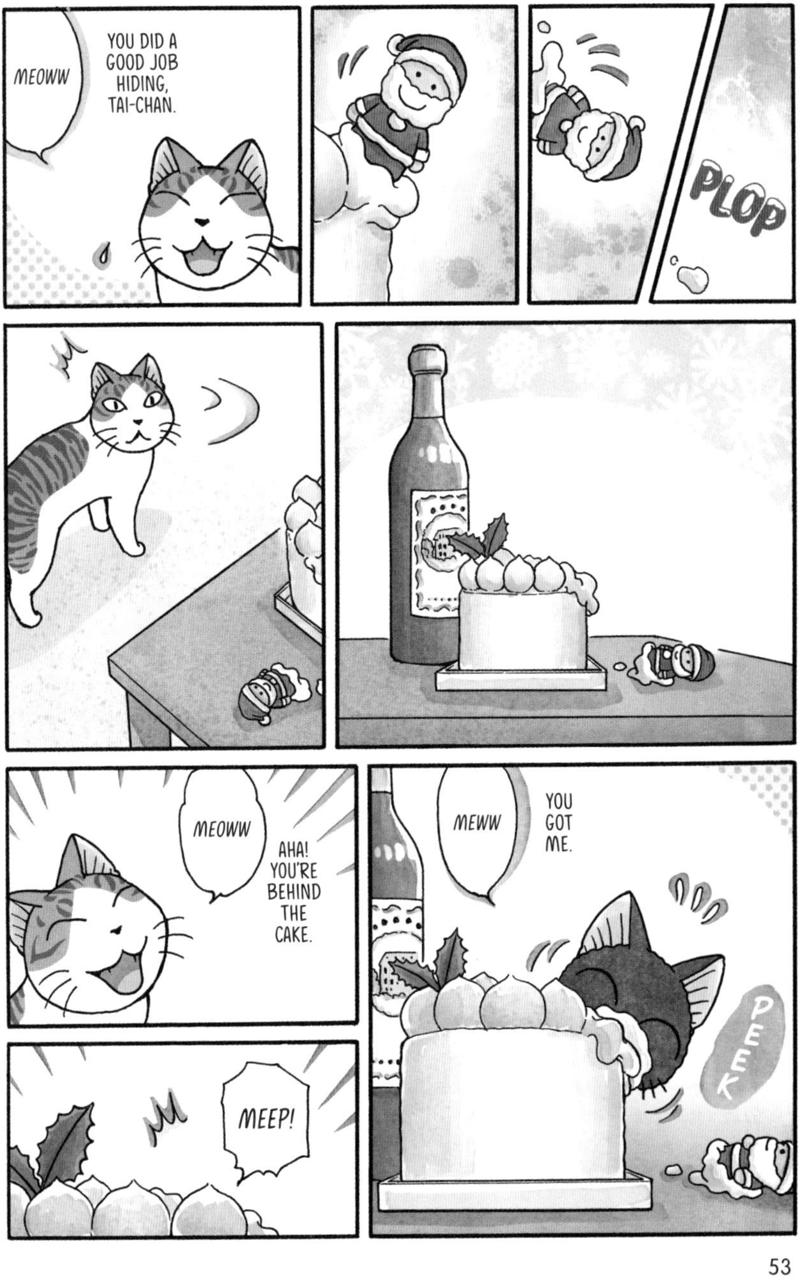
MEOWW
YOU DID A GOOD JOB HIDING, TAI-CHAN.
PLOP
MEOWW
AHA! YOU'RE BEHIND THE CAKE.
MEEP!
MEWW
YOU GOT ME.
PEEK

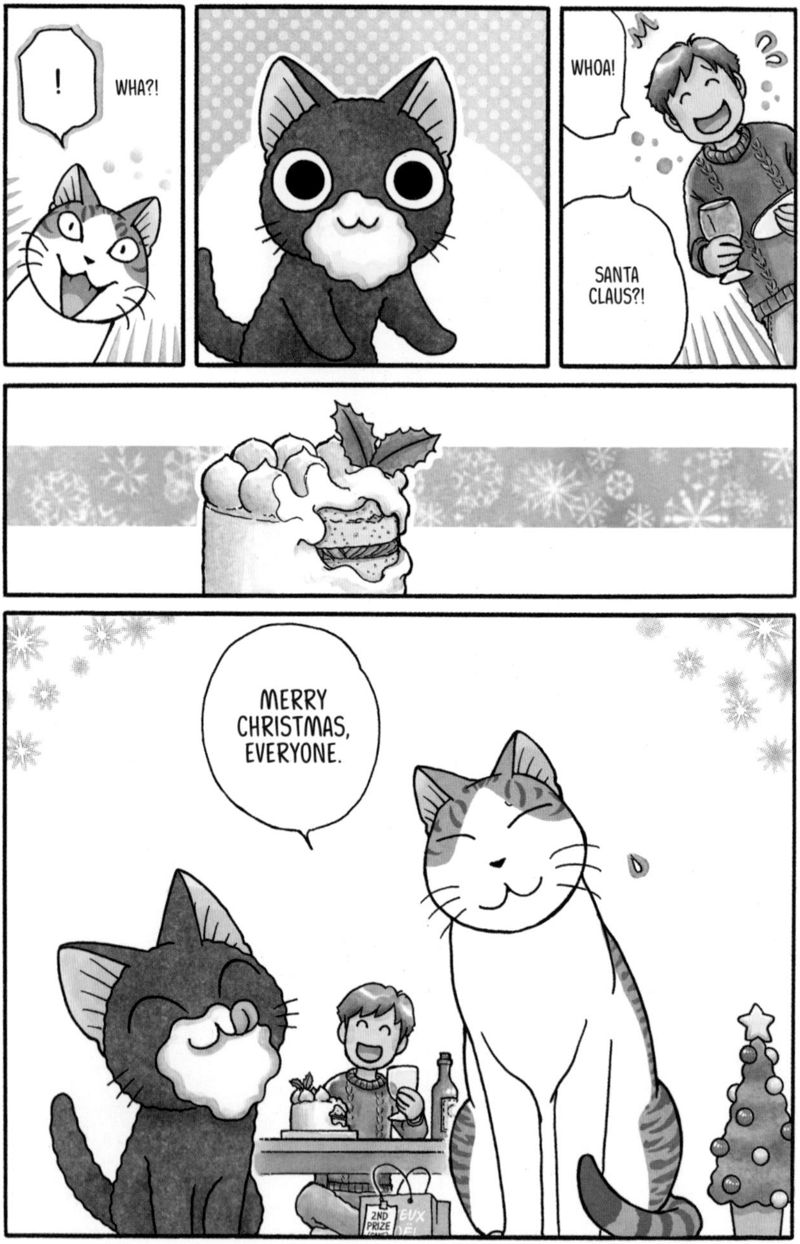
!
WHA?!
WHOA!
SANTA CLAUS?!
MERRY CHRISTMAS, EVERYONE.
2ND PRIZE

CHAPTER 60 Winter for Kittens

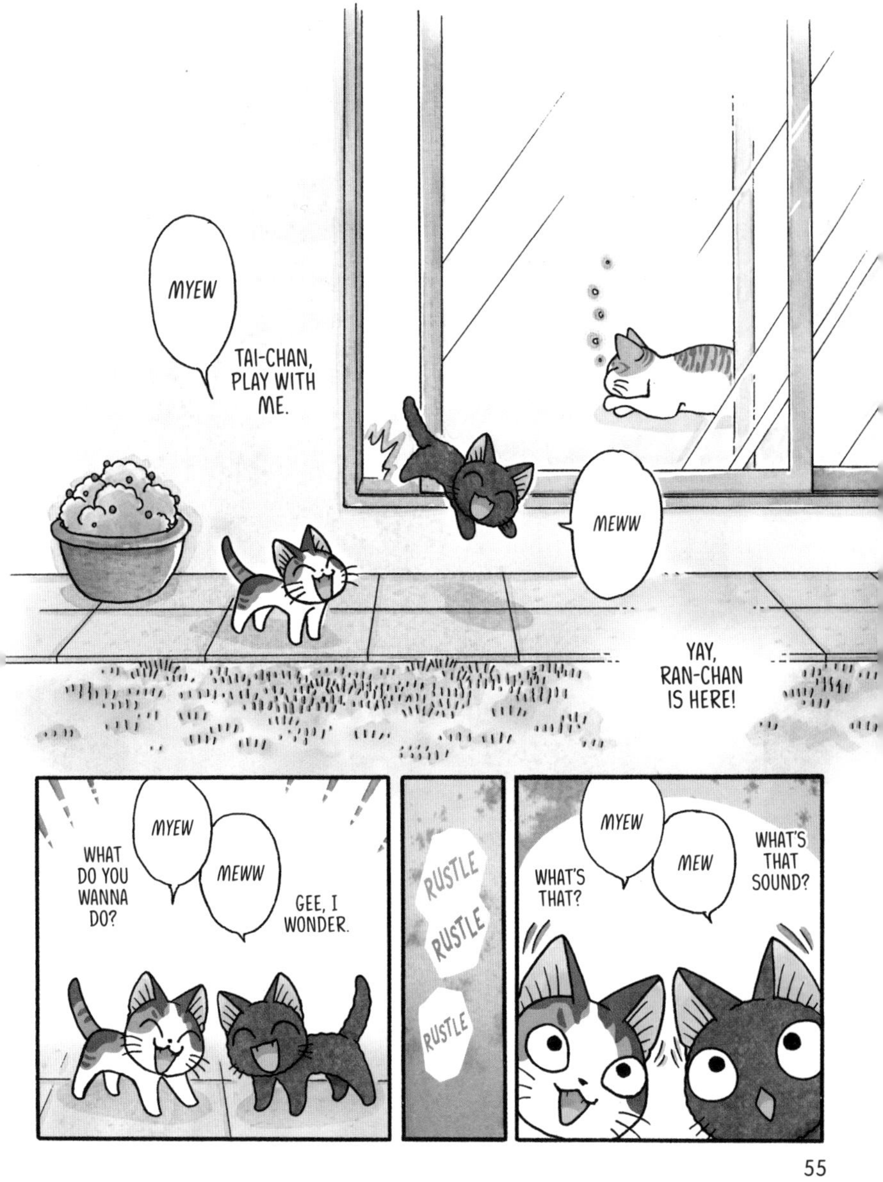
MYEW
TAI-CHAN, PLAY WITH ME.
MEWW
YAY, RAN-CHAN IS HERE!
MYEW
WHAT DO YOU WANNA DO?
MEWW
GEE, I WONDER.
RUSTLE
RUSTLE
RUSTLE
MYEW
WHAT'S THAT?
MEW
WHAT'S THAT SOUND?

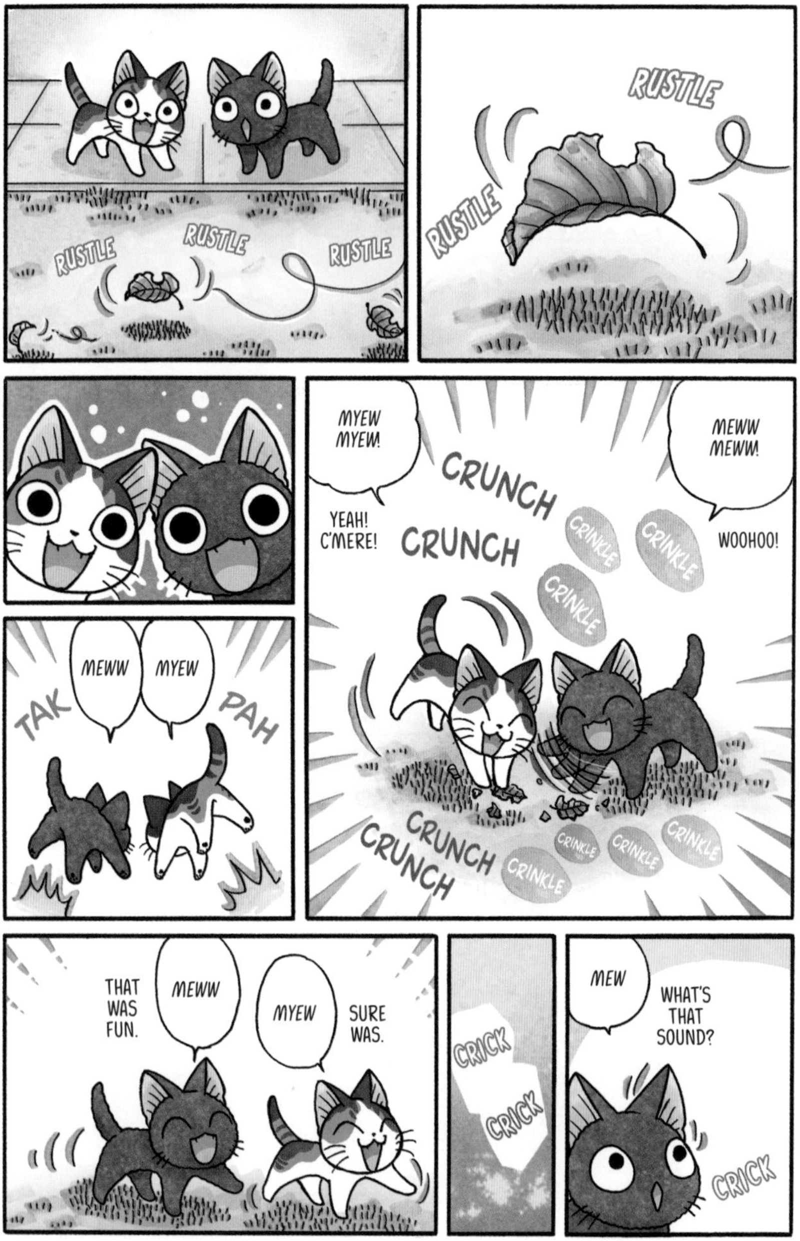
RUSTLE
RUSTLE
RUSTLE
RUSTLE
RUSTLE
MYEW MYEW!
YEAH! C'MERE!
MEWW MEWW!
WOOHOO!
CRUNCH
CRUNCH
CRINKLE
CRINKLE
CRINKLE
CRUNCH
CRUNCH
CRINKLE
CRINKLE
CRINKLE
CRINKLE
TAK
MEWW
MYEW
PAH
THAT WAS FUN.
MEWW
MYEW
SURE WAS.
CRICK
CRICK
MEW
WHAT'S THAT SOUND?
CRICK

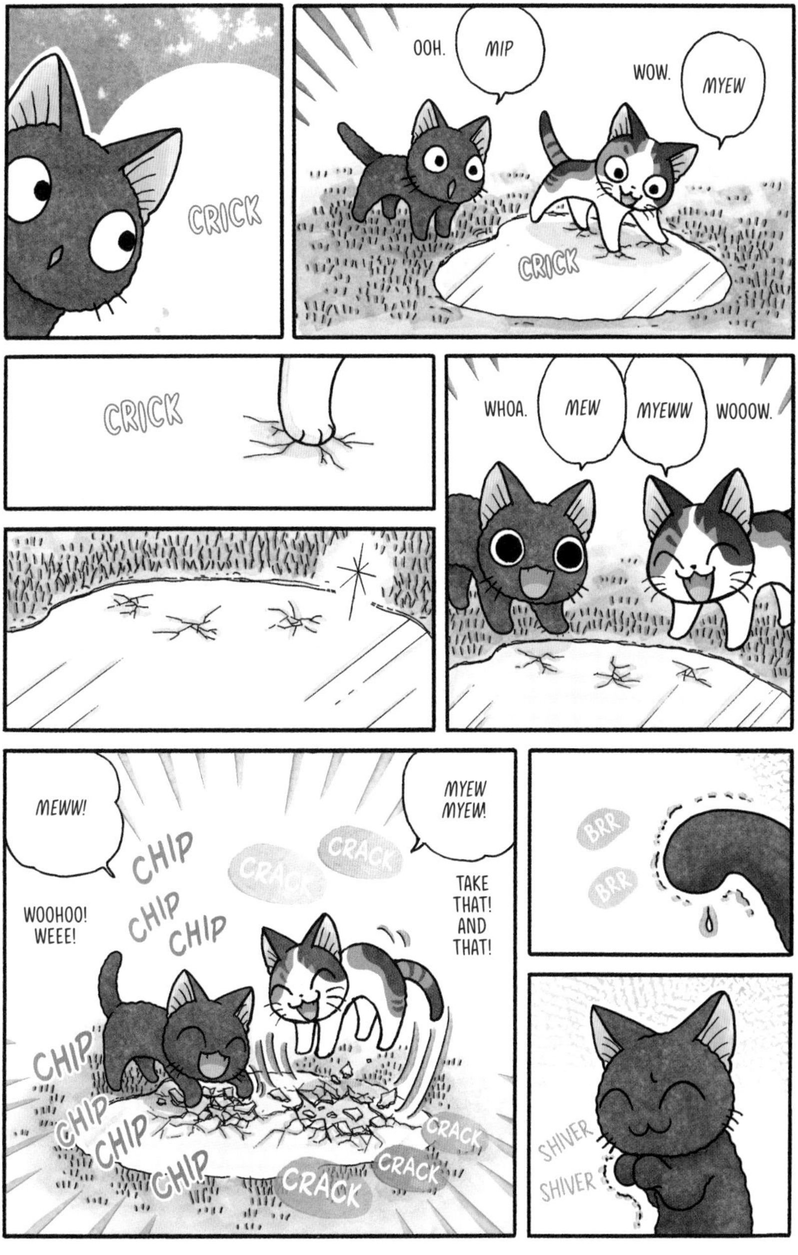
MYEW
WOW.
MIP
OOH.
CRICK
CRICK
WOOOW.
MYEWW
MEW
WHOA.
CRICK
BRR
BRR
SHIVER
SHIVER
MYEW MYEW!
TAKE THAT! AND THAT!
CRACK
CRACK
MEWW!
WOOHOO! WEEE!
CHIP
CHIP
CHIP
CHIP
CHIP
CHIP
CHIP
CRACK
CRACK
CRACK

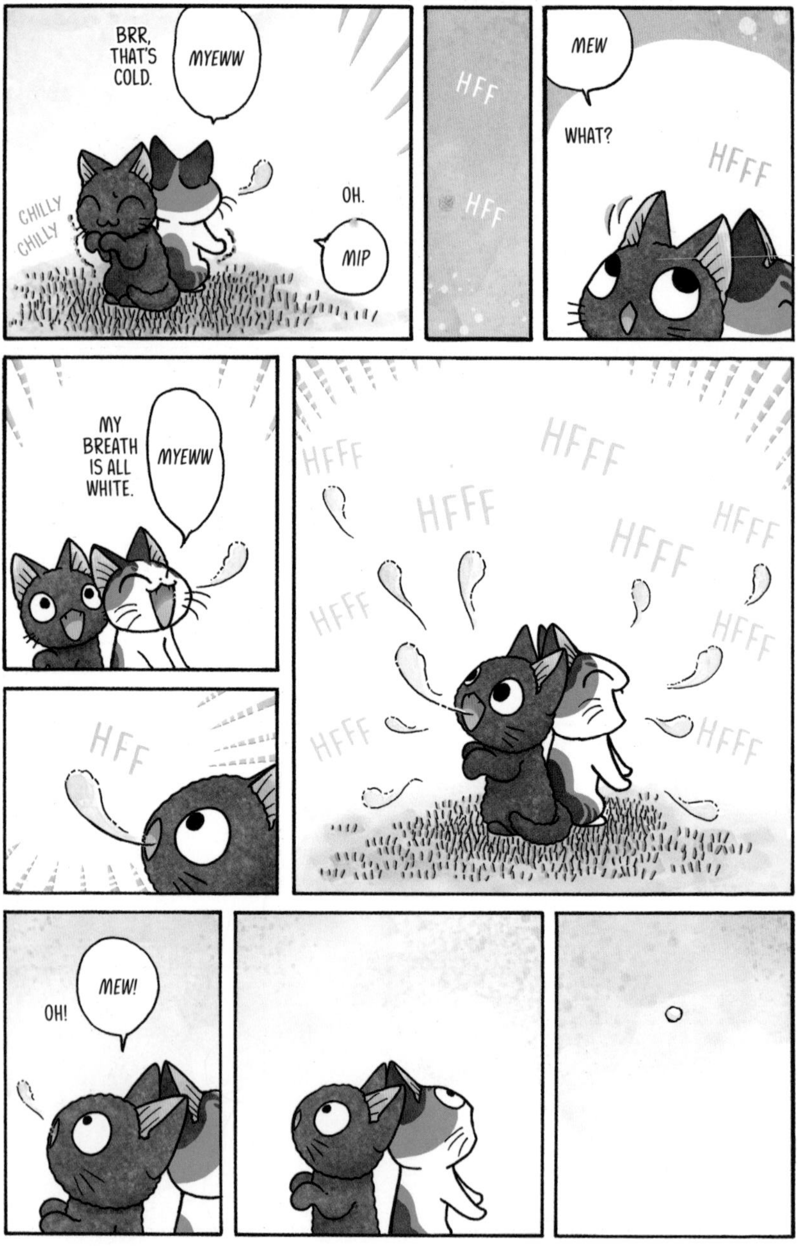
BRR, THAT'S COLD.
MYEWW
CHILLY CHILLY
OH.
MIP
HFF
HFF
MEW
WHAT?
HFFF
MY BREATH IS ALL WHITE.
MYEWW
HFF
HFFF
HFFF
HFFF
HFFF
HFFF
HFFF
HFFF
HFFF
HFFF
MEW!
OH!

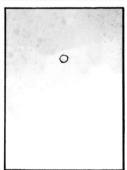

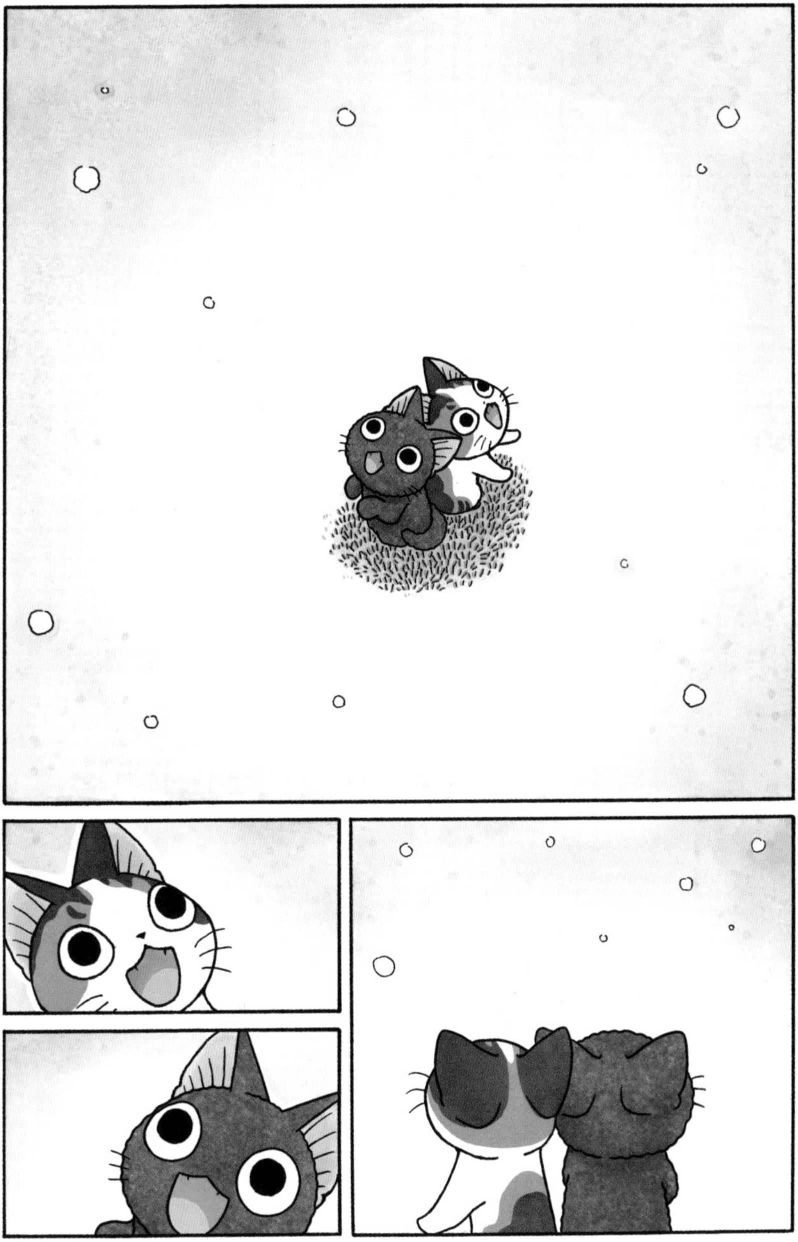

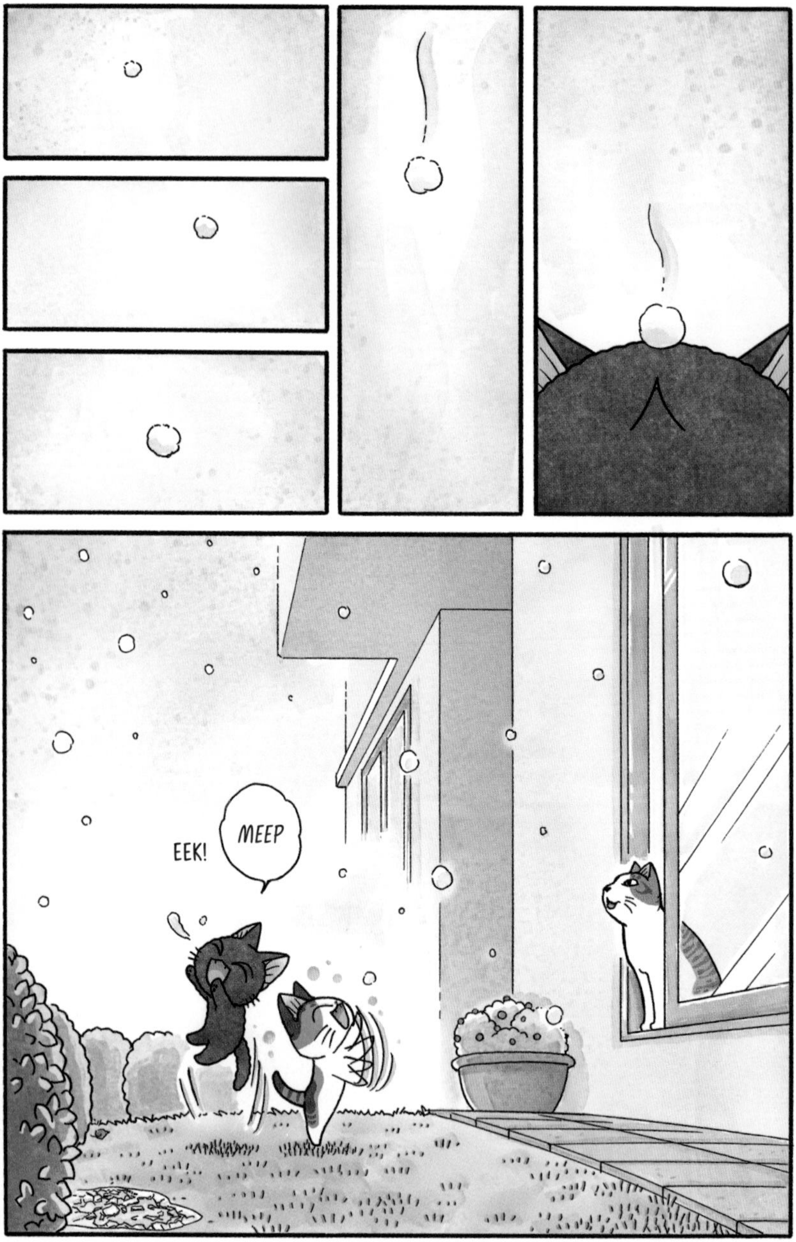
MEEP
EEK!

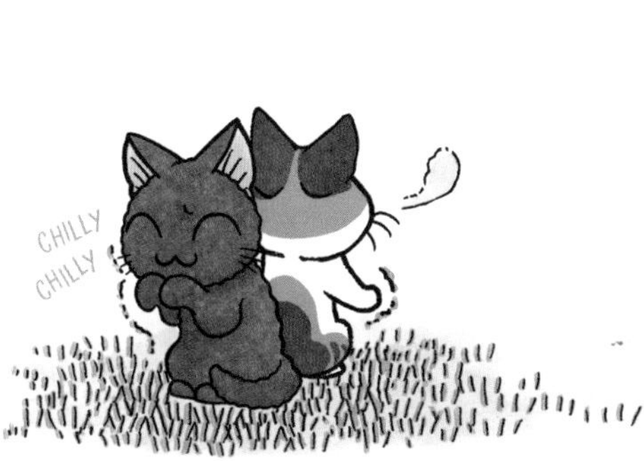
CHILLY
CHILLY

Sue & Tai-chan

CHAPTER 61 Kittens Are Tough

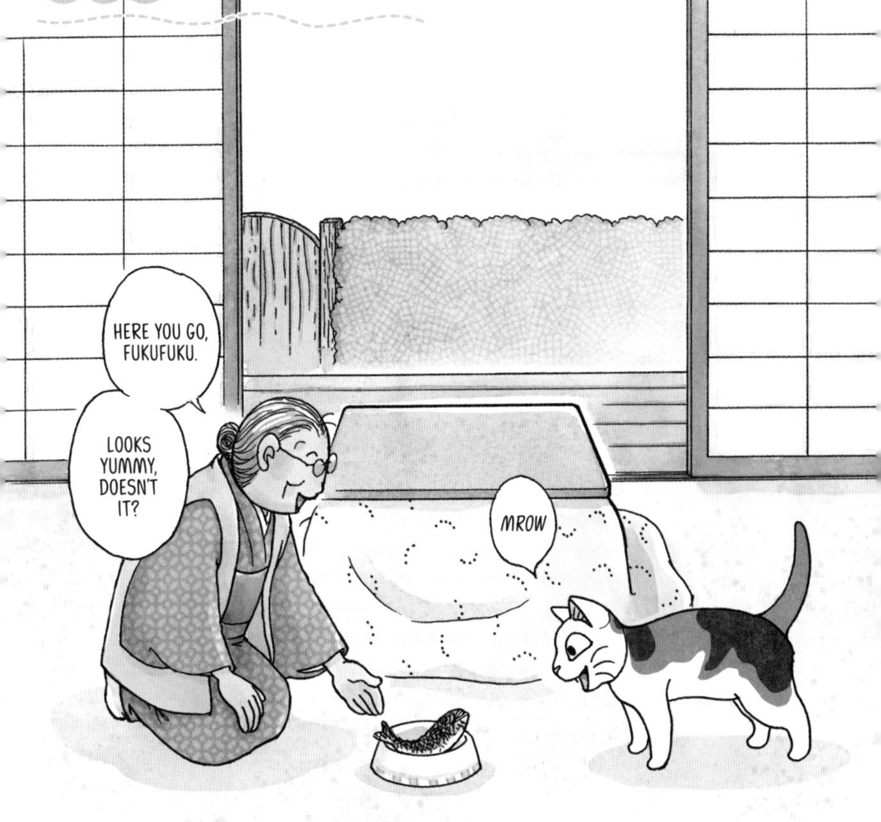
HERE YOU GO, FUKUFUKU.
LOOKS YUMMY, DOESN'T IT?
MROW

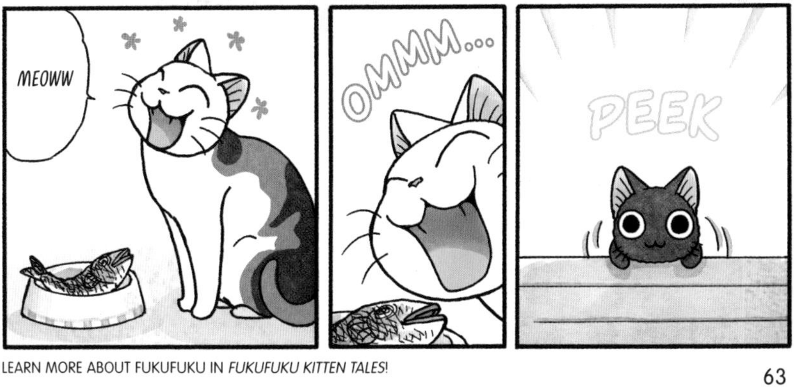
MEOWW
OMMM...
PEEK

LEARN MORE ABOUT FUKUFUKU IN *FUKUFUKU KITTEN TALES*!

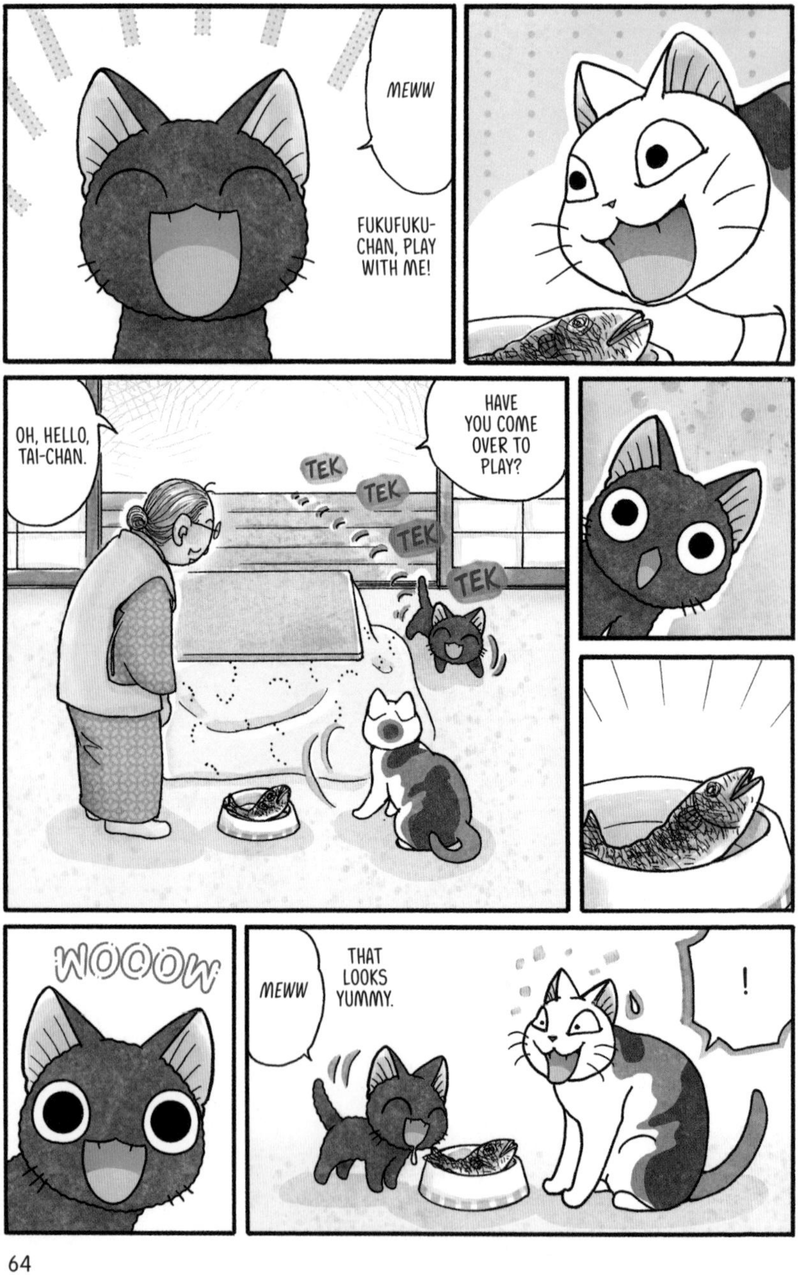
MEWW
FUKUFUKU-CHAN, PLAY WITH ME!
OH, HELLO, TAI-CHAN.
HAVE YOU COME OVER TO PLAY?
TEK
TEK
TEK
TEK
WOOOW
MEWW
THAT LOOKS YUMMY.
!

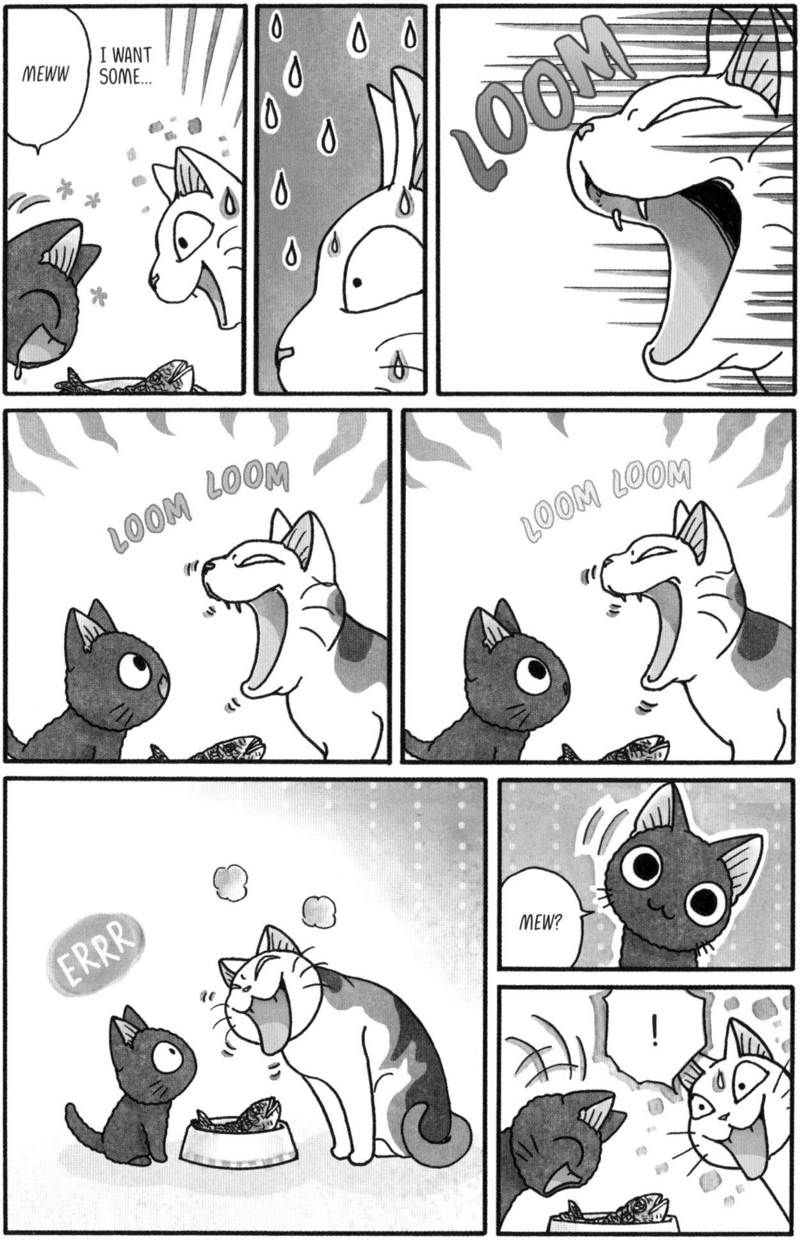
LOOM
I WANT SOME...
MEWW
LOOM LOOM
LOOM LOOM
MEW?
!
ERRR

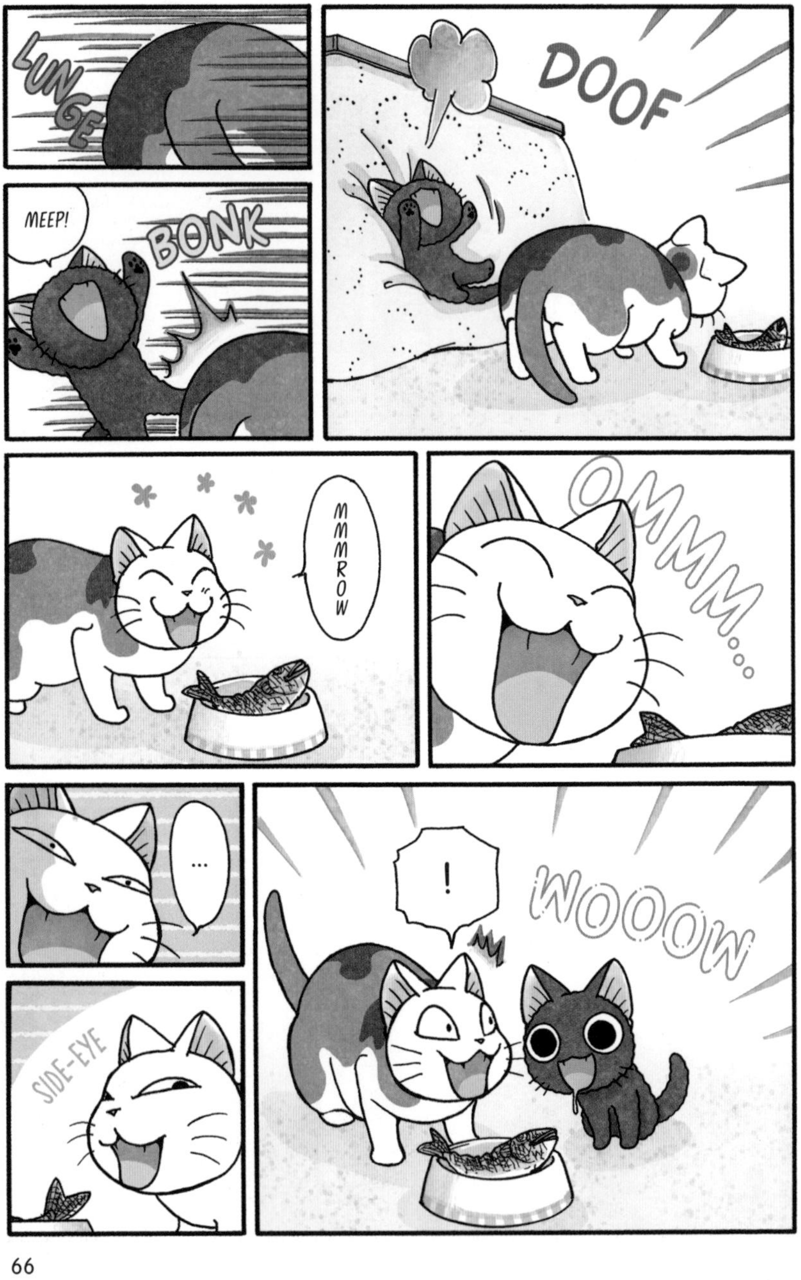
LUNGE
MEEP!
BONK
DOOF
MMMROW
OMMMM...
...
SIDE-EYE
!
WOOOW

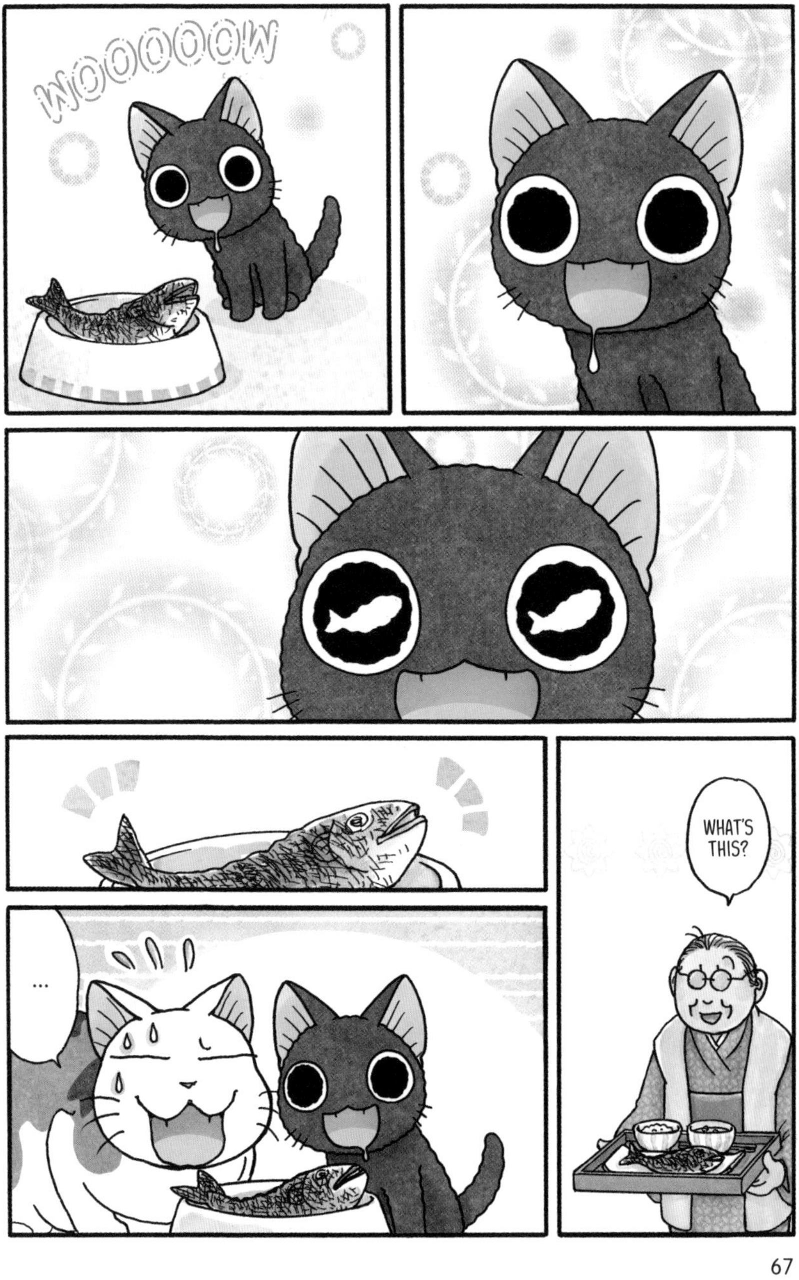
WOOOOOW
WHAT'S THIS?
...

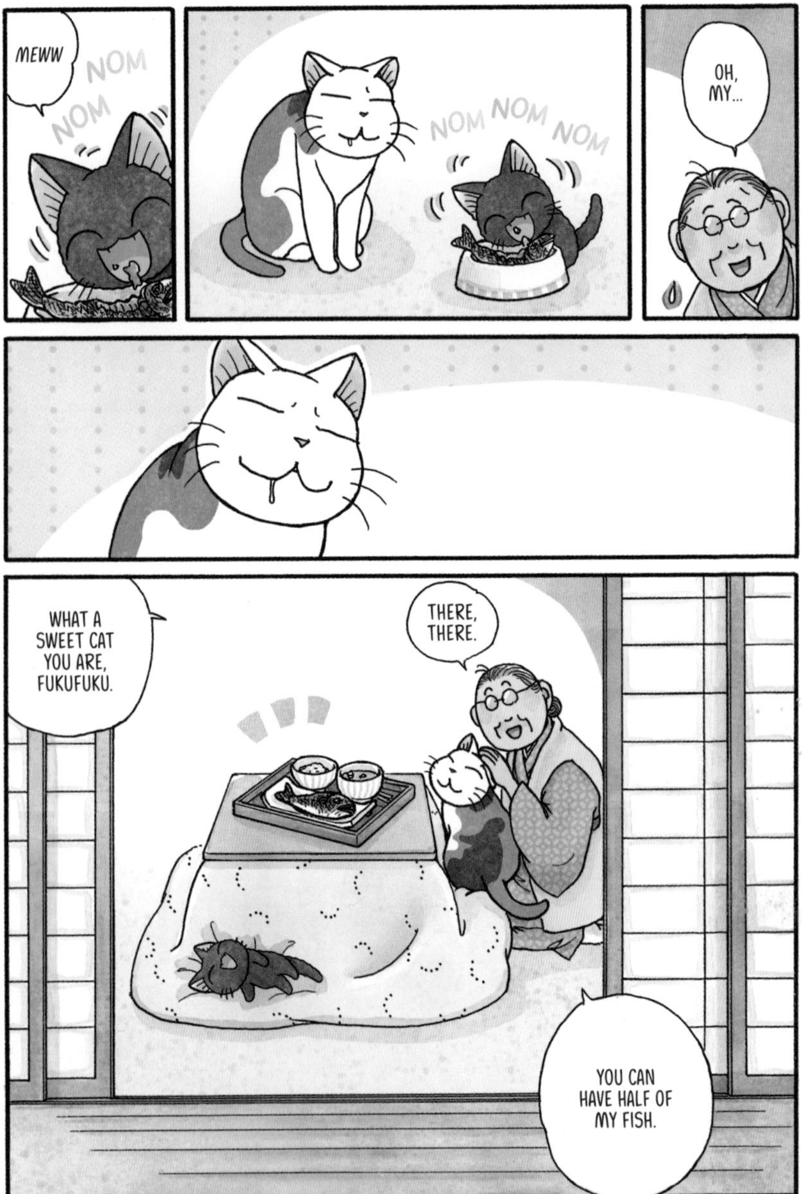
OH, MY...
NOM NOM NOM
MEWW
NOM NOM
THERE, THERE.
WHAT A SWEET CAT YOU ARE, FUKUFUKU.
YOU CAN HAVE HALF OF MY FISH.

CHAPTER 62 Treasure Hunter ☆

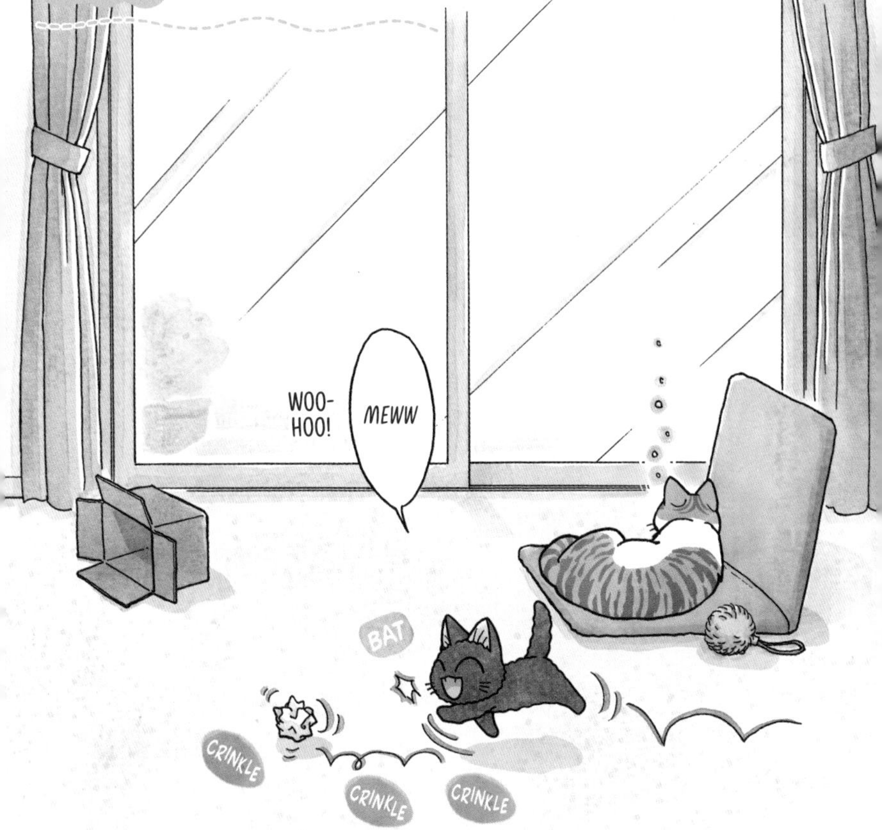
MEWW
WOO-HOO!
BAT
CRINKLE
CRINKLE
CRINKLE

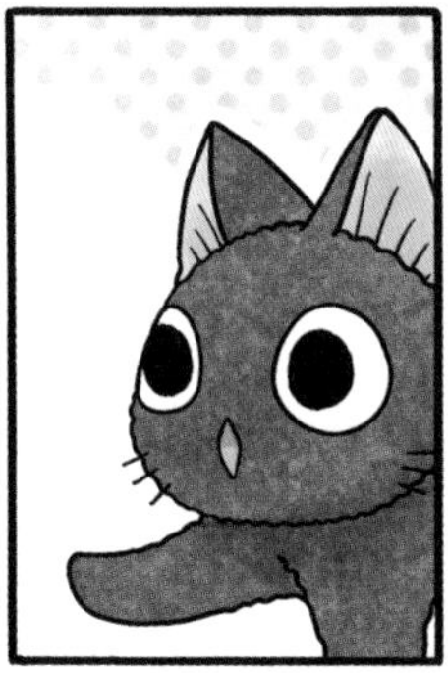

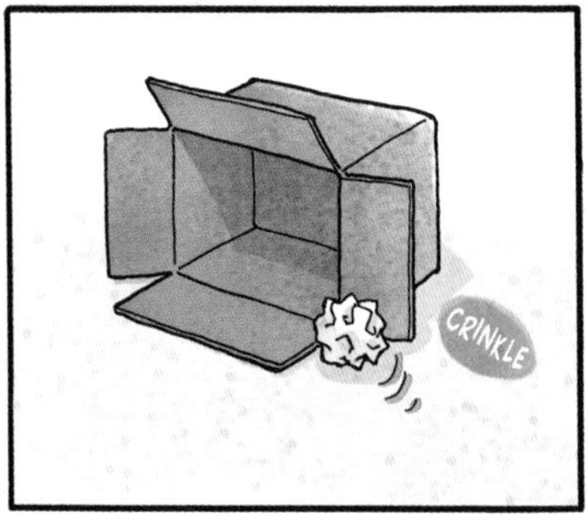
CRINKLE

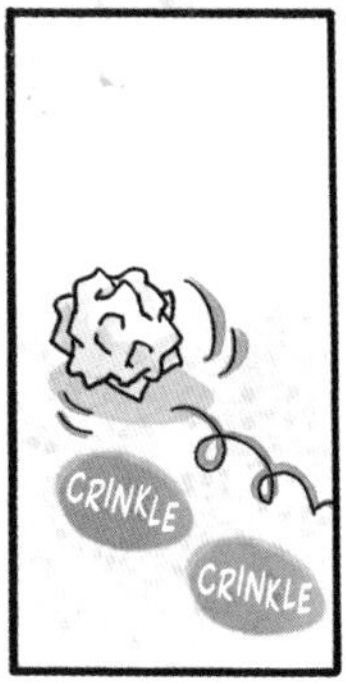
CRINKLE
CRINKLE

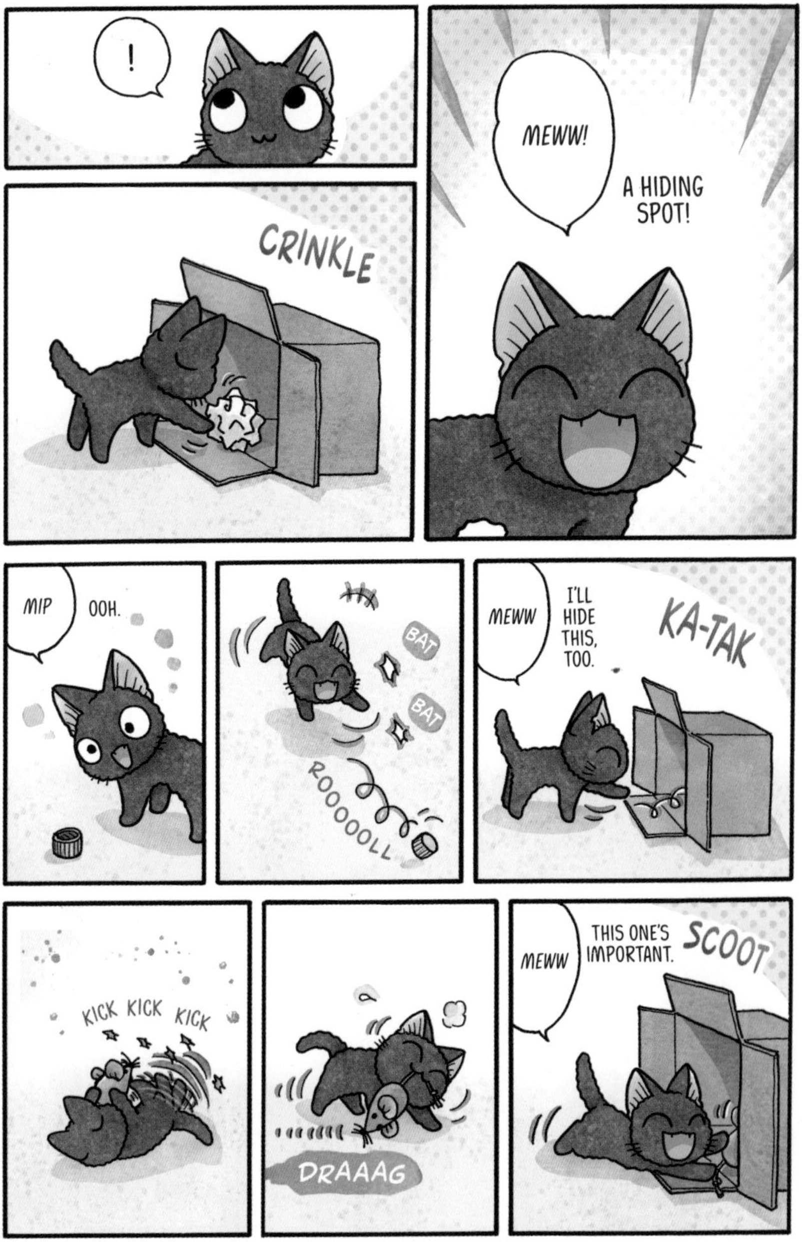
!
MEWW!
A HIDING SPOT!
CRINKLE
MIP
OOH.
BAT
BAT
ROOOOOLL
MEWW
I'LL HIDE THIS, TOO.
KA-TAK
KICK KICK KICK
DRAAAG
MEWW
THIS ONE'S IMPORTANT.
SCOOT

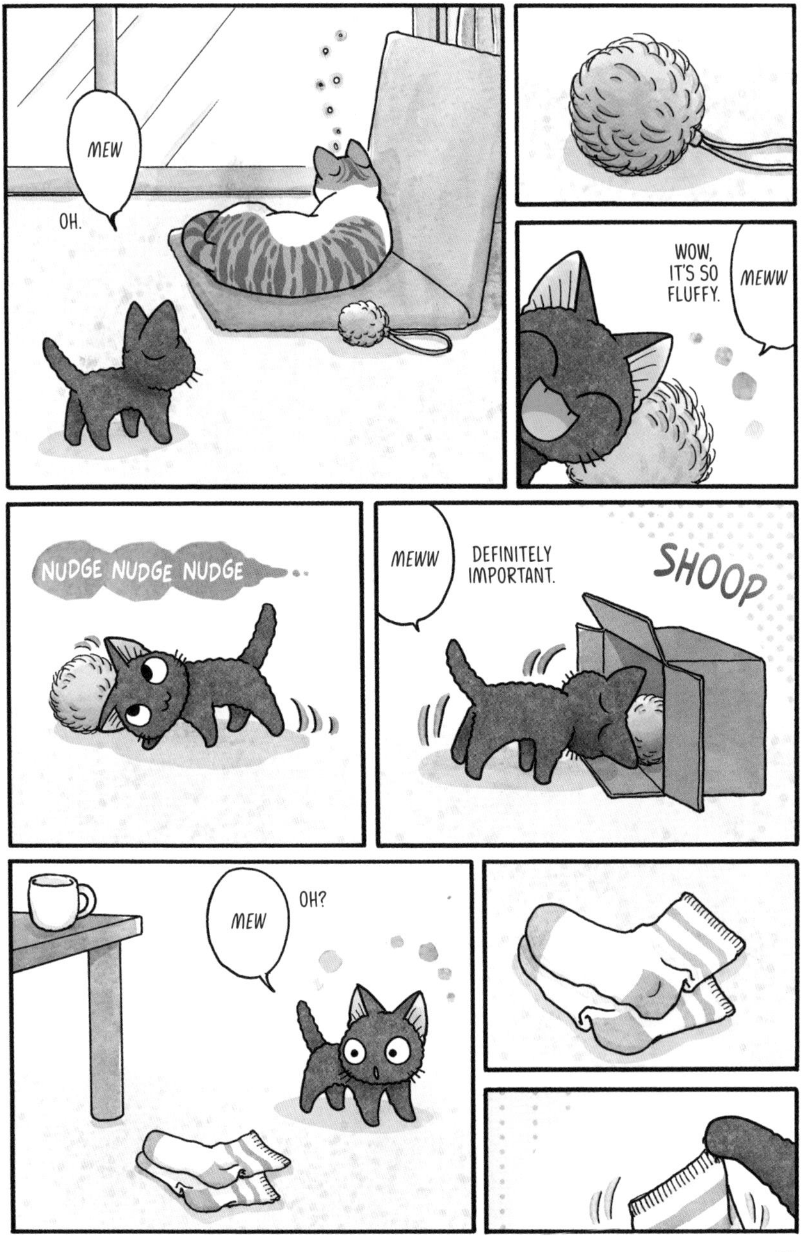
MEW
OH.
WOW, IT'S SO FLUFFY.
MEWW
NUDGE NUDGE NUDGE
MEWW
DEFINITELY IMPORTANT.
SHOOP
MEW
OH?

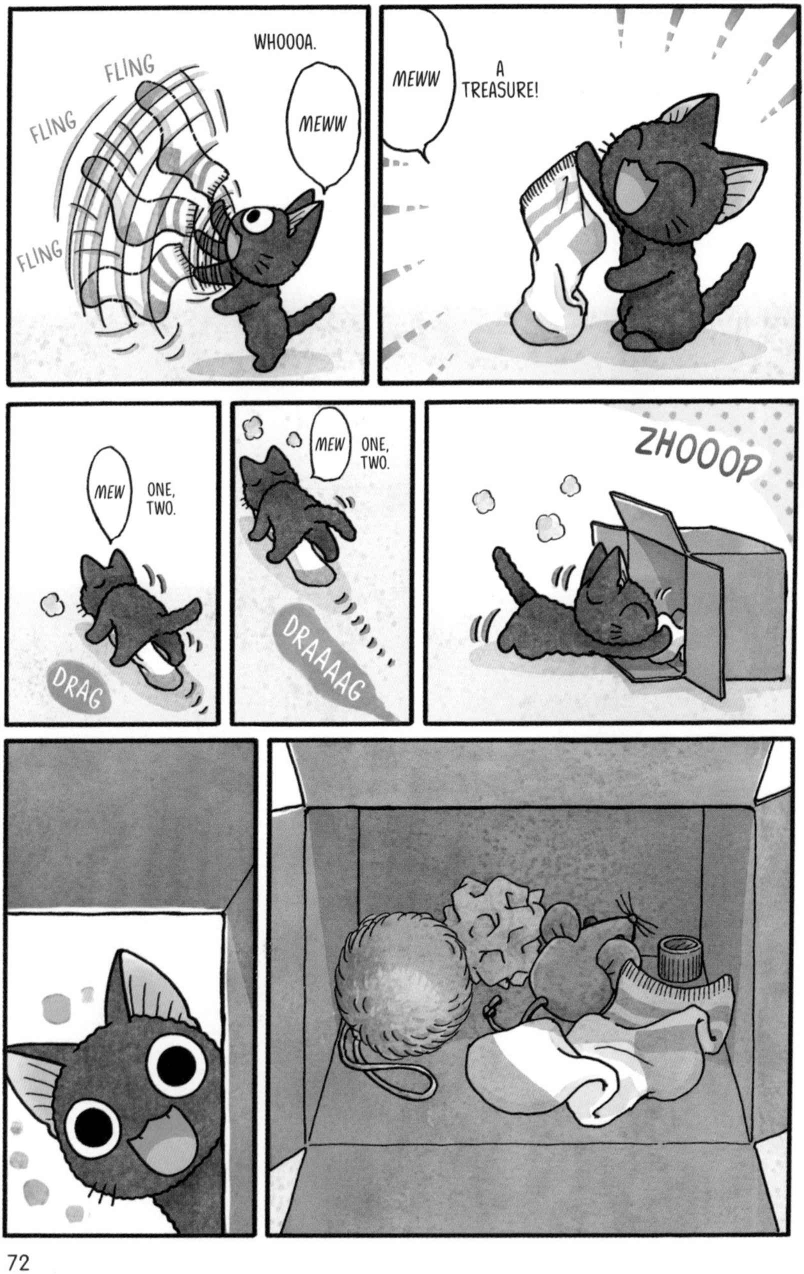
FLING
FLING
FLING
MEWW
WHOOOA.
MEWW
A TREASURE!
MEW
ONE, TWO.
DRAG
MEW
ONE, TWO.
DRAAAAG
ZHOOOP

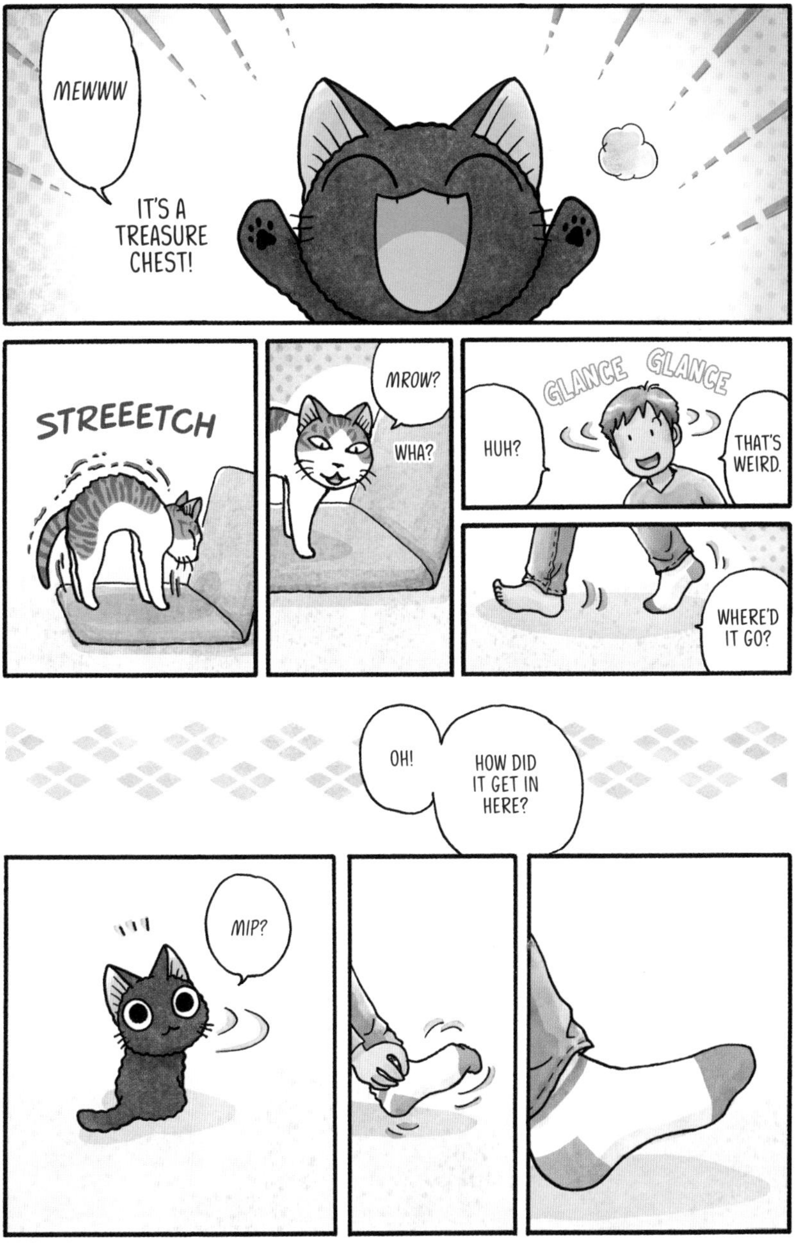
MEWWW
IT'S A TREASURE CHEST!
STREEETCH
MROW?
WHA?
GLANCE GLANCE
HUH?
THAT'S WEIRD.
WHERE'D IT GO?
OH!
HOW DID IT GET IN HERE?
MIP?

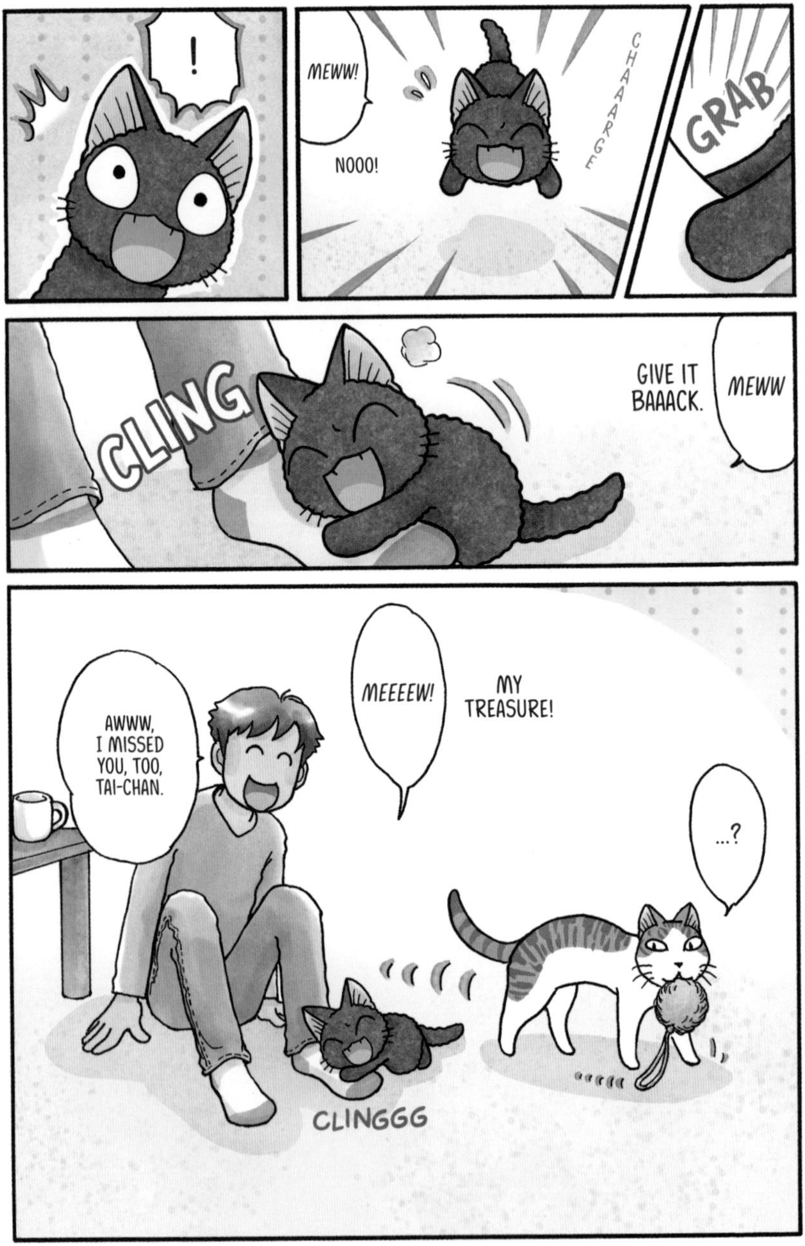
!
MEWW!
NOOO!
CHAAAARGE
GRAB
CLING
GIVE IT BAAACK.
MEWW
MEEEEW!
MY TREASURE!
AWWW, I MISSED YOU, TOO, TAI-CHAN.
...?
CLINGGG

CHAPTER 63 Good Napping Weather

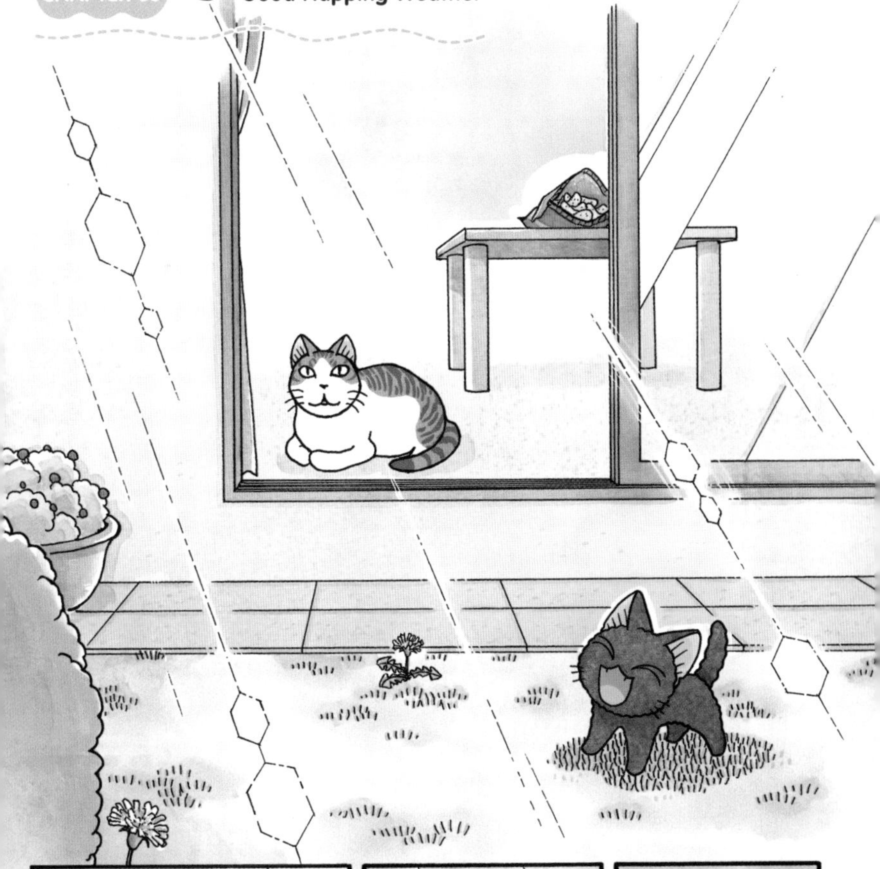

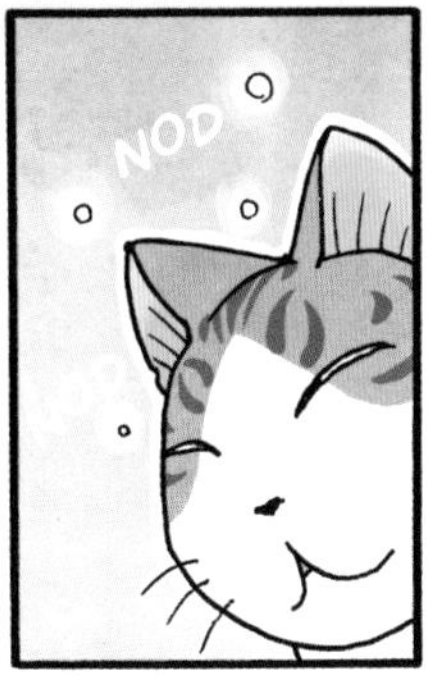
NOD

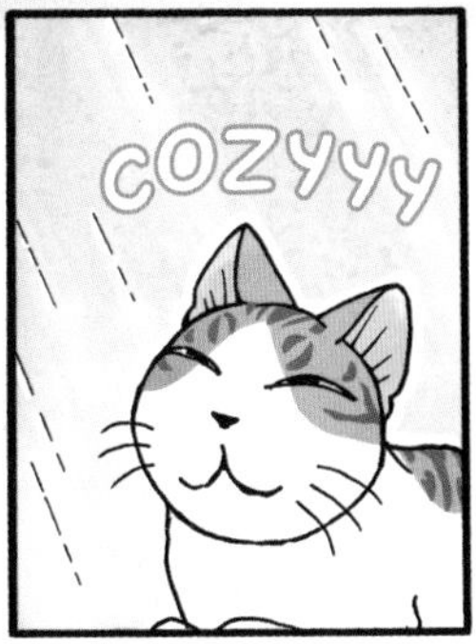
COZYYY

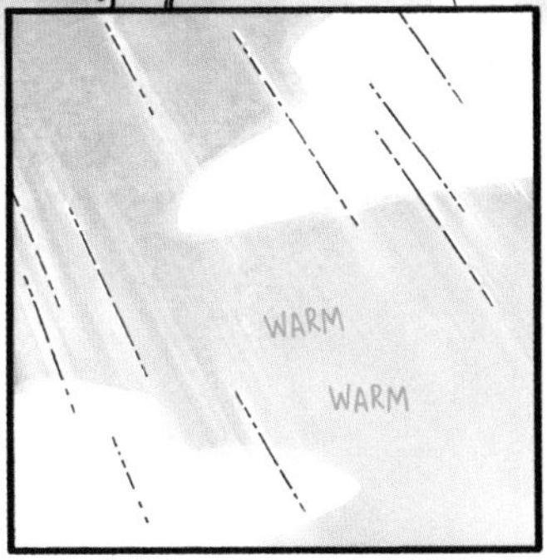
WARM
WARM

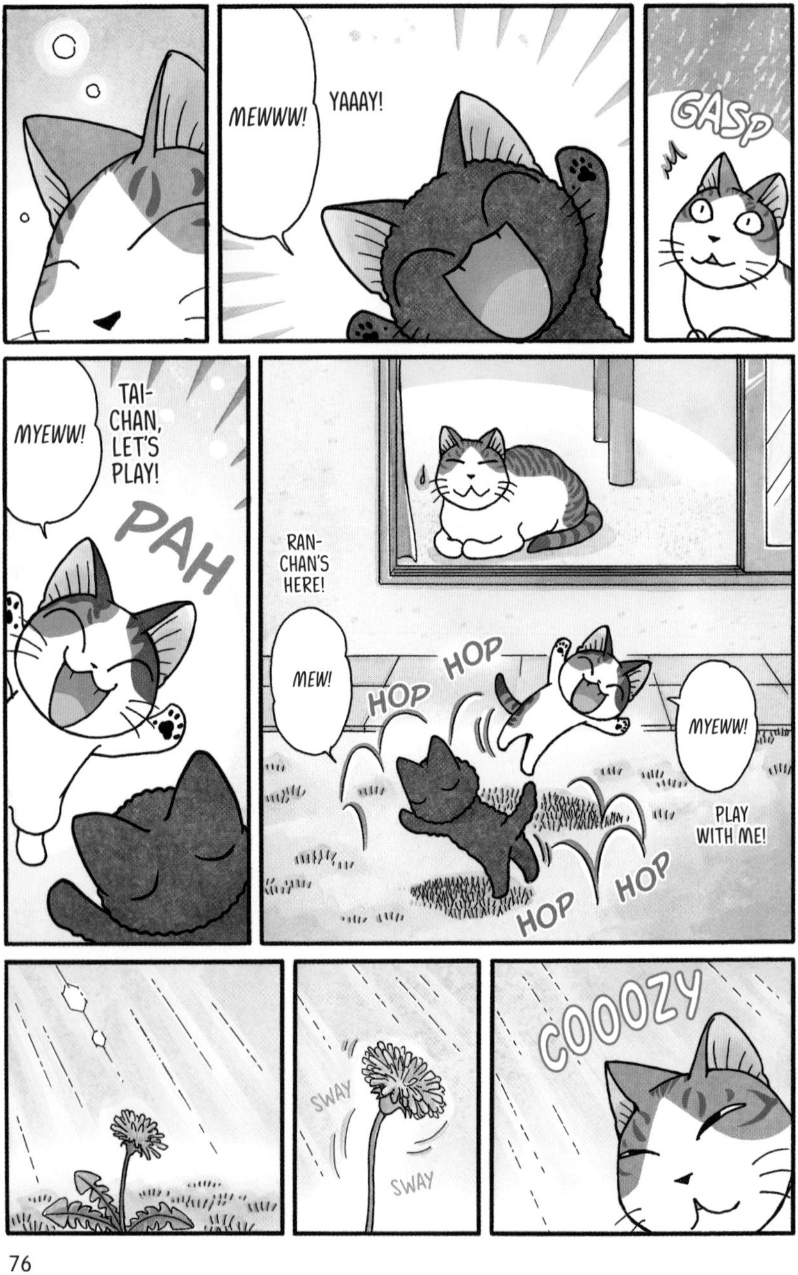
GASP
YAAAY!
MEWWW!
RAN-CHAN'S HERE!
MEW!
HOP HOP
HOP
MYEWW!
PLAY WITH ME!
HOP HOP
TAI-CHAN, LET'S PLAY!
MYEWW!
PAH
COOOZY
SWAY
SWAY

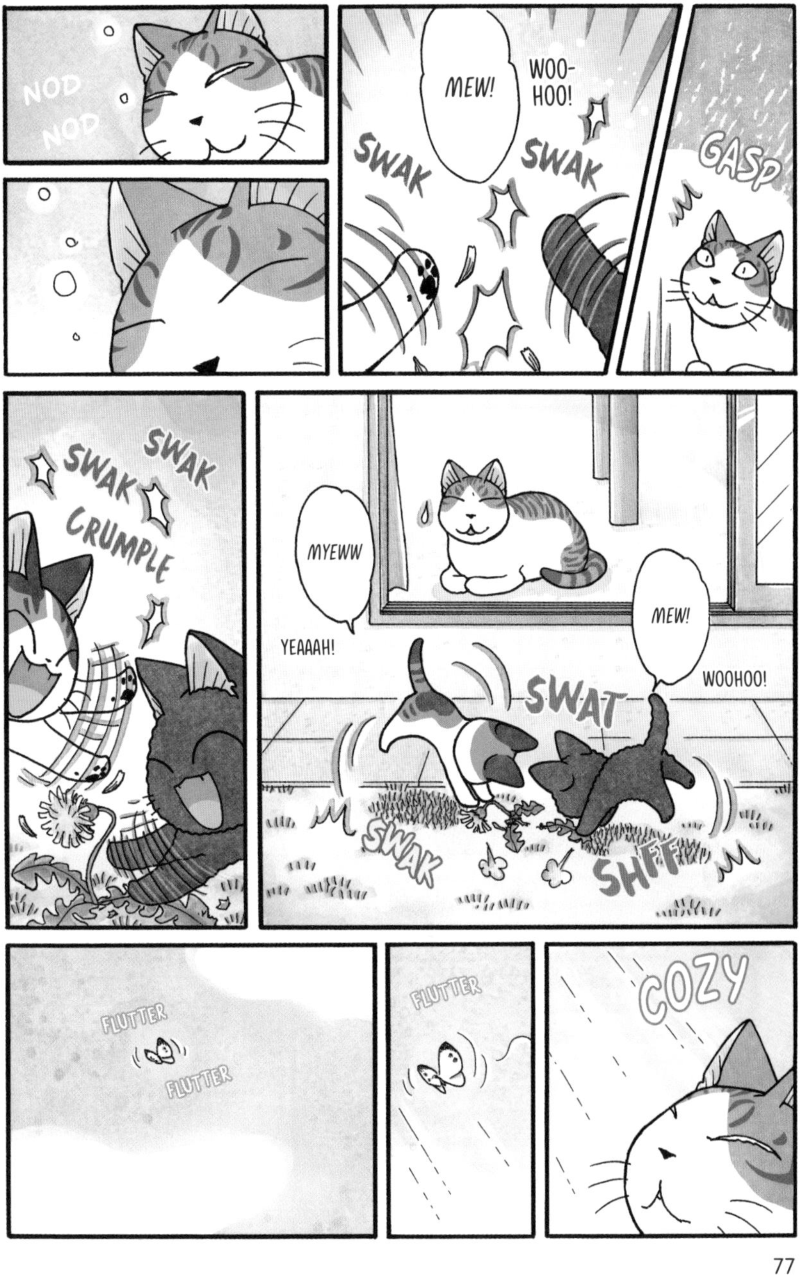
GASP
MEW!
WOO-HOO!
SWAK
SWAK
NOD
NOD
MYEWW
YEAAAH!
MEW!
WOOHOO!
SWAT
SWAK
SHFF
SWAK
SWAK
CRUMPLE
COZY
FLUTTER
FLUTTER
FLUTTER

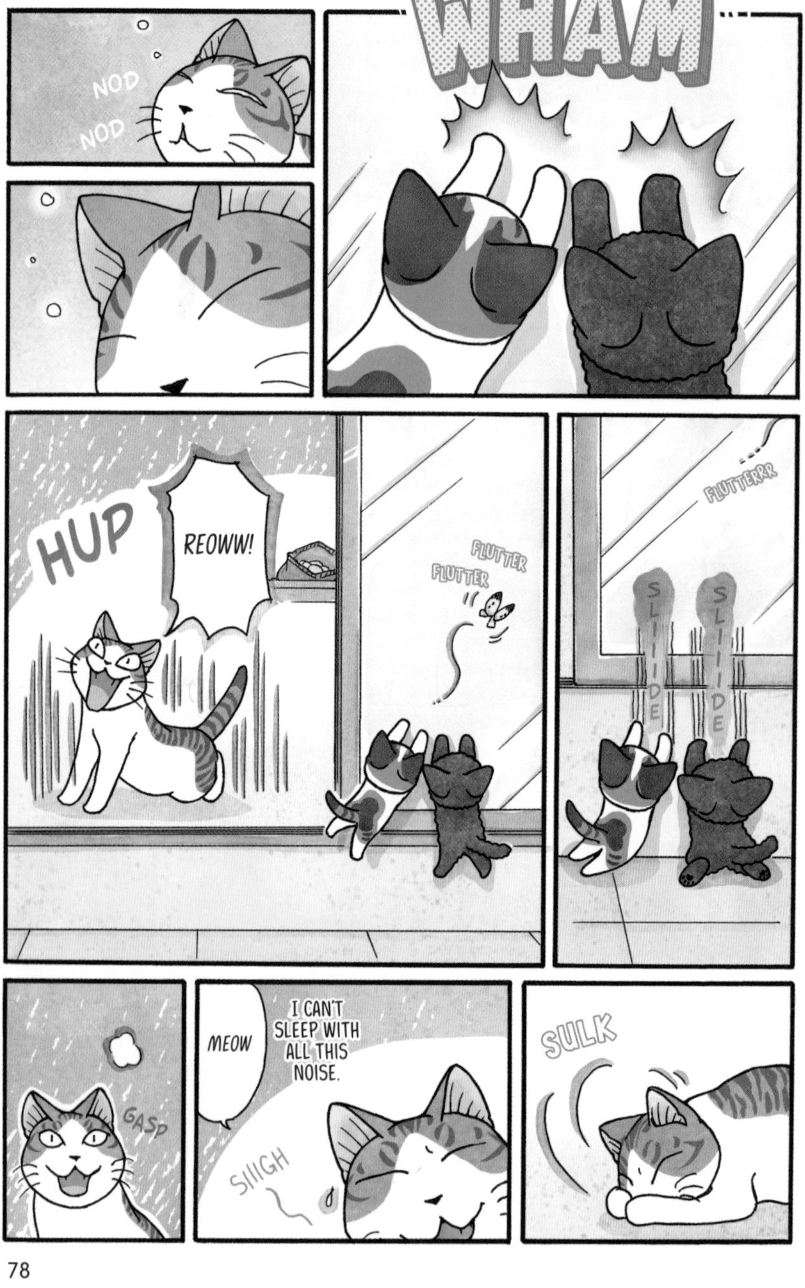
NOD
NOD
WHAM
HUP
REOWW!
FLUTTER
FLUTTER
FLUTTERRR
SLIIIDE
SLIIIDE
GASP
MEOW
I CAN'T SLEEP WITH ALL THIS NOISE.
SIIIGH
SULK

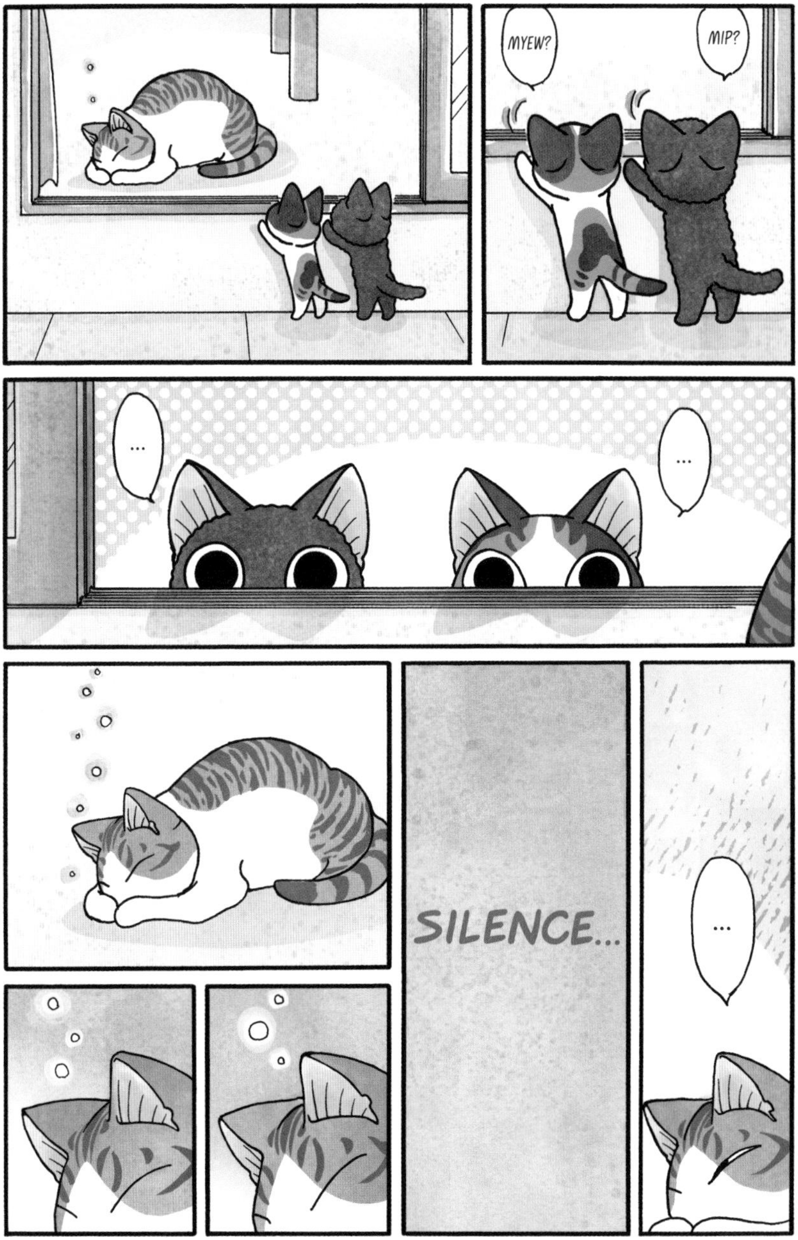
MIP?
MYEW?
...
...
...
SILENCE...

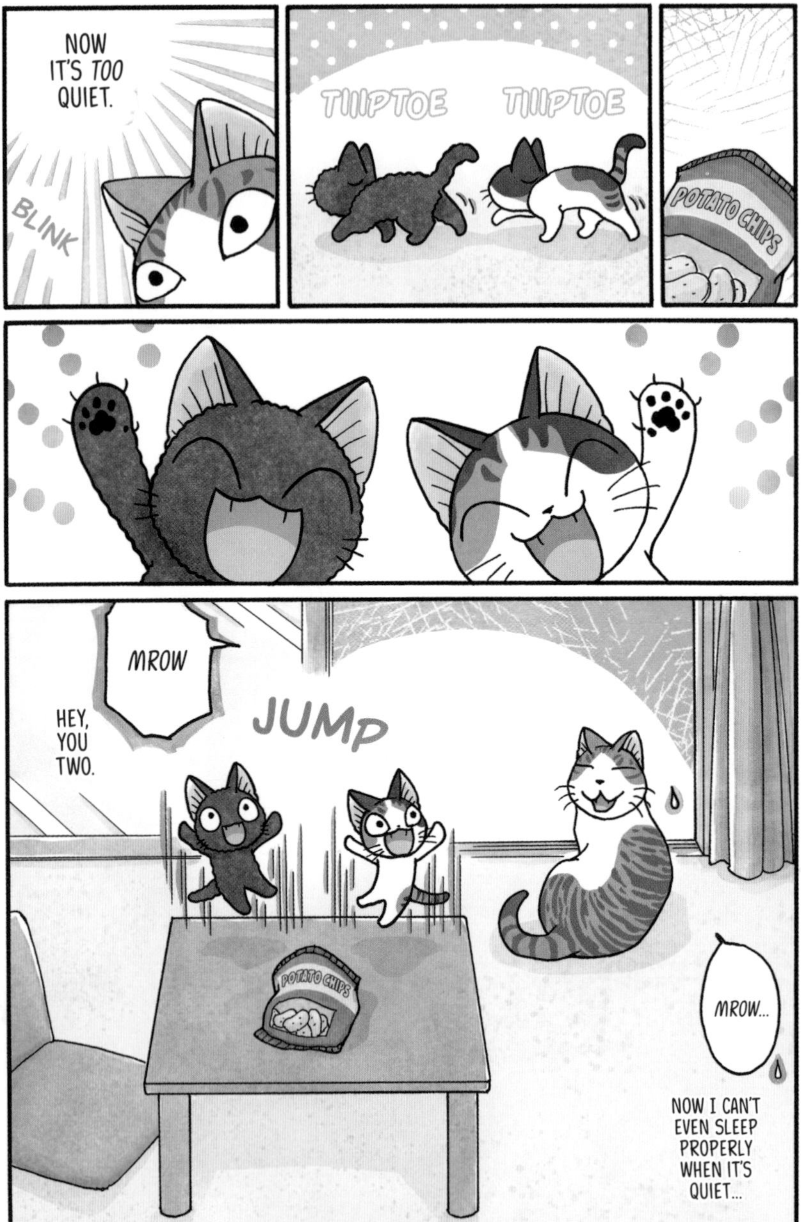
NOW IT'S *TOO* QUIET.
BLINK
TIIIPTOE
TIIIPTOE
POTATO CHIPS
MROW
HEY, YOU TWO.
JUMP
POTATO CHIPS
MROW...
NOW I CAN'T EVEN SLEEP PROPERLY WHEN IT'S QUIET...

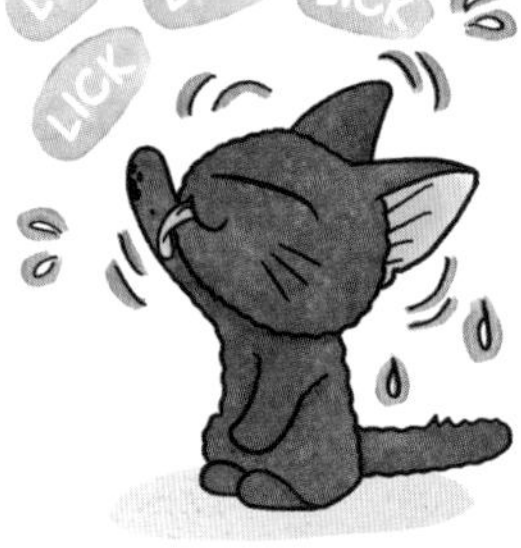
LICK
LICK
LICK
LICK

Sue & Tai-chan

CHAPTER 64 Senior Cat Power

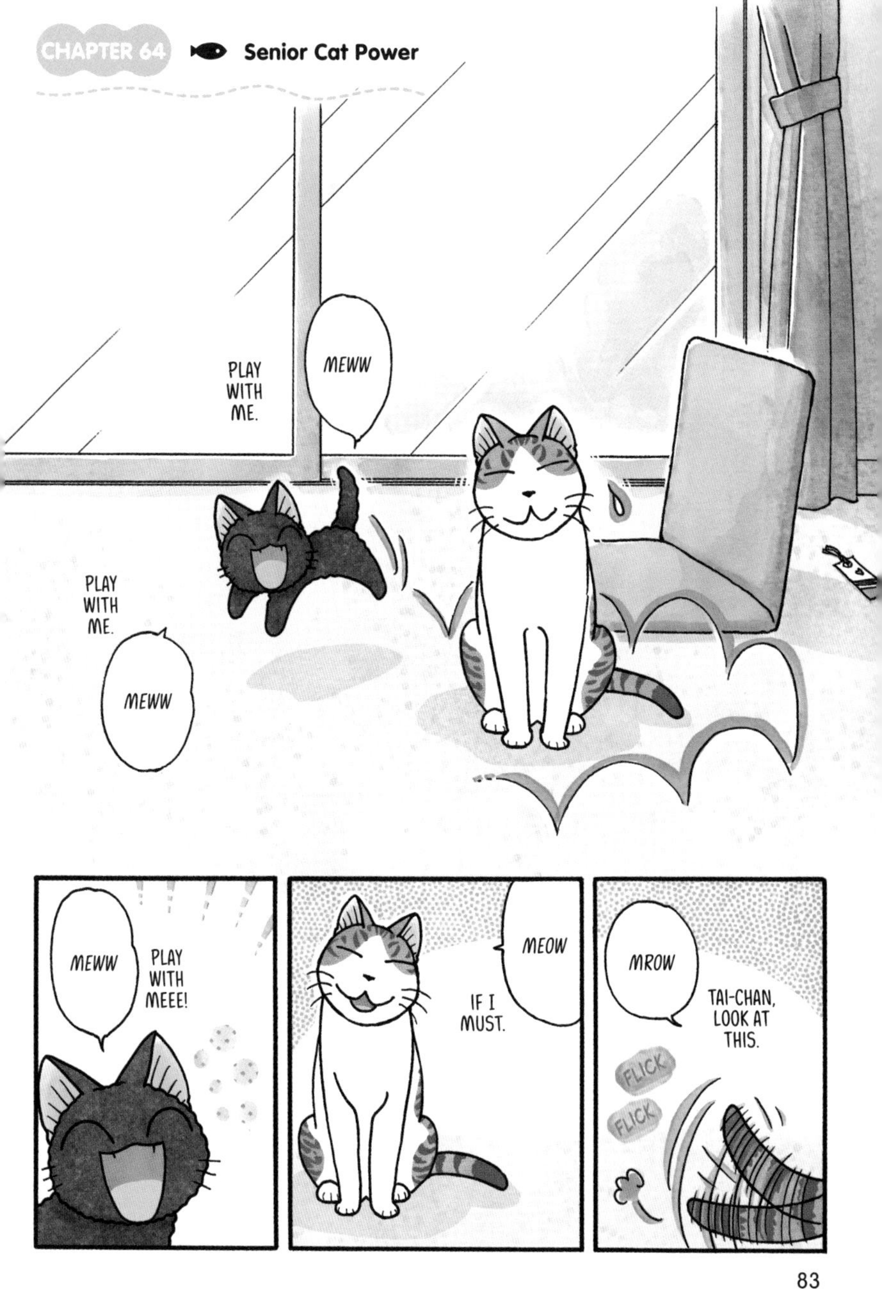

MEWW
PLAY WITH ME.
PLAY WITH ME.
MEWW
MROW
TAI-CHAN, LOOK AT THIS.
FLICK
FLICK
MEOW
IF I MUST.
MEWW
PLAY WITH MEEE!

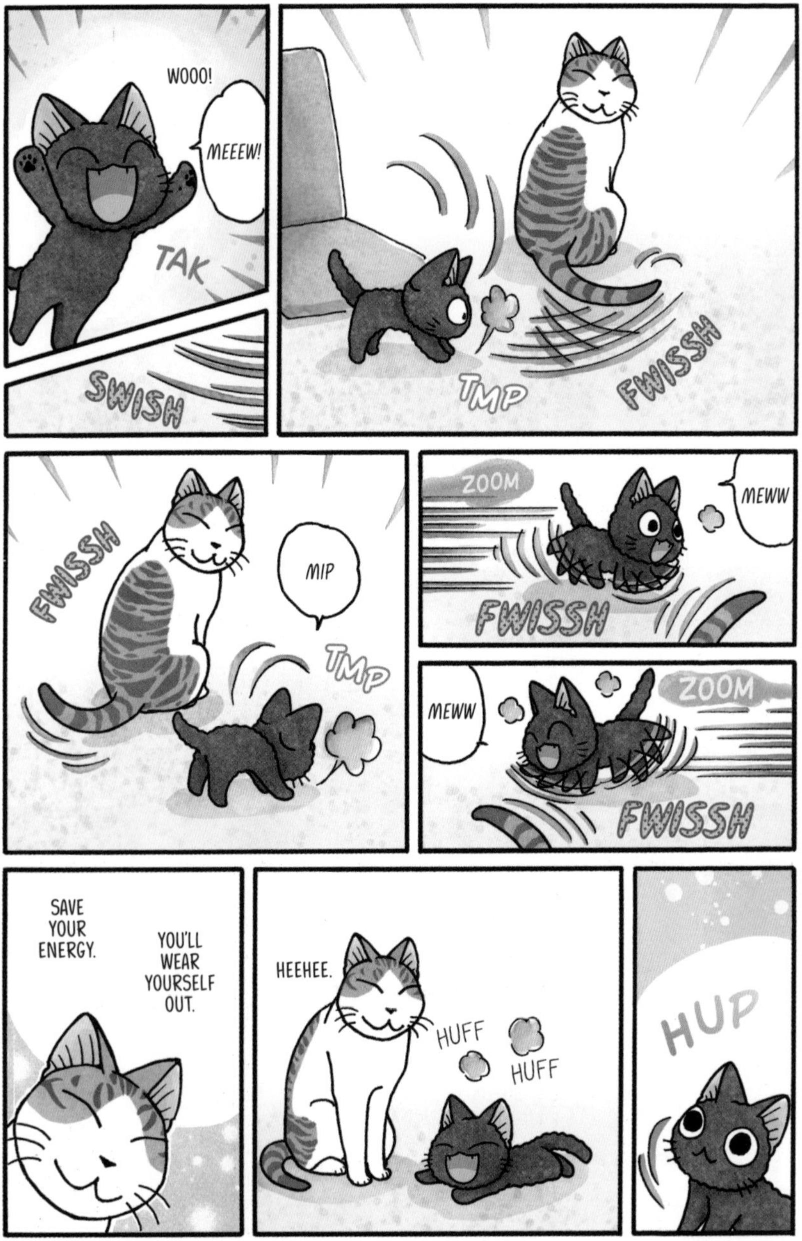
WOOO!
MEEEW!
TAK
SWISH
TMP
FWISSH
FWISSH
MIP
TMP
ZOOM
MEWW
FWISSH
MEWW
ZOOM
FWISSH
SAVE YOUR ENERGY.
YOU'LL WEAR YOURSELF OUT.
HEEHEE.
HUFF
HUFF
HUP

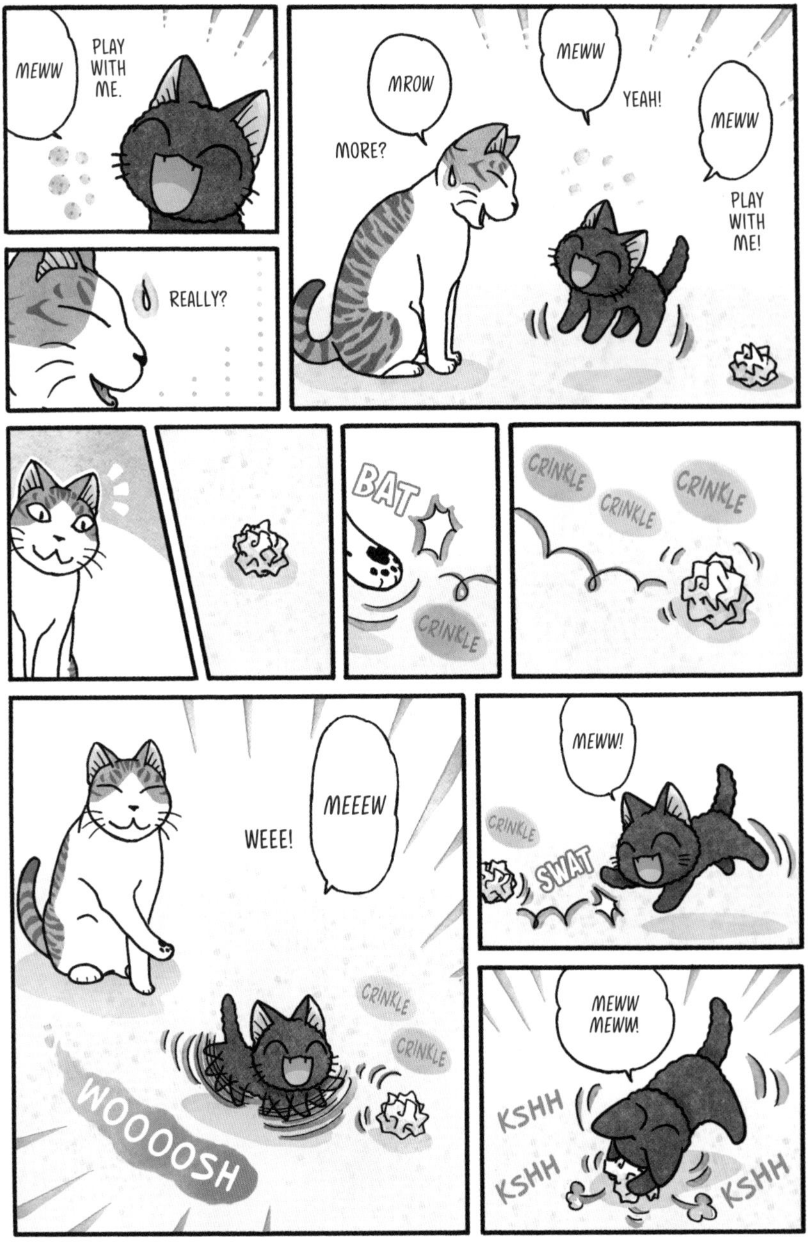
MEWW
PLAY WITH ME.
REALLY?
MROW
MORE?
MEWW
YEAH!
MEWW
PLAY WITH ME!
BAT
CRINKLE
CRINKLE
CRINKLE
CRINKLE
MEEEW
WEEE!
CRINKLE
CRINKLE
WOOOOSH
MEWW!
CRINKLE
SWAT
MEWW MEWW!
KSHH
KSHH
KSHH

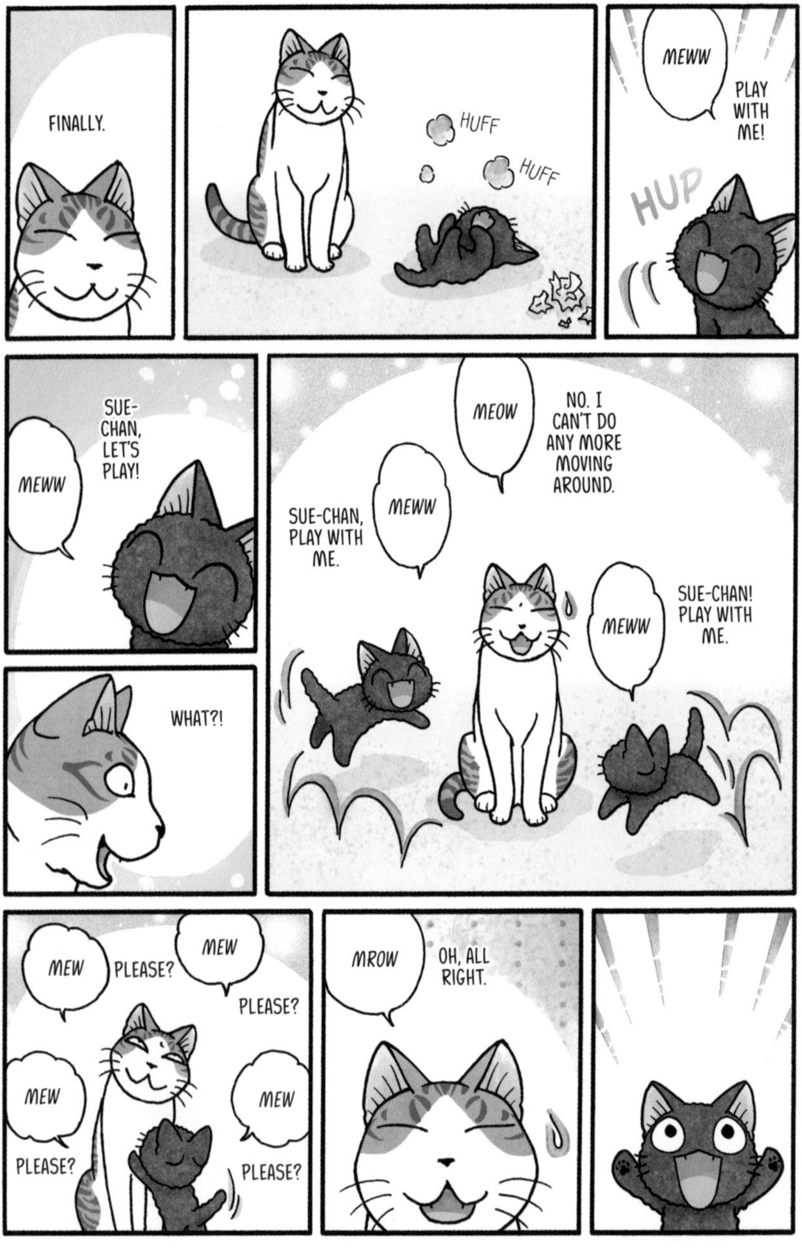
FINALLY.
HUFF
HUFF
MEWW
PLAY WITH ME!
HUP
MEWW
SUE-CHAN, LET'S PLAY!
WHAT?!
MEOW
NO. I CAN'T DO ANY MORE MOVING AROUND.
MEWW
SUE-CHAN, PLAY WITH ME.
MEWW
SUE-CHAN! PLAY WITH ME.
MEW
PLEASE?
MEW
PLEASE?
MEW
PLEASE?
MEW
PLEASE?
MROW
OH, ALL RIGHT.

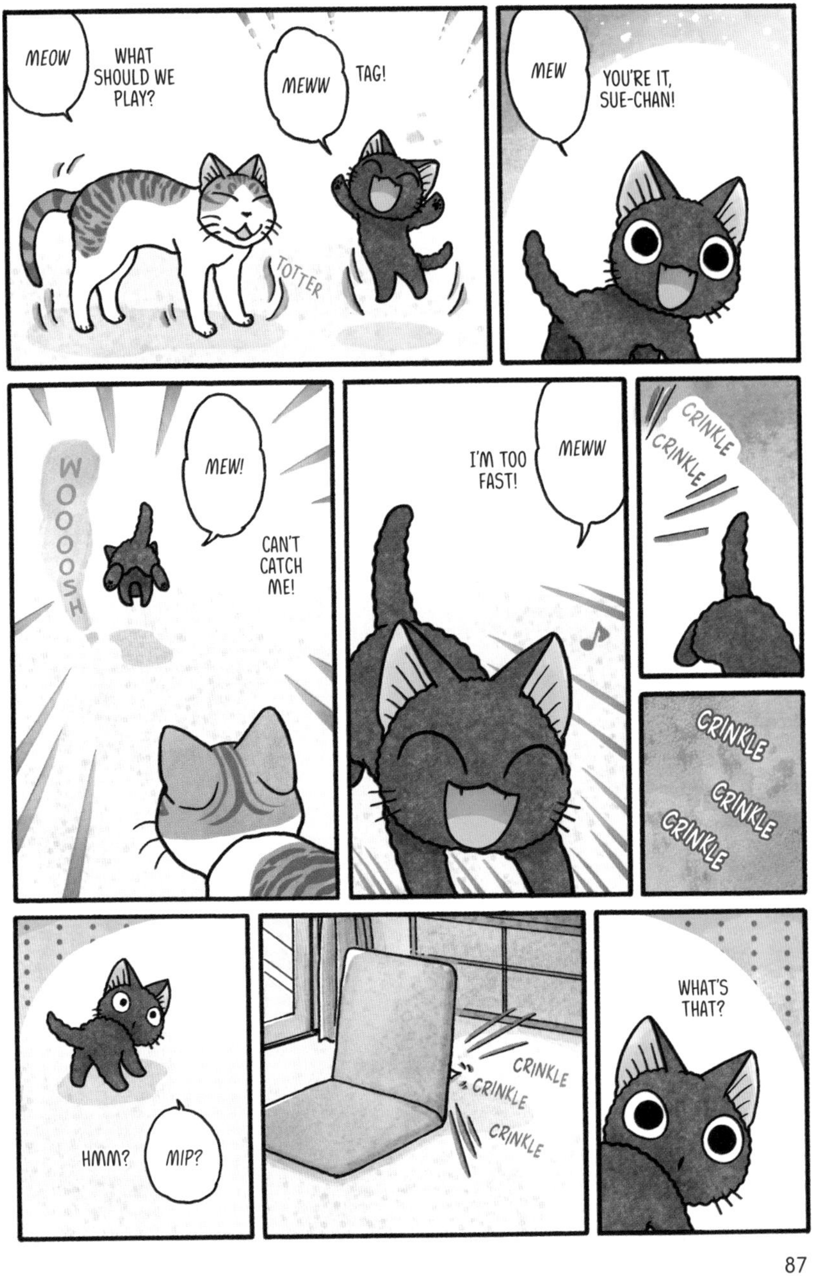
MEOW
WHAT SHOULD WE PLAY?
MEWW
TAG!
TOTTER
MEW
YOU'RE IT, SUE-CHAN!
MEW!
WOOOOOSH
CAN'T CATCH ME!
MEWW
I'M TOO FAST!
CRINKLE
CRINKLE
CRINKLE
CRINKLE
CRINKLE
HMM?
MIP?
CRINKLE
CRINKLE
CRINKLE
WHAT'S THAT?

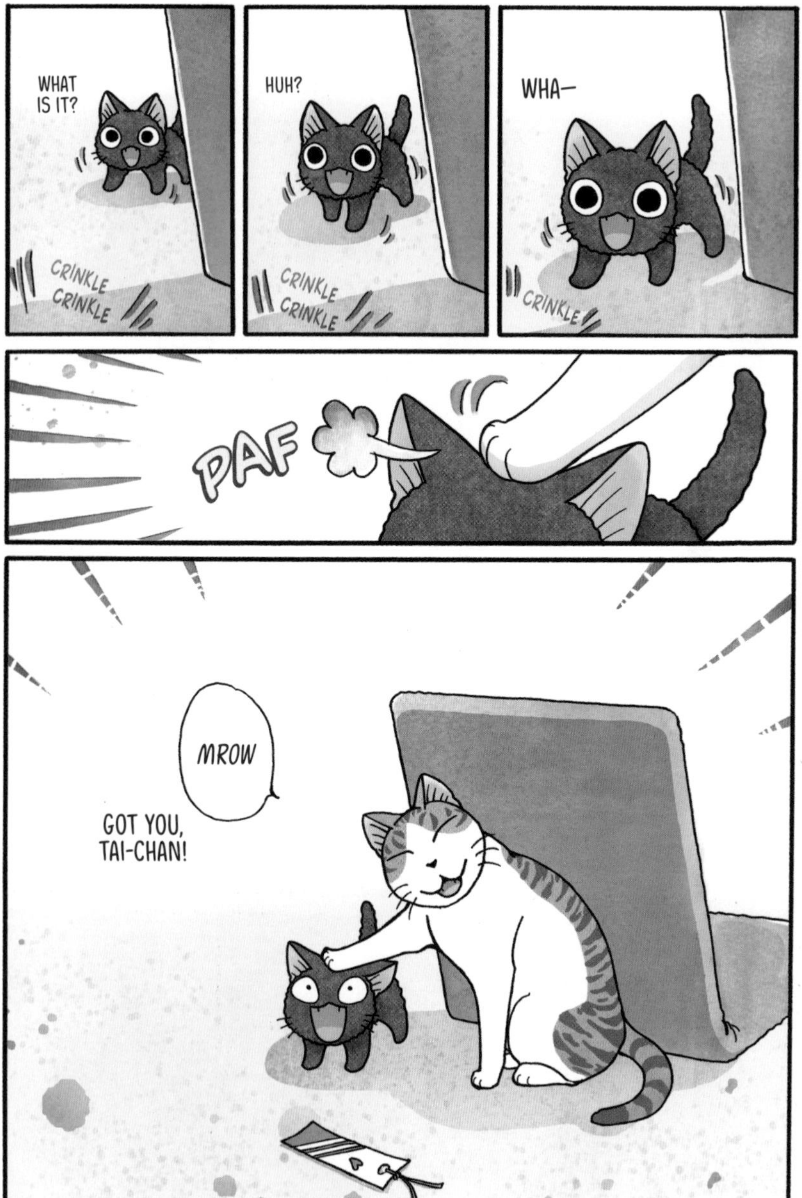
WHAT IS IT?
CRINKLE CRINKLE
HUH?
CRINKLE CRINKLE
WHA—
CRINKLE
PAF
MROW
GOT YOU, TAI-CHAN!

CHAPTER 65 CUTE ☆

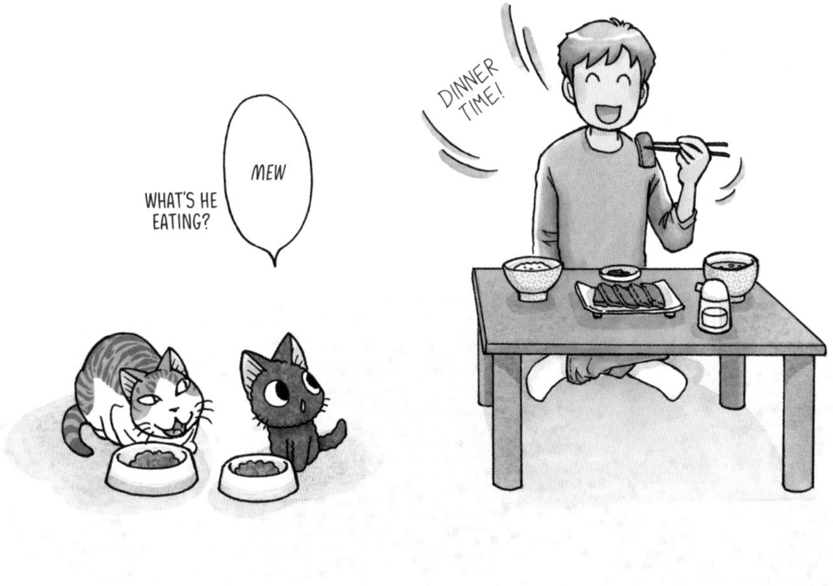
DINNER TIME!
MEW
WHAT'S HE EATING?

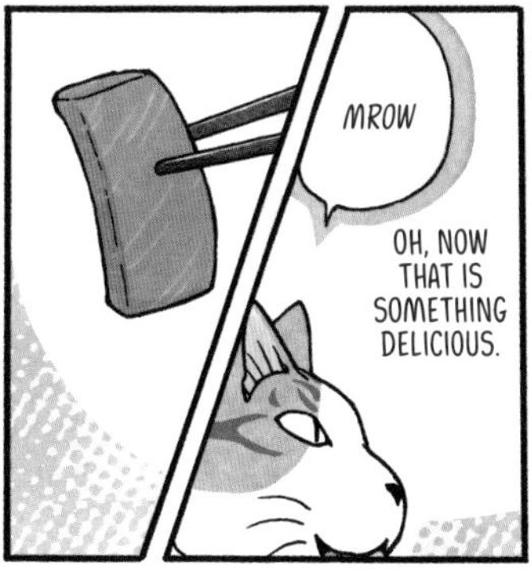
MROW
OH, NOW THAT IS SOMETHING DELICIOUS.

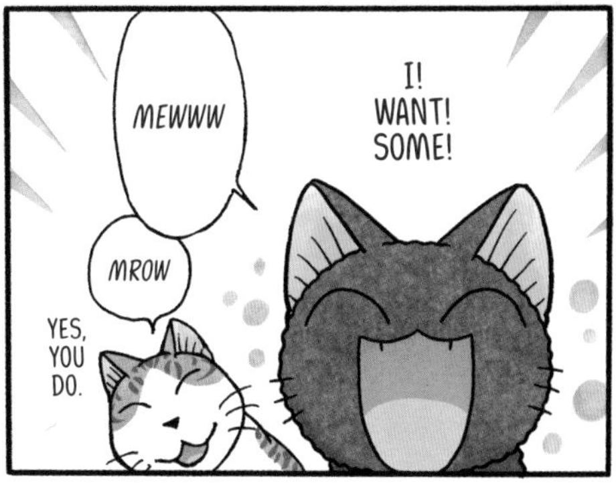
MEWWW
I! WANT! SOME!
MROW
YES, YOU DO.

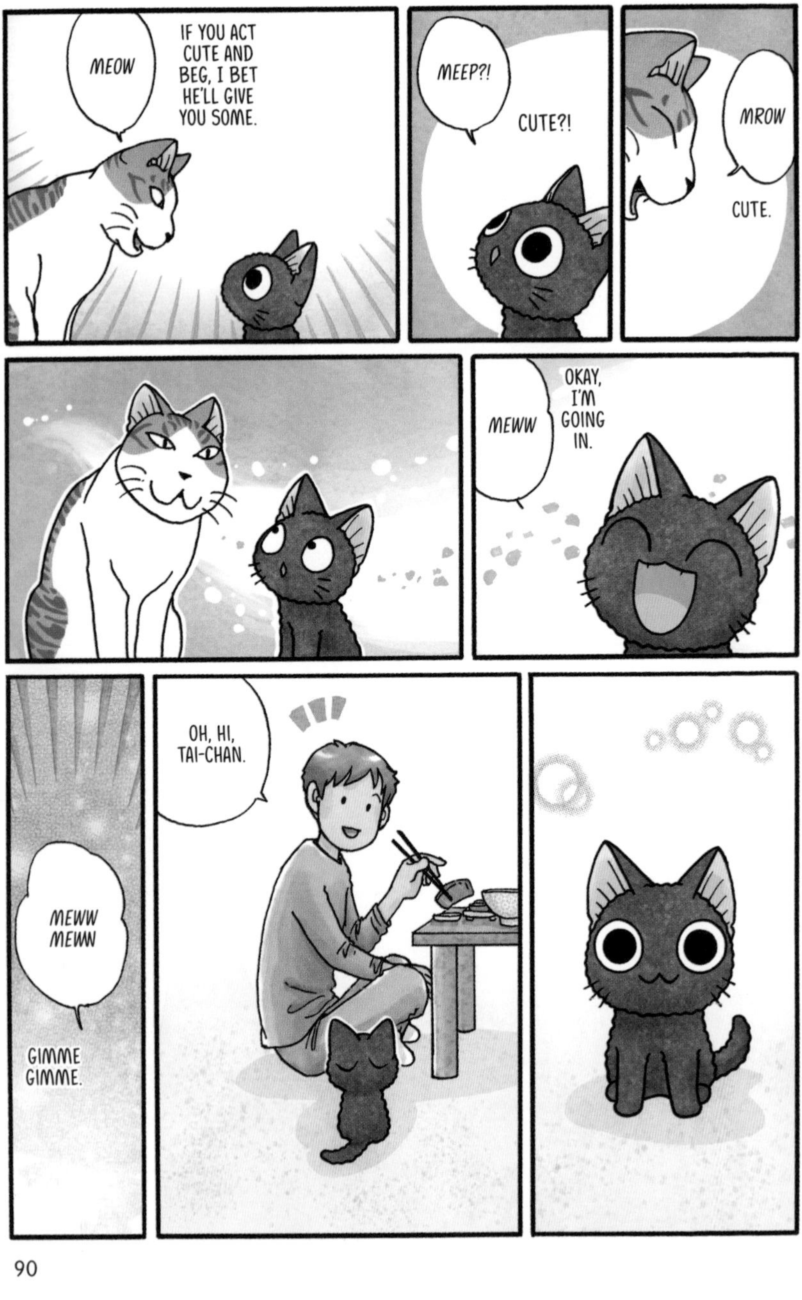
MEOW
IF YOU ACT CUTE AND BEG, I BET HE'LL GIVE YOU SOME.
MEEP?!
CUTE?!
MROW
CUTE.
MEWW
OKAY, I'M GOING IN.
MEWW MEWW
GIMME GIMME.
OH, HI, TAI-CHAN.

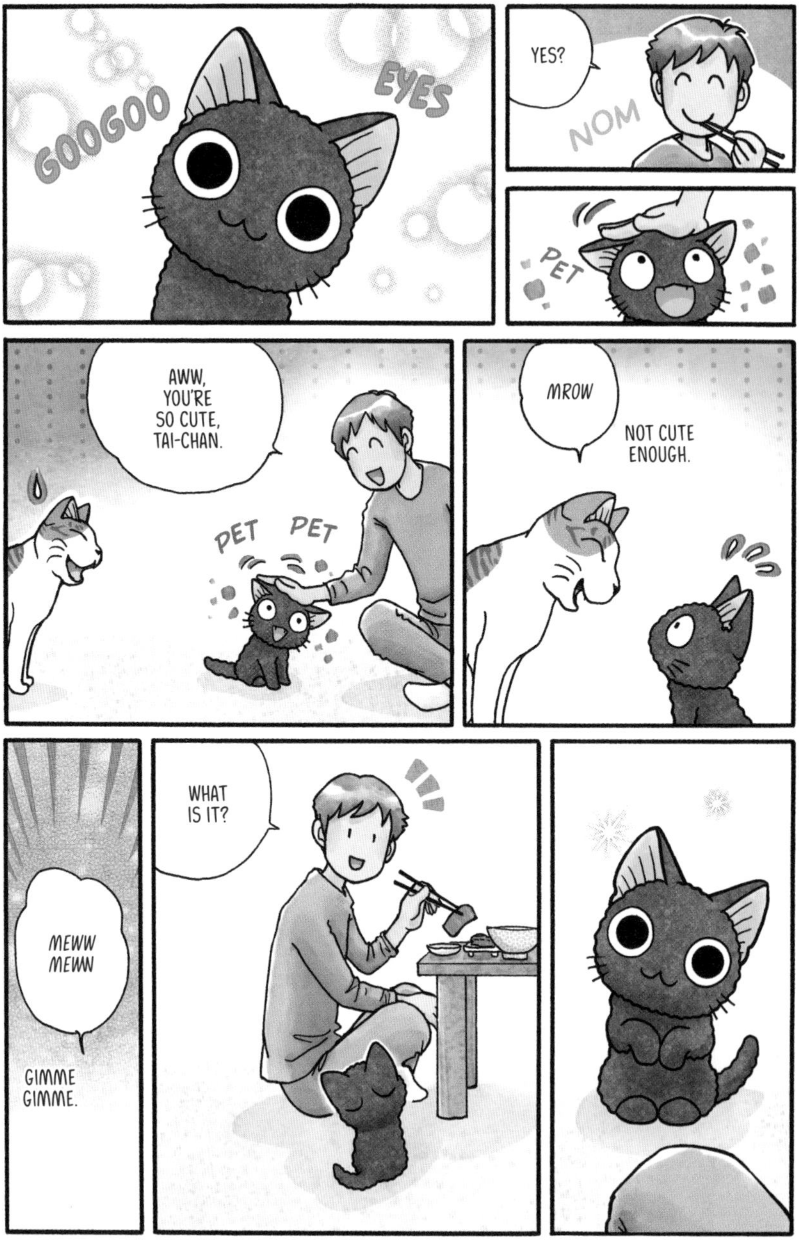
GOOGOO
EYES
YES?
NOM
PET
AWW, YOU'RE SO CUTE, TAI-CHAN.
PET PET
MROW
NOT CUTE ENOUGH.
MEWW MEWW
GIMME GIMME.
WHAT IS IT?

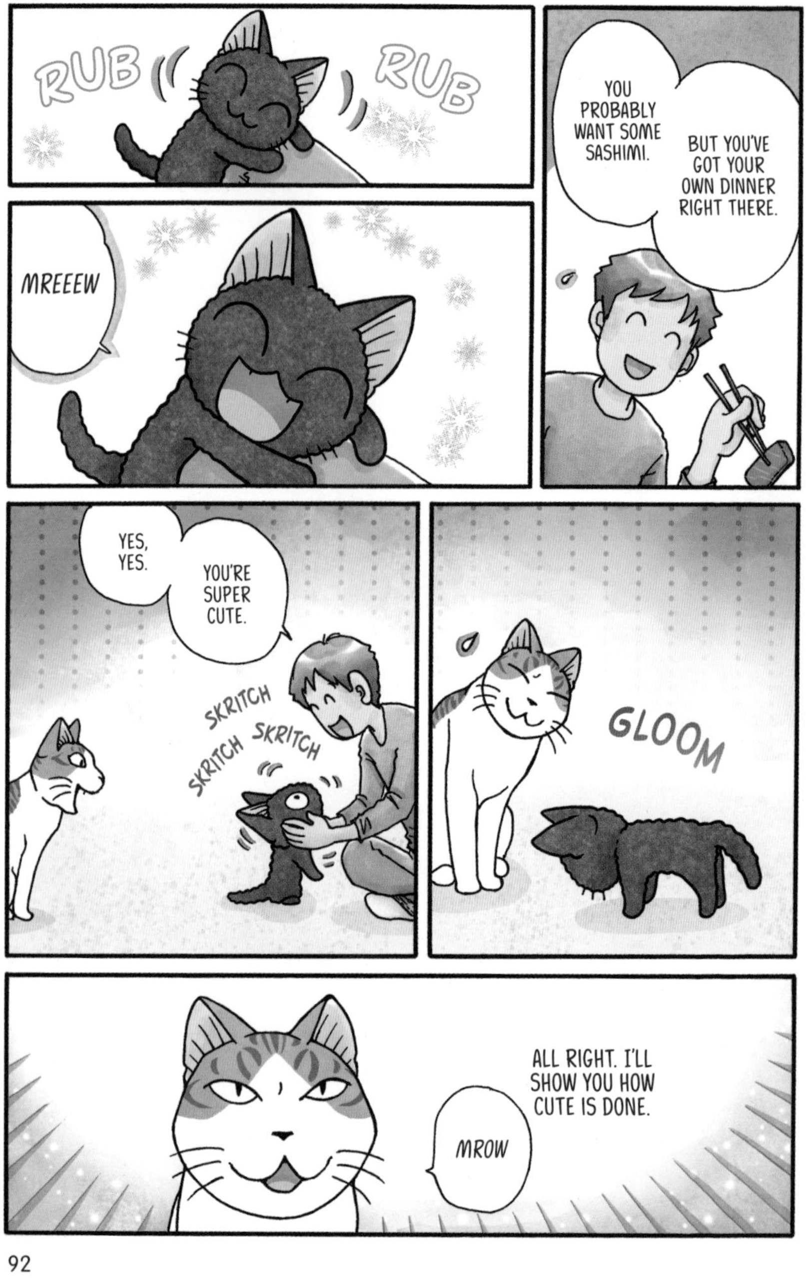
RUB RUB
MREEEW
YOU PROBABLY WANT SOME SASHIMI.
BUT YOU'VE GOT YOUR OWN DINNER RIGHT THERE.
YES, YES.
YOU'RE SUPER CUTE.
SKRITCH SKRITCH SKRITCH
GLOOM
MROW
ALL RIGHT. I'LL SHOW YOU HOW CUTE IS DONE.

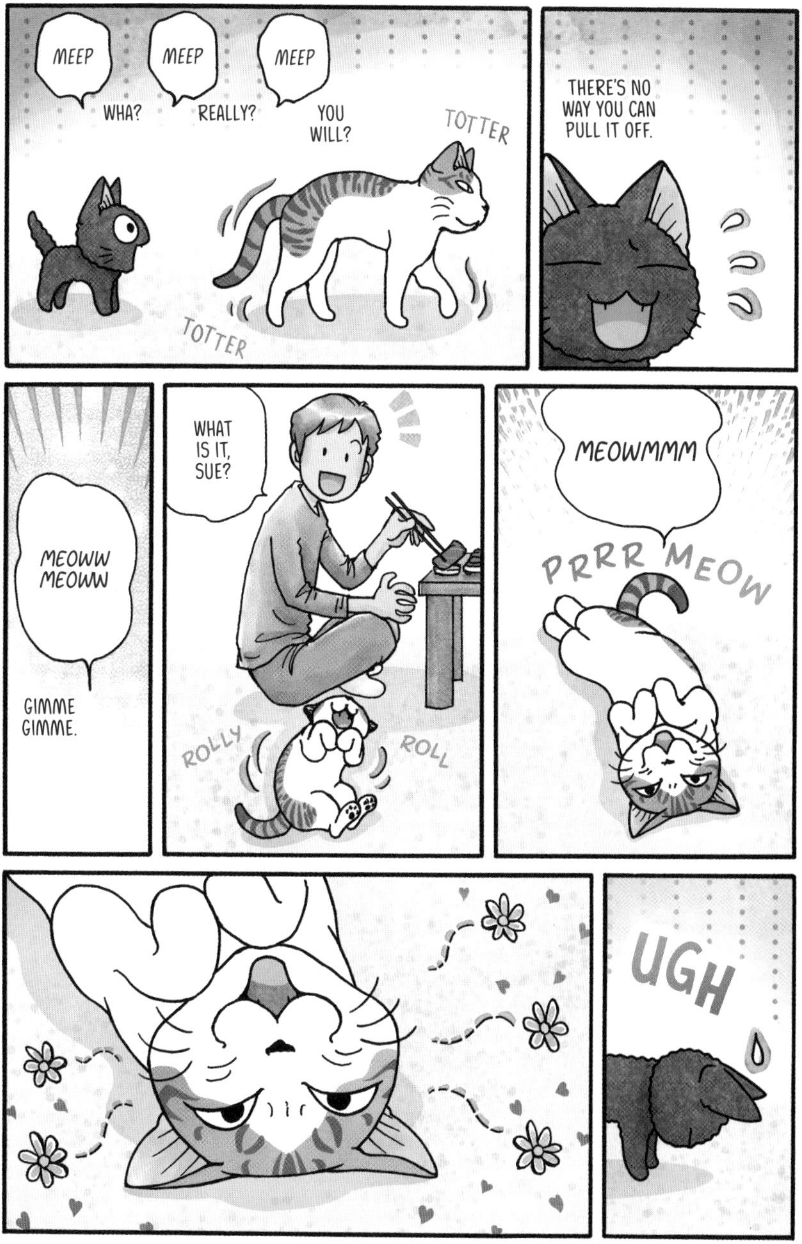
MEEP
WHA?
MEEP
REALLY?
MEEP
YOU WILL?
TOTTER
TOTTER
THERE'S NO WAY YOU CAN PULL IT OFF.
MEOWW MEOWW
GIMME GIMME.
WHAT IS IT, SUE?
ROLLY
ROLL
MEOWMMM
PRRR MEOW
UGH

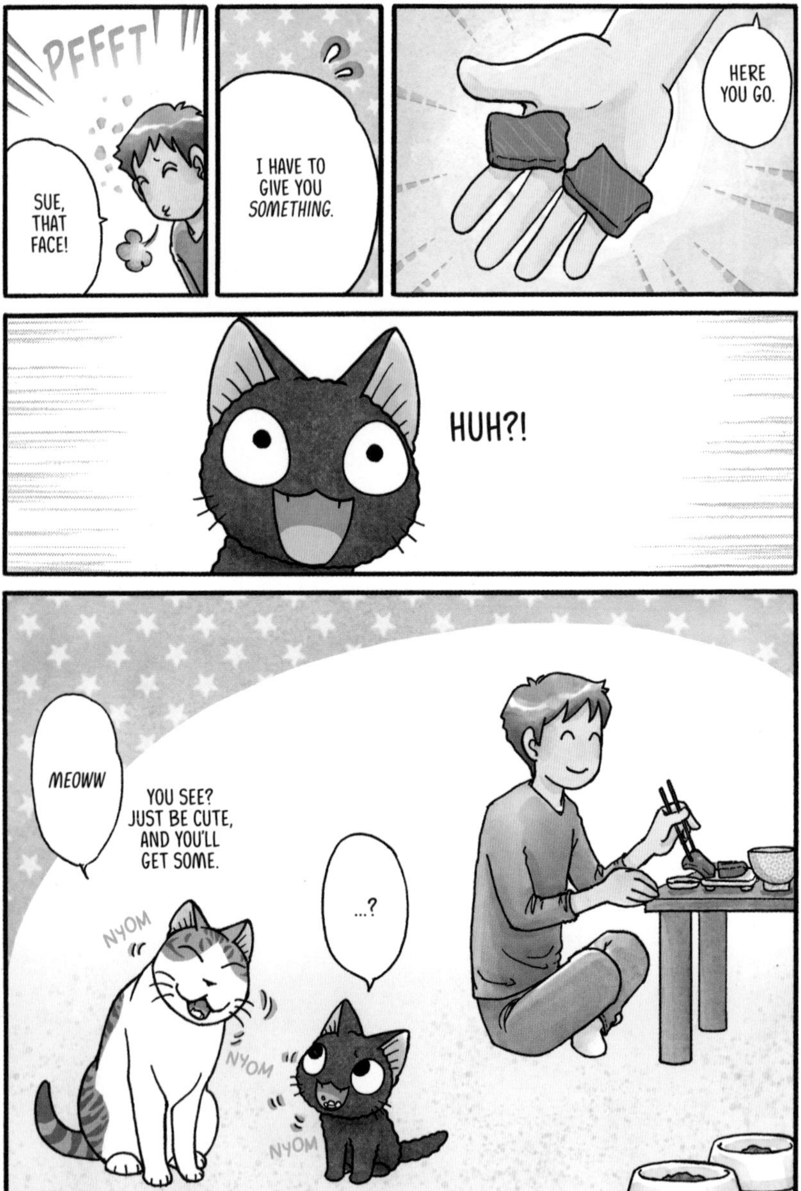
PFFFT
SUE, THAT FACE!
I HAVE TO GIVE YOU *SOMETHING*.
HERE YOU GO.
HUH?!
MEOWW
YOU SEE? JUST BE CUTE, AND YOU'LL GET SOME.
...?
NYOM
NYOM
NYOM

CHAPTER 66 Grown-Ups...

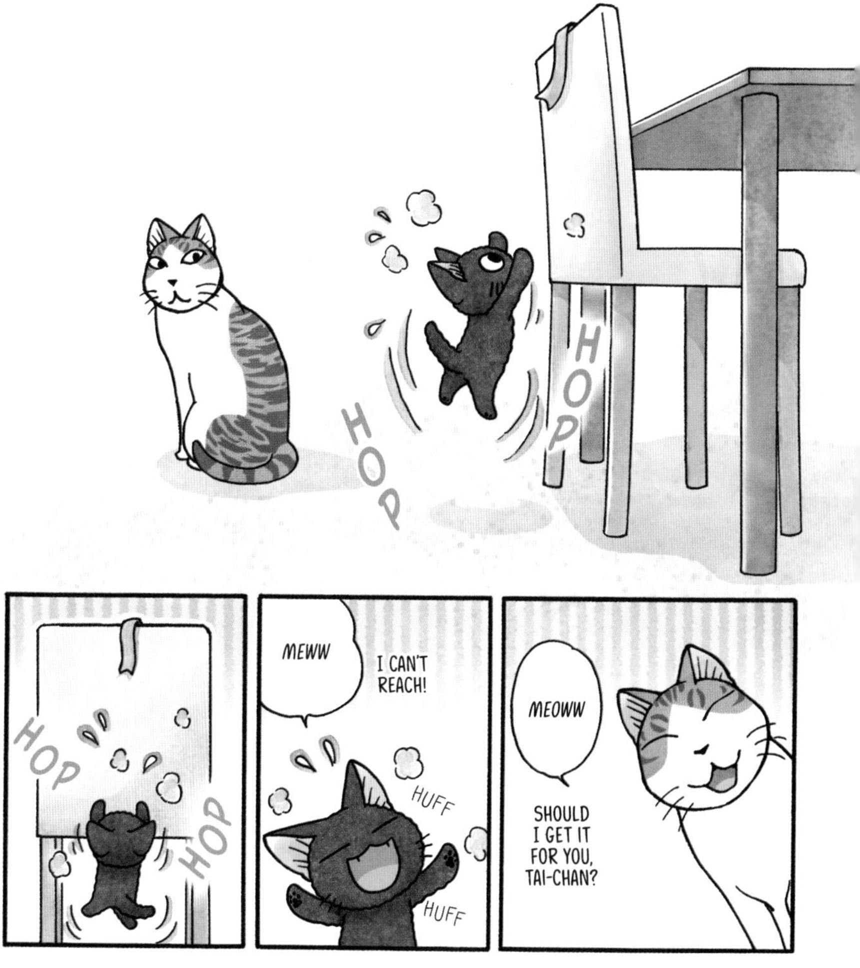
HOP
HOP
HOP
HOP
MEWW
I CAN'T REACH!
HUFF
HUFF
MEOWW
SHOULD I GET IT FOR YOU, TAI-CHAN?

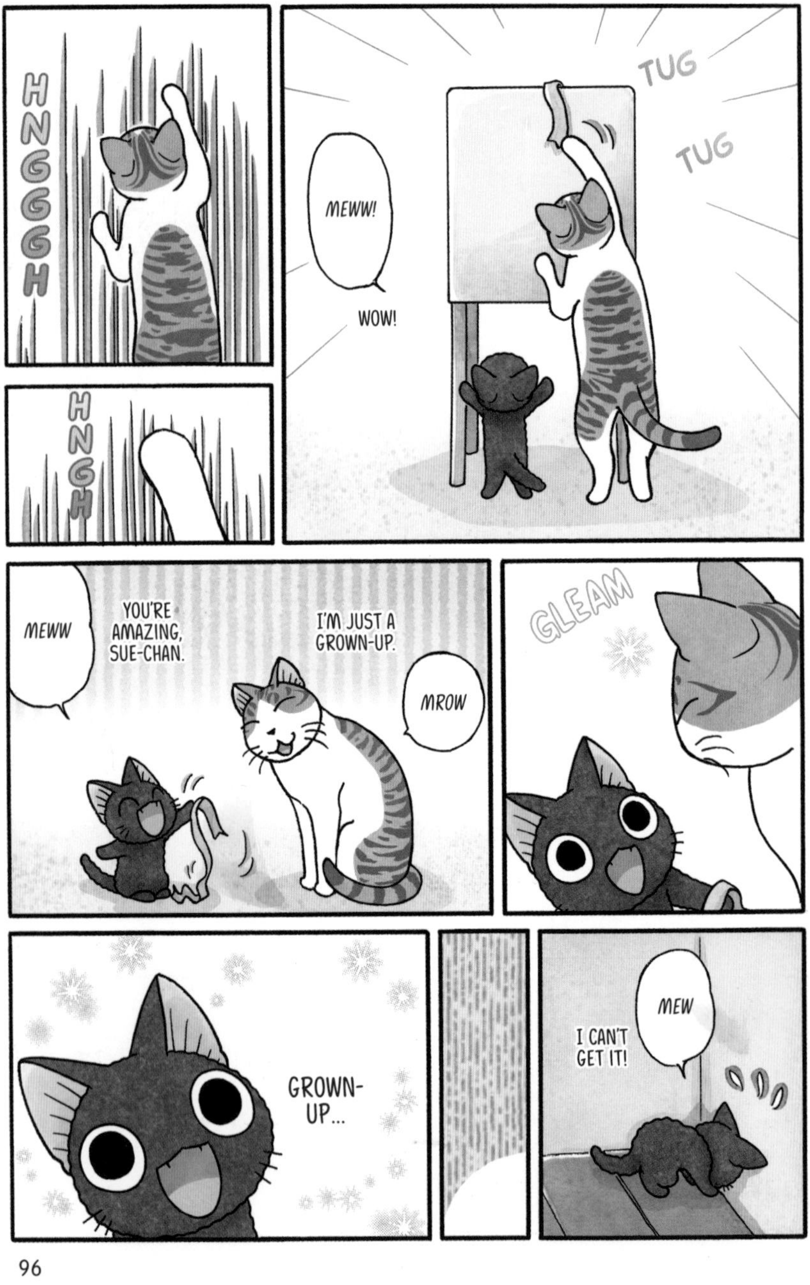
HNGGGGH
HNGH
TUG
TUG
MEWW!
WOW!
MEWW
YOU'RE AMAZING, SUE-CHAN.
I'M JUST A GROWN-UP.
MROW
GLEAM
GROWN-UP...
MEW
I CAN'T GET IT!

WHAT IS IT, TAI-CHAN?

MROW?

MEW

IT'S BEHIND THE BOX.

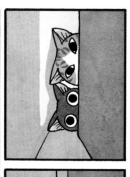

NGH

SHOVE SHOVE

"SCOOOOT"

WOW!

MEW!

MEWW

YOU'RE AMAZING, SUE-CHAN.

MROW

HUFF

HUFF

I'M JUST A GROWN-UP.

GROWN-UP...

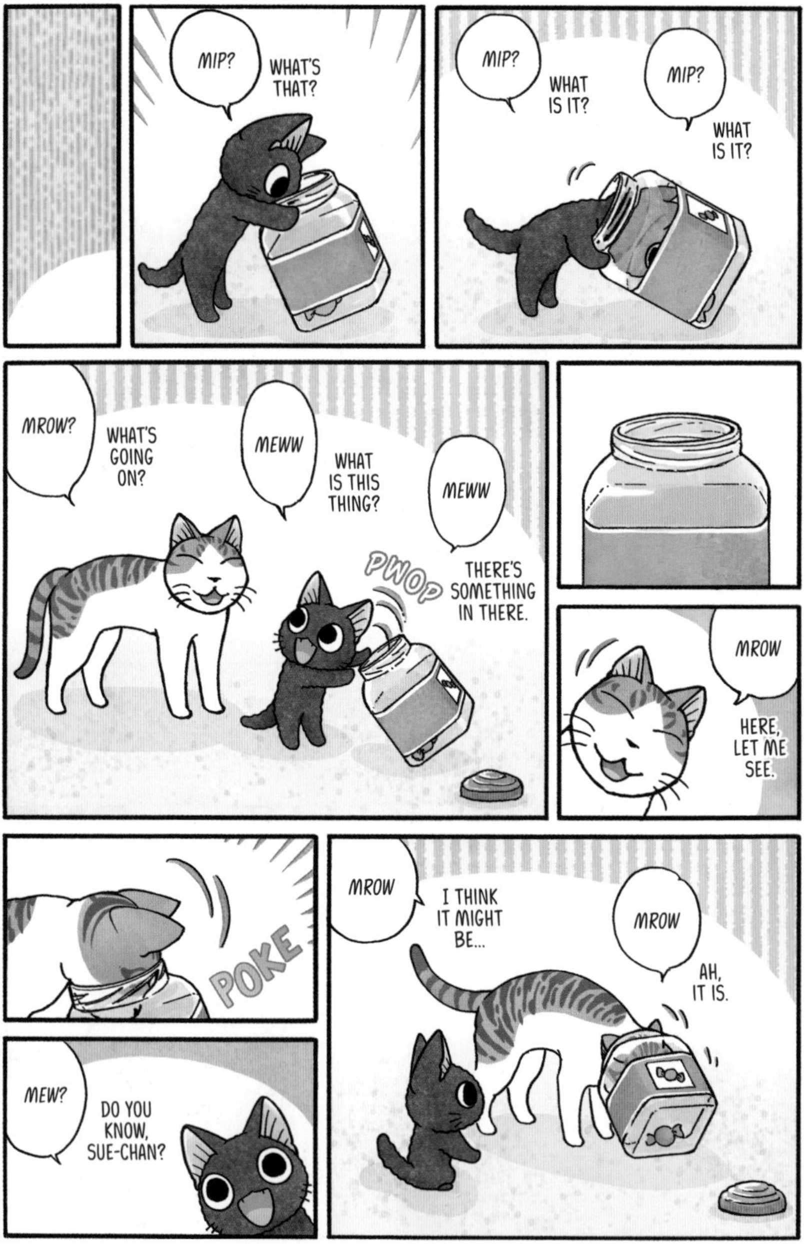
MIP?
WHAT'S THAT?
MIP?
WHAT IS IT?
MIP?
WHAT IS IT?
MROW?
WHAT'S GOING ON?
MEWW
WHAT IS THIS THING?
MEWW
PWOP
THERE'S SOMETHING IN THERE.
MROW
HERE, LET ME SEE.
POKE
MEW?
DO YOU KNOW, SUE-CHAN?
MROW
I THINK IT MIGHT BE...
MROW
AH, IT IS.

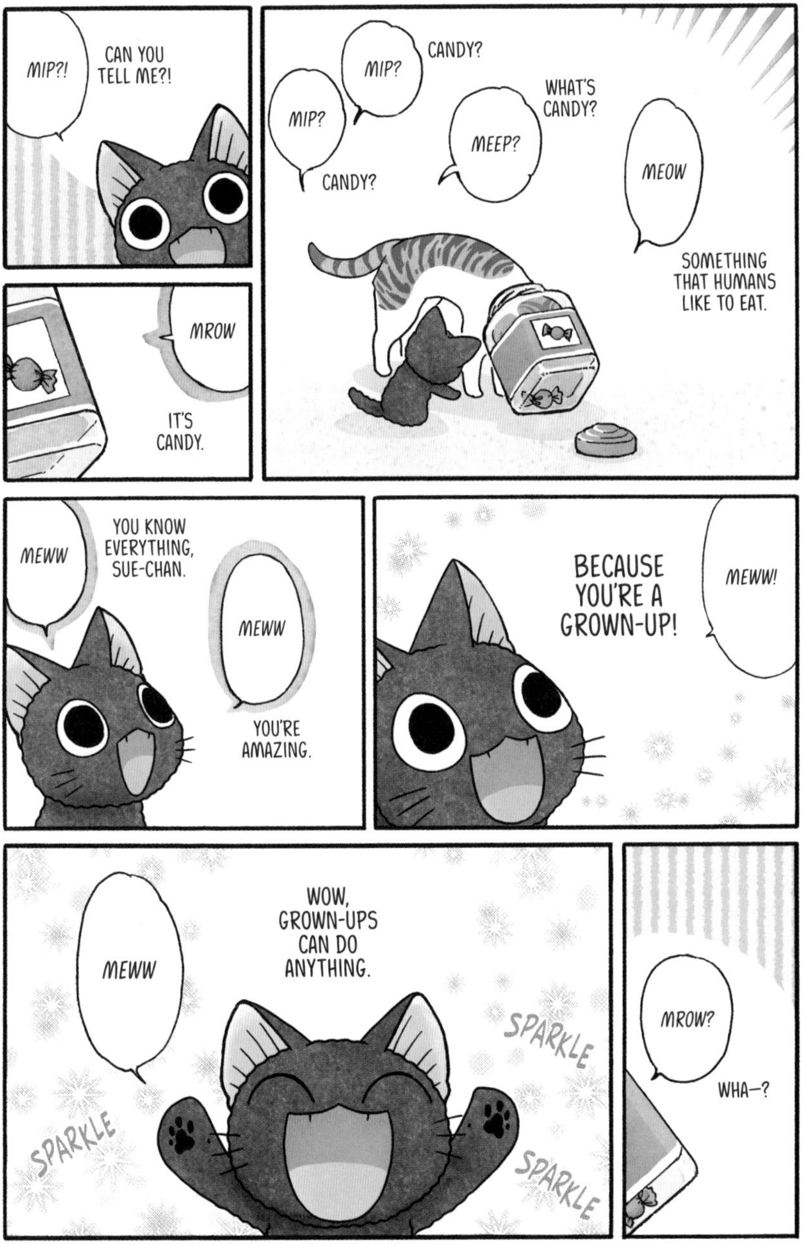
MIP?!
CAN YOU TELL ME?!
MROW
IT'S CANDY.
MIP?
CANDY?
MIP?
CANDY?
MEEP?
WHAT'S CANDY?
MEOW
SOMETHING THAT HUMANS LIKE TO EAT.
MEWW
YOU KNOW EVERYTHING, SUE-CHAN.
MEWW
YOU'RE AMAZING.
BECAUSE YOU'RE A GROWN-UP!
MEWW!
MEWW
WOW, GROWN-UPS CAN DO ANYTHING.
SPARKLE
SPARKLE
SPARKLE
MROW?
WHA—?

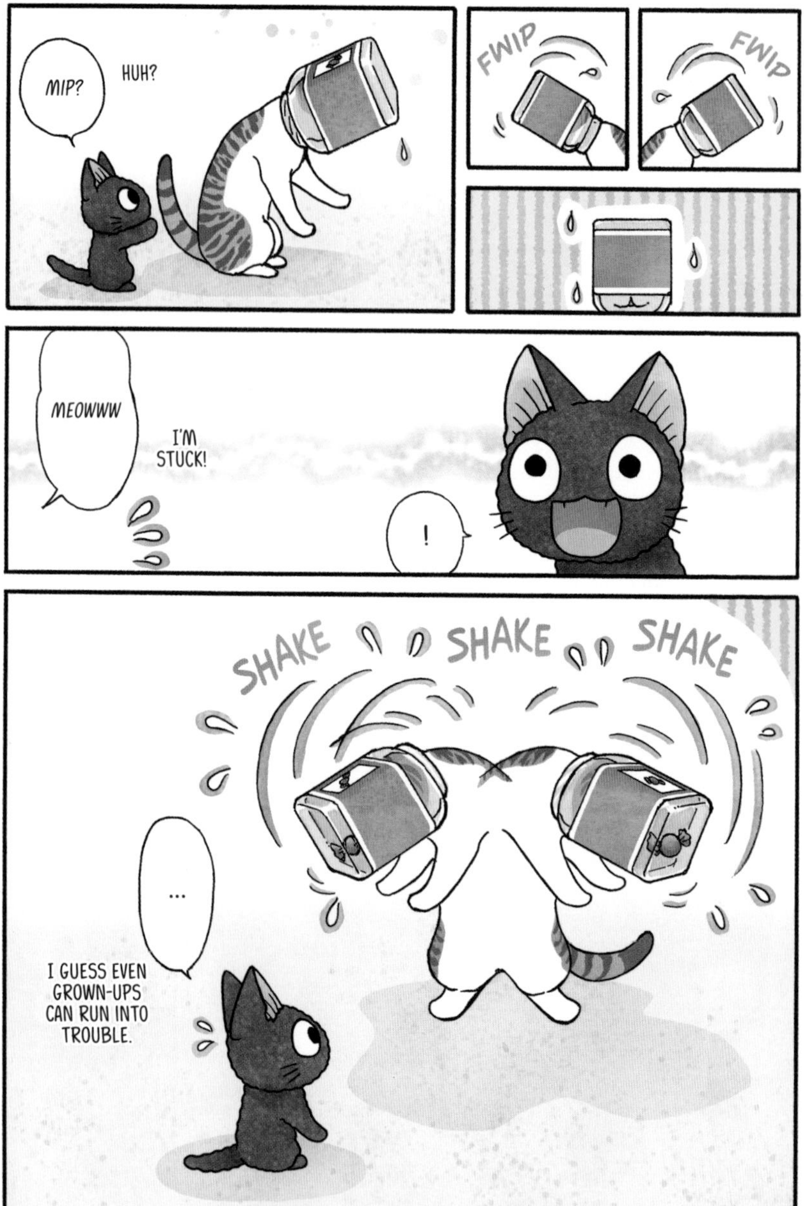
FWIP
FWIP
MIP?
HUH?
MEOWWW
I'M STUCK!
!
SHAKE SHAKE SHAKE
...
I GUESS EVEN GROWN-UPS CAN RUN INTO TROUBLE.

Sue & Tai-chan

CHAPTER 67 Ice Magic ☆

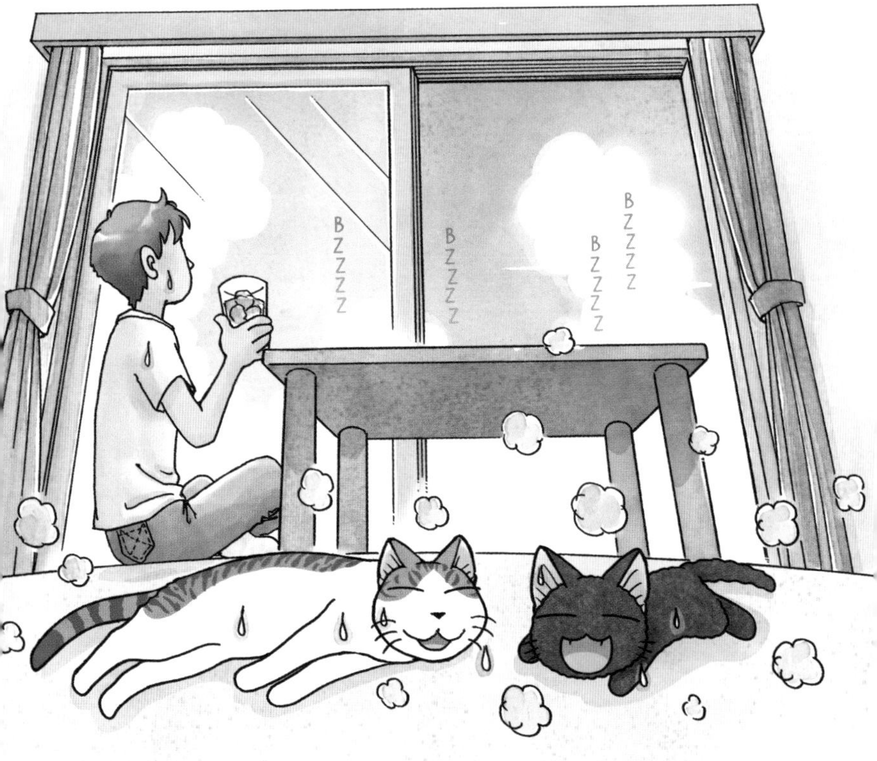
BZZZZ
BZZZZZ
BZZZZZ
BZZZZ

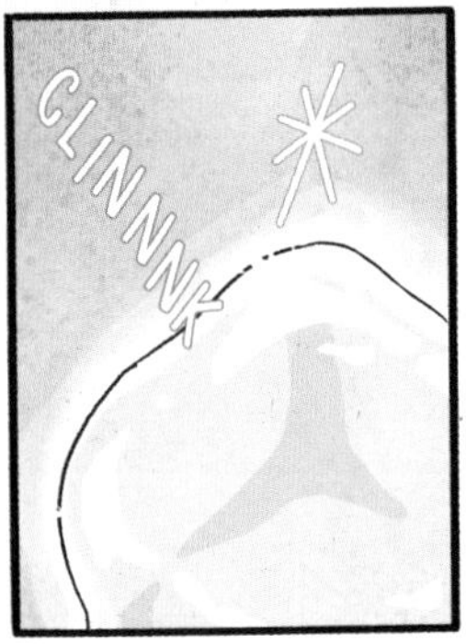
CLINNNK

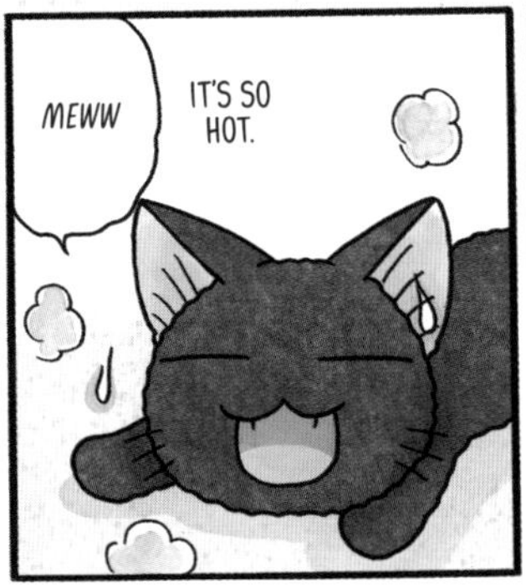
IT'S SO HOT.
MEWW

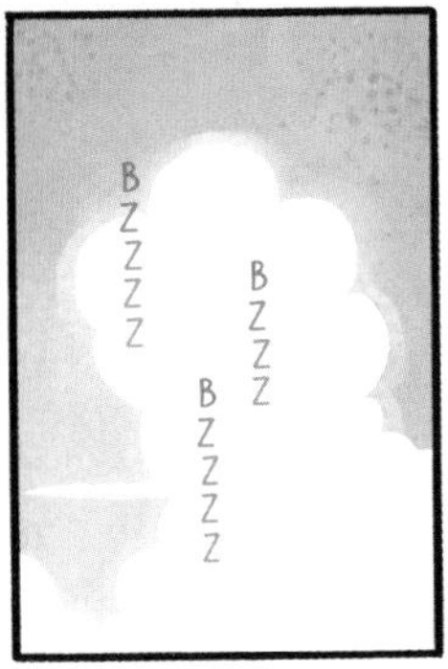
BZZZ
BZZZZZ
BZZZZ

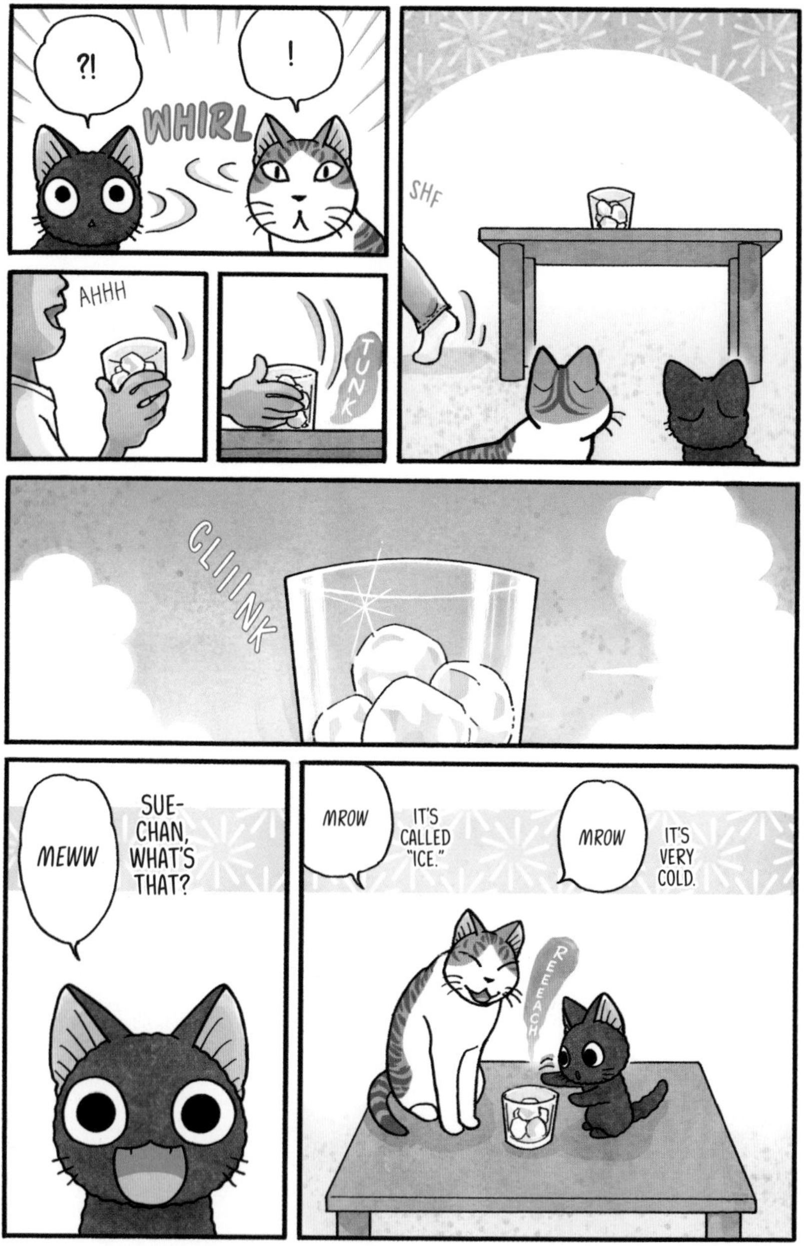
?!
!
WHIRL
AHHH
TUNK
SHF
CLIIINK
MEWW
SUE-CHAN, WHAT'S THAT?
MROW
IT'S CALLED "ICE."
MROW
IT'S VERY COLD.
REEEACH

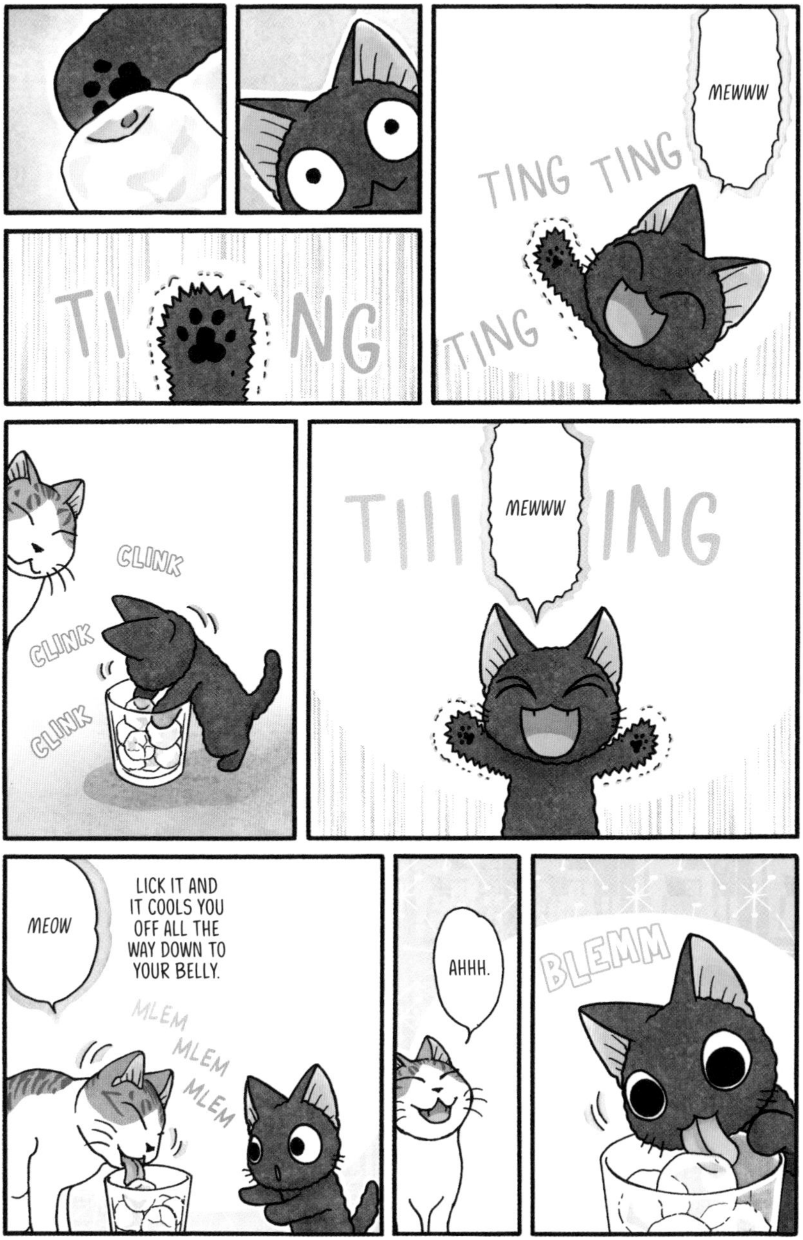
TI NG
TING TING
MEWWW
TING
CLINK
CLINK
CLINK
TIII ING
MEWWW
MEOW
LICK IT AND IT COOLS YOU OFF ALL THE WAY DOWN TO YOUR BELLY.
MLEM
MLEM
MLEM
AHHH.
BLEMM

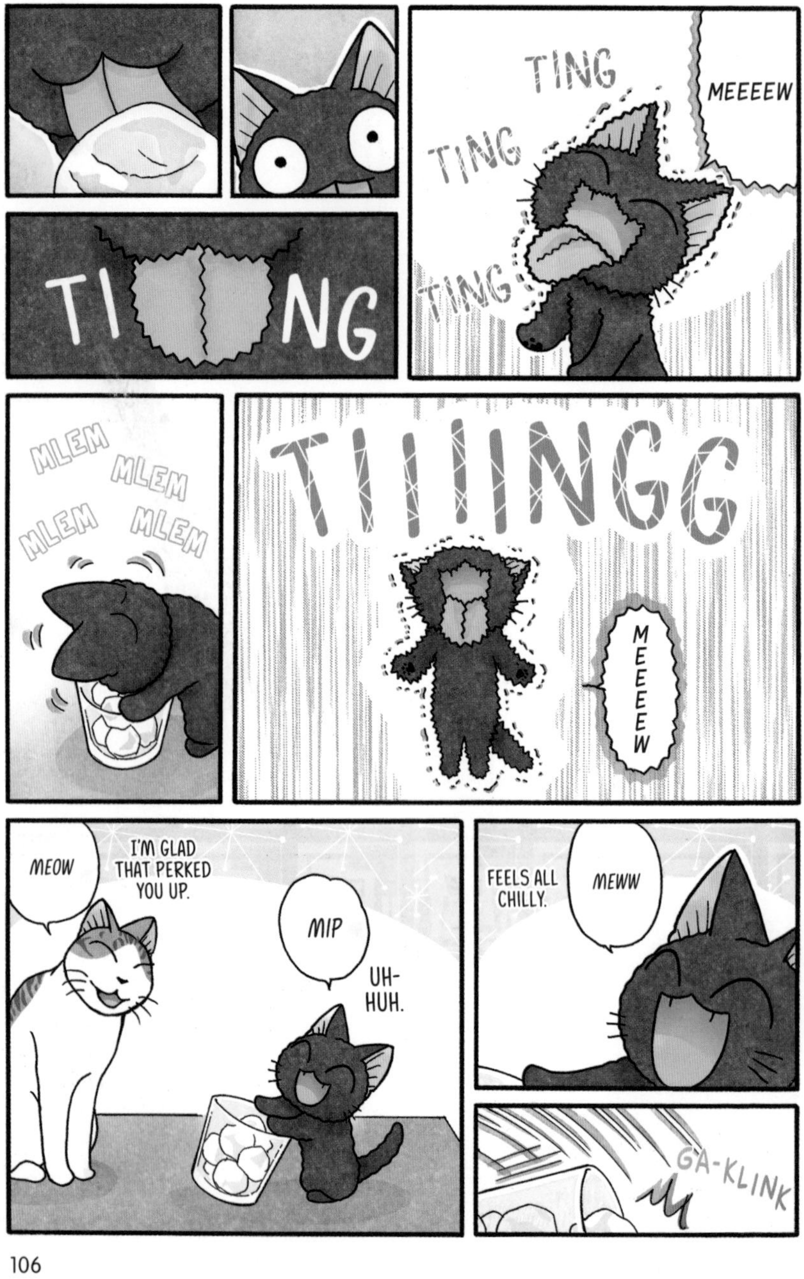
TI NG
TING
TING
TING
MEEEEW
MLEM
MLEM
MLEM
MLEM
TIIINGG
MEEEEW
MEOW
I'M GLAD THAT PERKED YOU UP.
MIP
UH-HUH.
FEELS ALL CHILLY.
MEWW
GA-KLINK

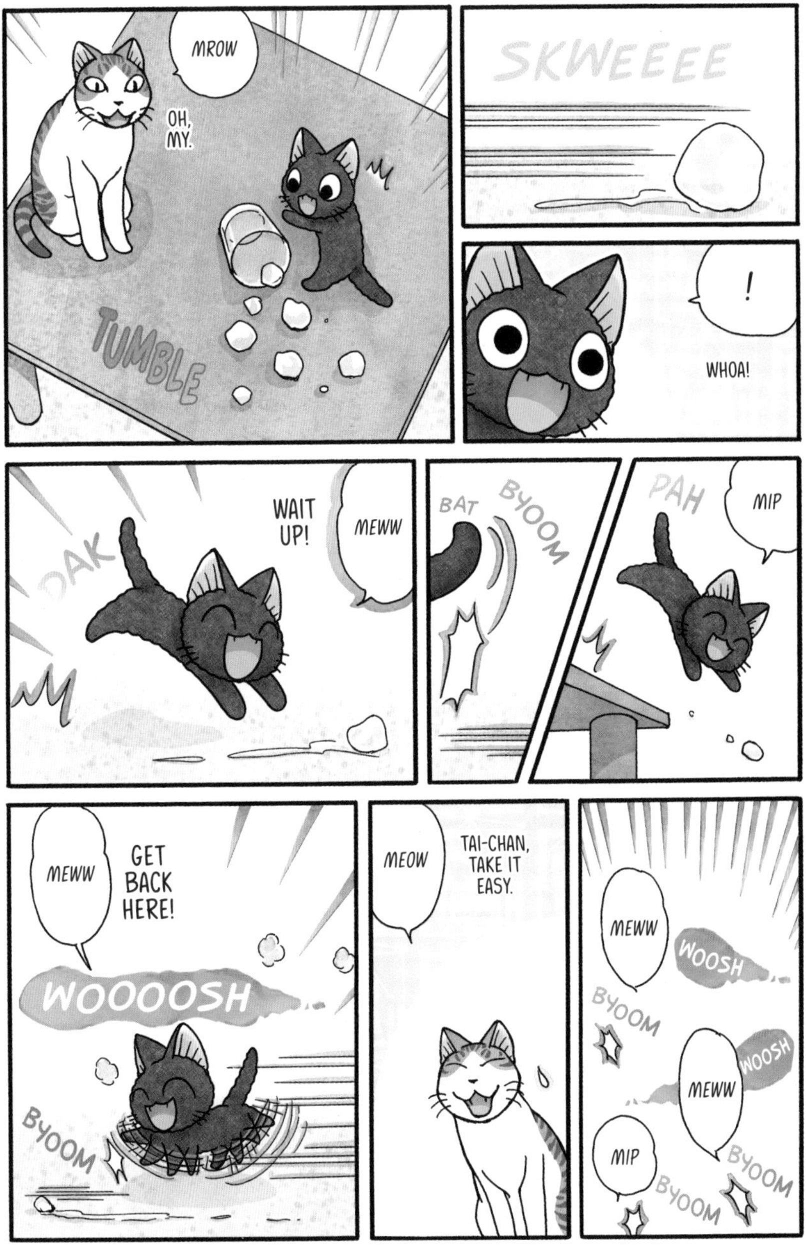
MROW
OH, MY.
TUMBLE
SKWEEEE
!
WHOA!
DAK
WAIT UP!
MEWW
BAT
BYOOM
PAH
MIP
MEWW
GET BACK HERE!
WOOOOSH
BYOOM
MEOW
TAI-CHAN, TAKE IT EASY.
MEWW
WOOSH
BYOOM
WOOSH
MEWW
MIP
BYOOM
BYOOM

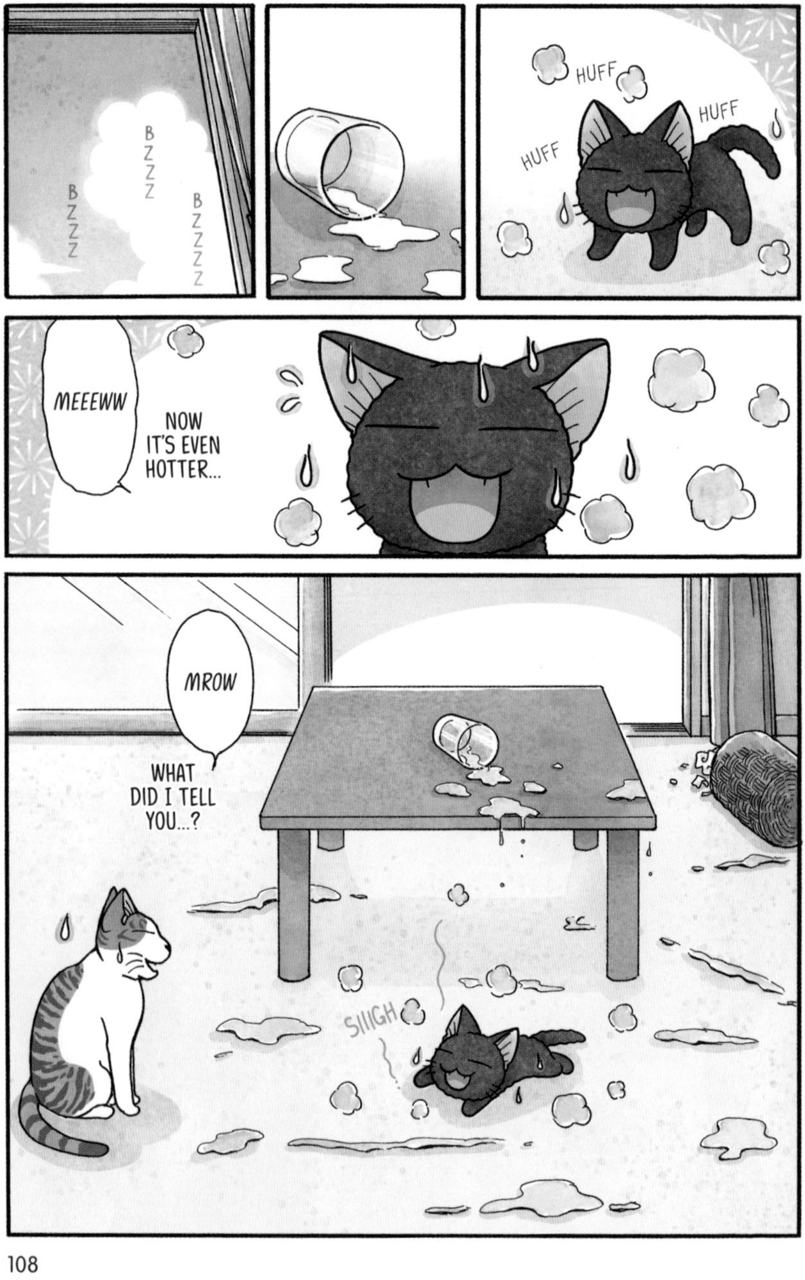
HUFF
HUFF
HUFF
BZZZ
BZZZ
BZZZZ
MEEEWW
NOW IT'S EVEN HOTTER...
MROW
WHAT DID I TELL YOU...?
SIIIGH

CHAPTER 68 The Scary Thing...

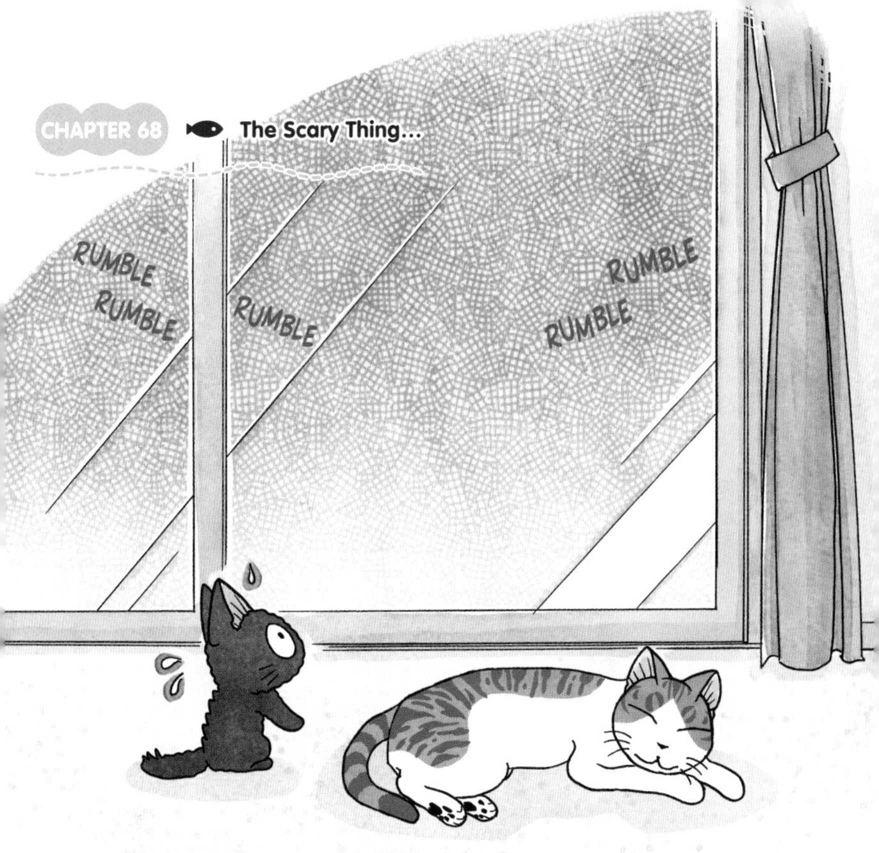
RUMBLE
RUMBLE
RUMBLE
RUMBLE
RUMBLE

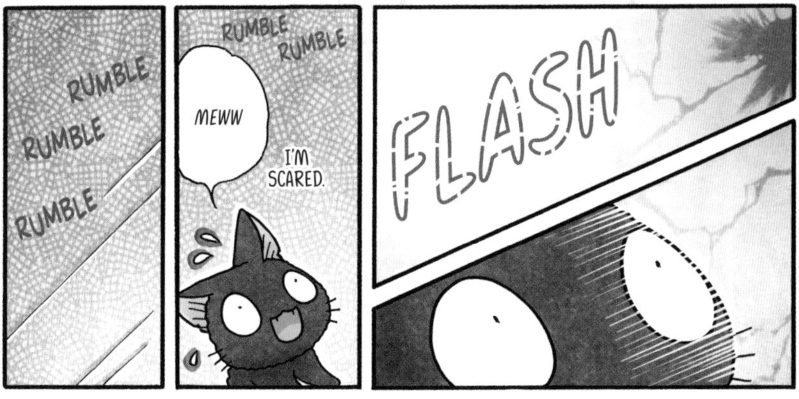
RUMBLE
RUMBLE
RUMBLE
RUMBLE
RUMBLE
MEWW
I'M SCARED.
FLASH

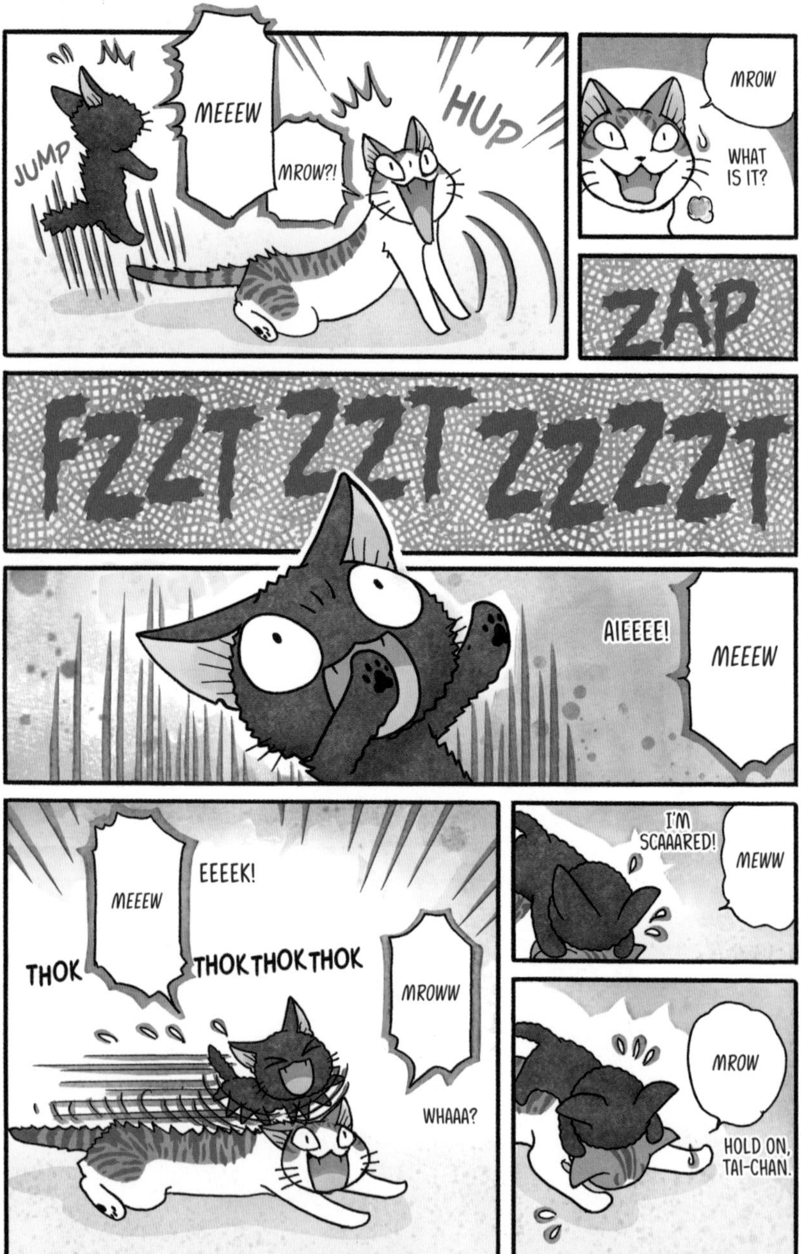
JUMP
MEEEW
MROW?!
HUP
MROW
WHAT IS IT?
ZAP
FZZT ZZT ZZZZT
AIEEEE!
MEEEW
MEEEW
EEEEK!
THOK
THOK THOK THOK
MROWW
WHAAA?
I'M SCAAARED!
MEWW
MROW
HOLD ON, TAI-CHAN.

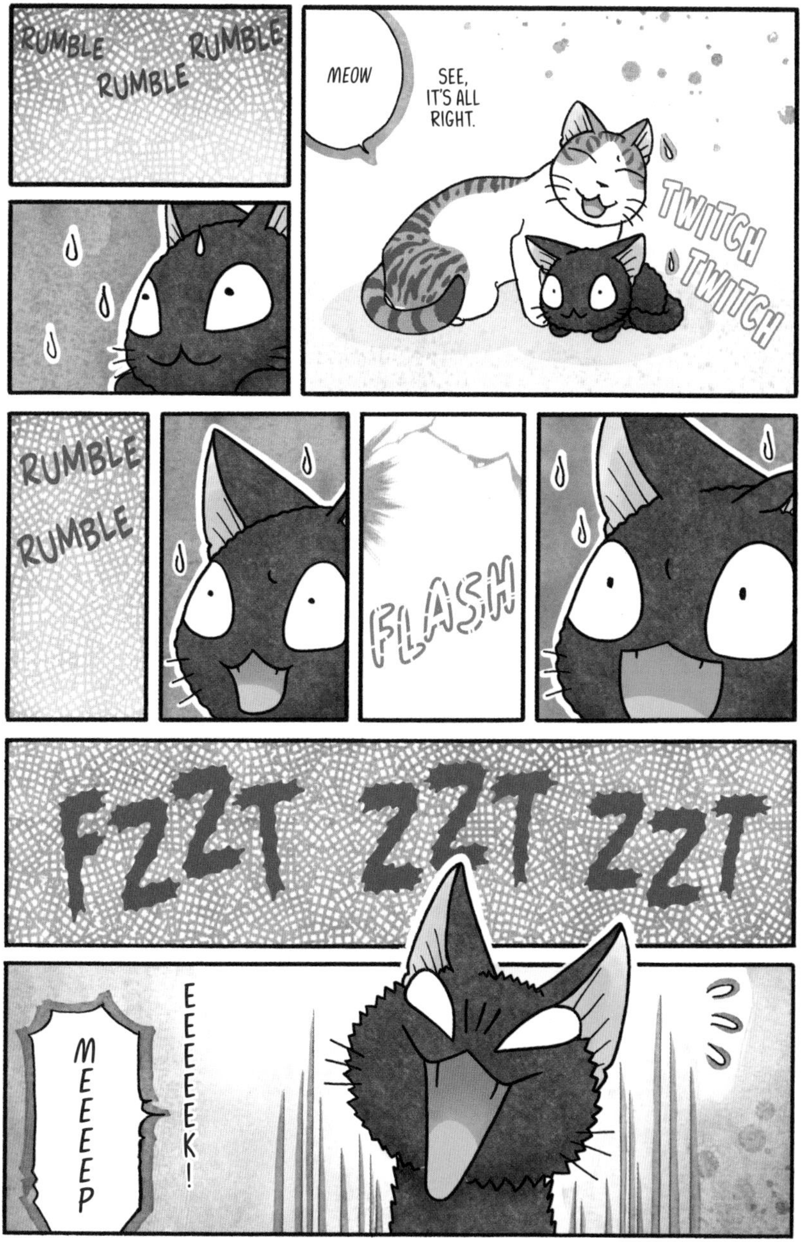
SEE, IT'S ALL RIGHT.
MEOW
TWITCH TWITCH
RUMBLE RUMBLE RUMBLE
FLASH
RUMBLE RUMBLE
FZZT ZZT ZZT
EEEEEEK!
MEEEEEP

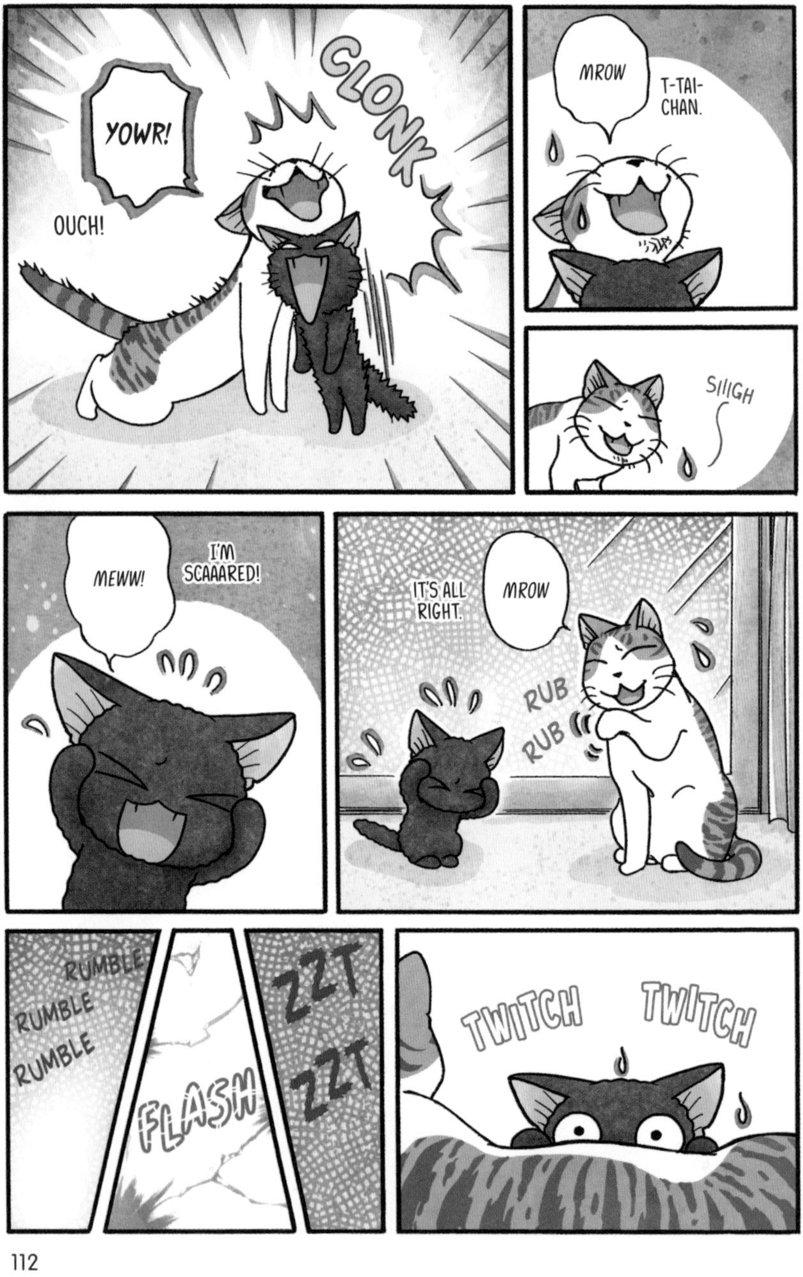
YOWR!
OUCH!
CLONK
MROW
T-TAI-CHAN.
SIIIGH
MEWW!
I'M SCAAARED!
IT'S ALL RIGHT.
MROW
RUB RUB
RUMBLE
RUMBLE
RUMBLE
FLASH
ZZT
ZZT
TWITCH
TWITCH

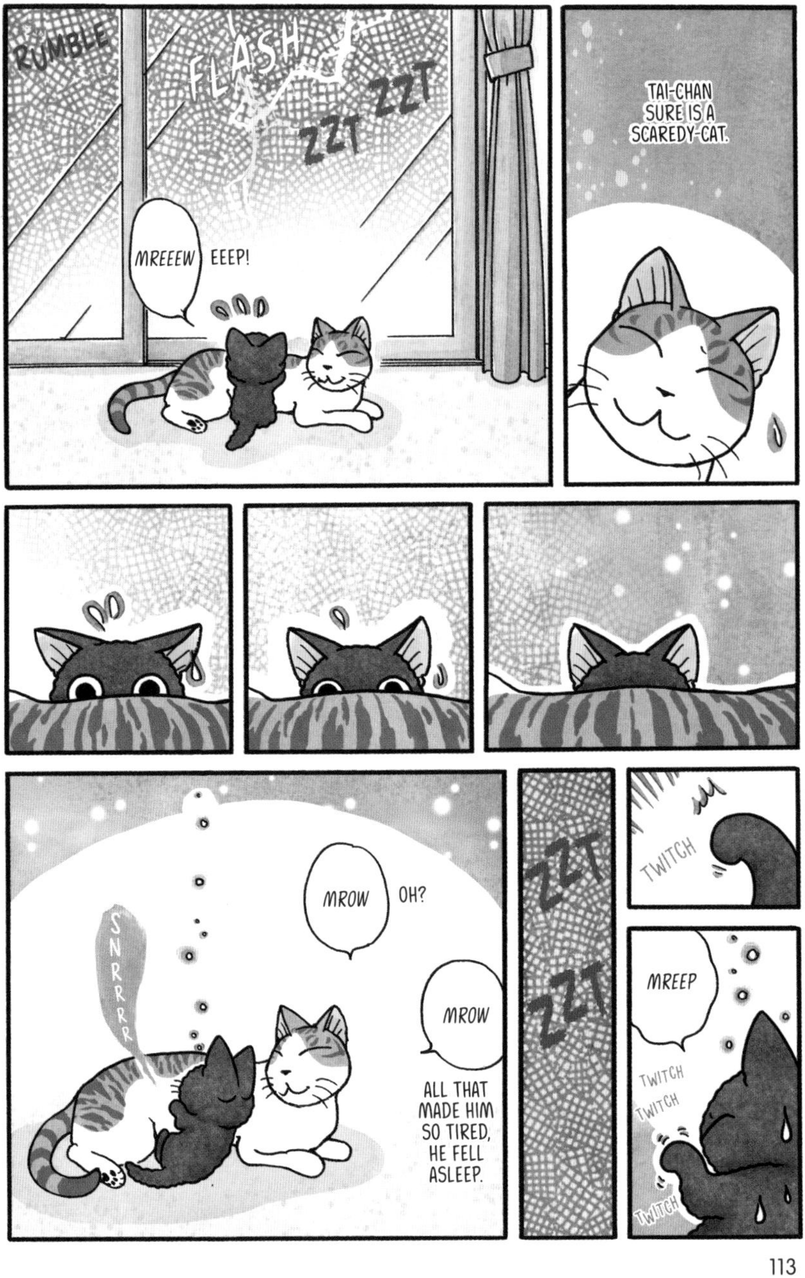
RUMBLE
FLASH
ZZT ZZT
MREEEW
EEEP!
TAI-CHAN SURE IS A SCAREDY-CAT.
SNRRRR
MROW
OH?
MROW
ALL THAT MADE HIM SO TIRED, HE FELL ASLEEP.
ZZT
ZZT
TWITCH
MREEP
TWITCH
TWITCH
TWITCH

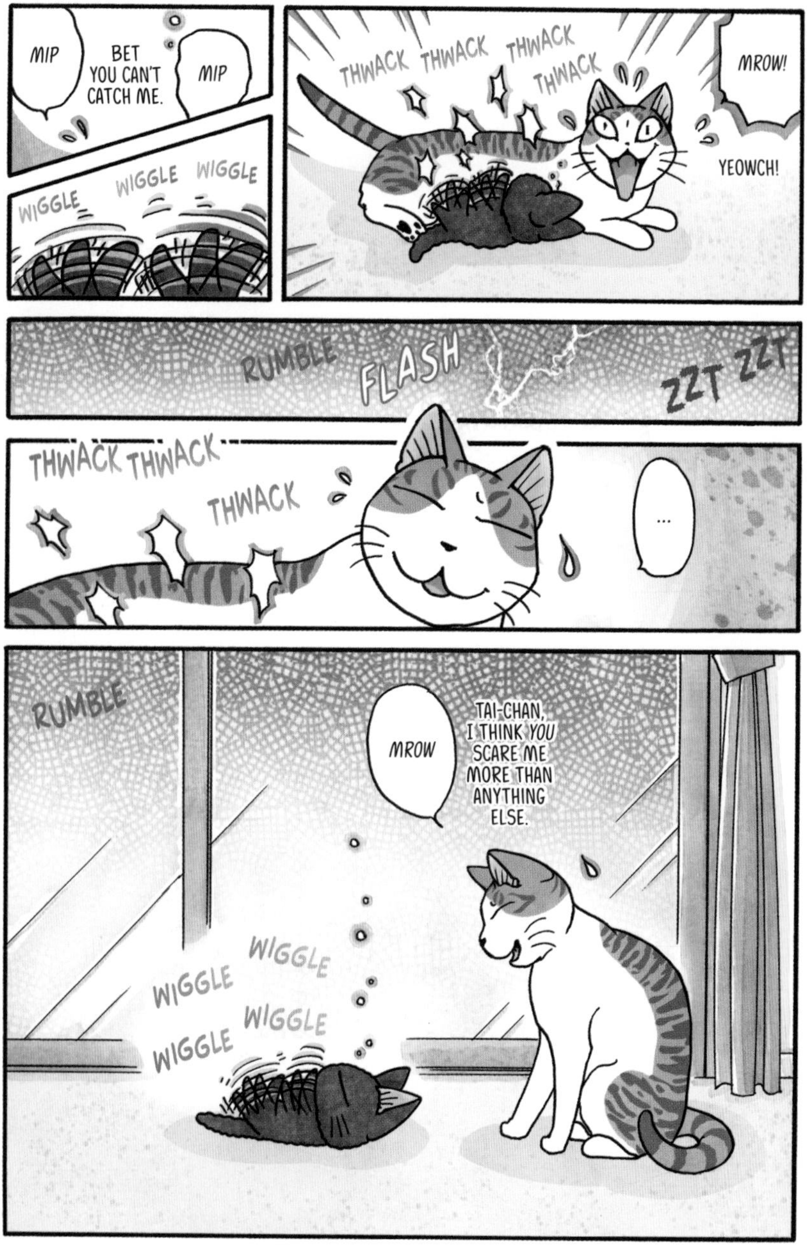
MIP
BET YOU CAN'T CATCH ME.
MIP
WIGGLE WIGGLE WIGGLE
THWACK THWACK THWACK THWACK
MROW!
YEOWCH!
RUMBLE
FLASH
ZZT ZZT
THWACK THWACK
THWACK
...
RUMBLE
MROW
TAI-CHAN, I THINK *YOU* SCARE ME MORE THAN ANYTHING ELSE.
WIGGLE WIGGLE
WIGGLE WIGGLE

CHAPTER 69 Trouble Brewing?!

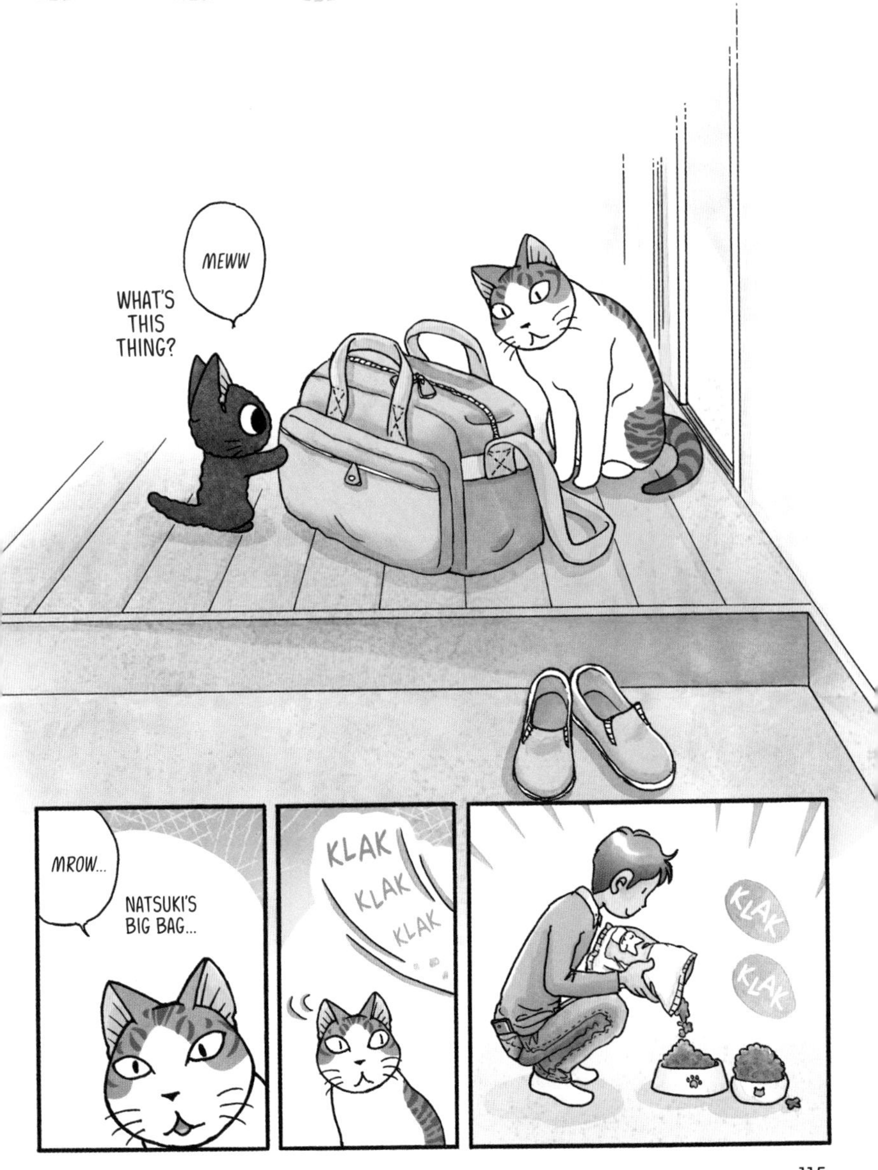
MEWW
WHAT'S THIS THING?
KLAK
KLAK
KLAK
KLAK
KLAK
MROW...
NATSUKI'S BIG BAG...

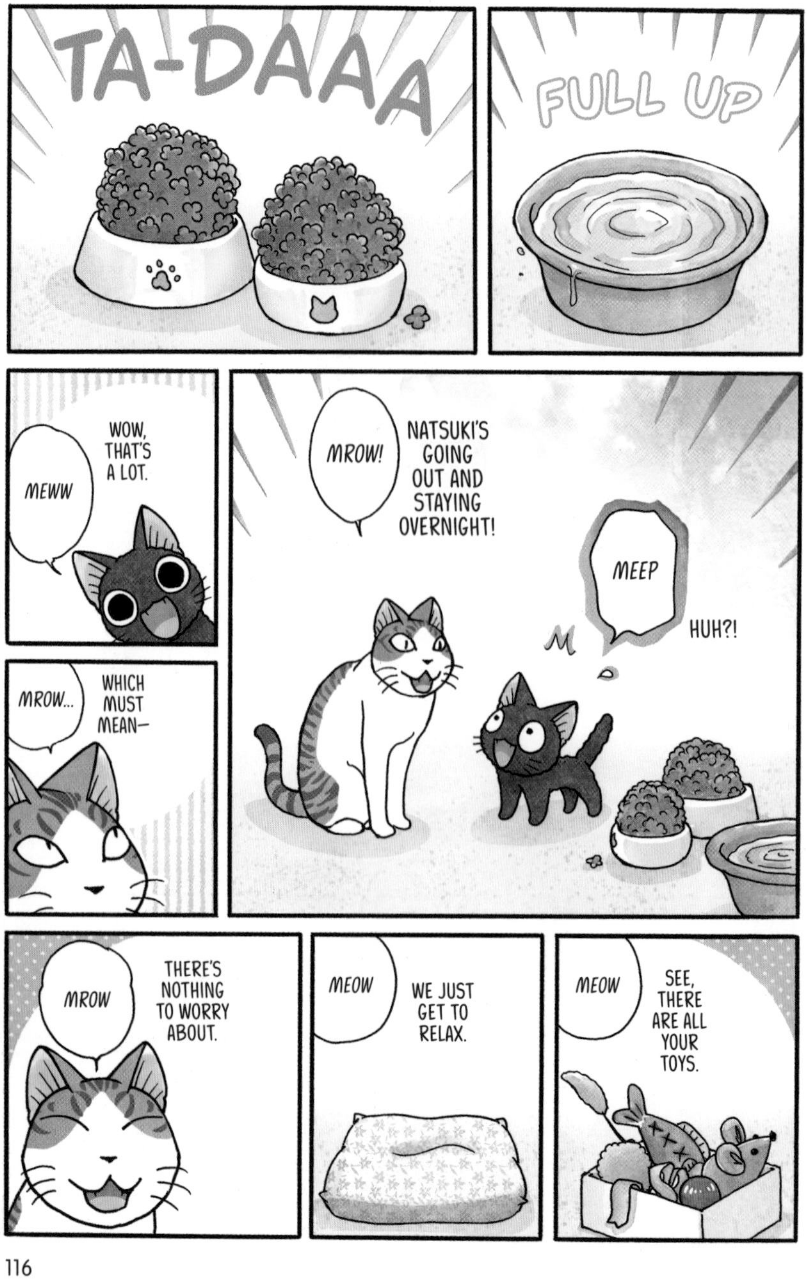

TA-DAAA
FULL UP
MEWW
WOW, THAT'S A LOT.
MROW...
WHICH MUST MEAN—
MROW!
NATSUKI'S GOING OUT AND STAYING OVERNIGHT!
MEEP
HUH?!
MROW
THERE'S NOTHING TO WORRY ABOUT.
MEOW
WE JUST GET TO RELAX.
MEOW
SEE, THERE ARE ALL YOUR TOYS.

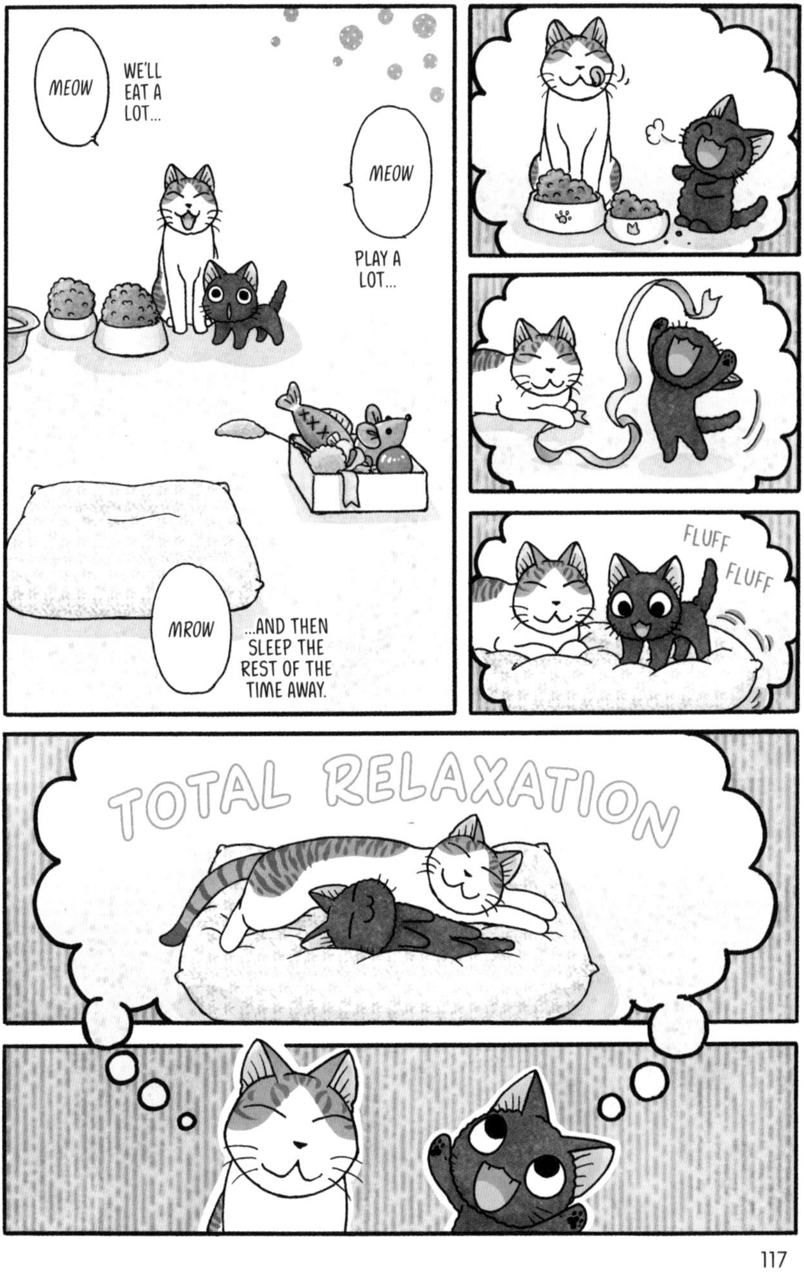
MEOW
WE'LL EAT A LOT...
MEOW
PLAY A LOT...
MROW
...AND THEN SLEEP THE REST OF THE TIME AWAY.
FLUFF
FLUFF
TOTAL RELAXATION

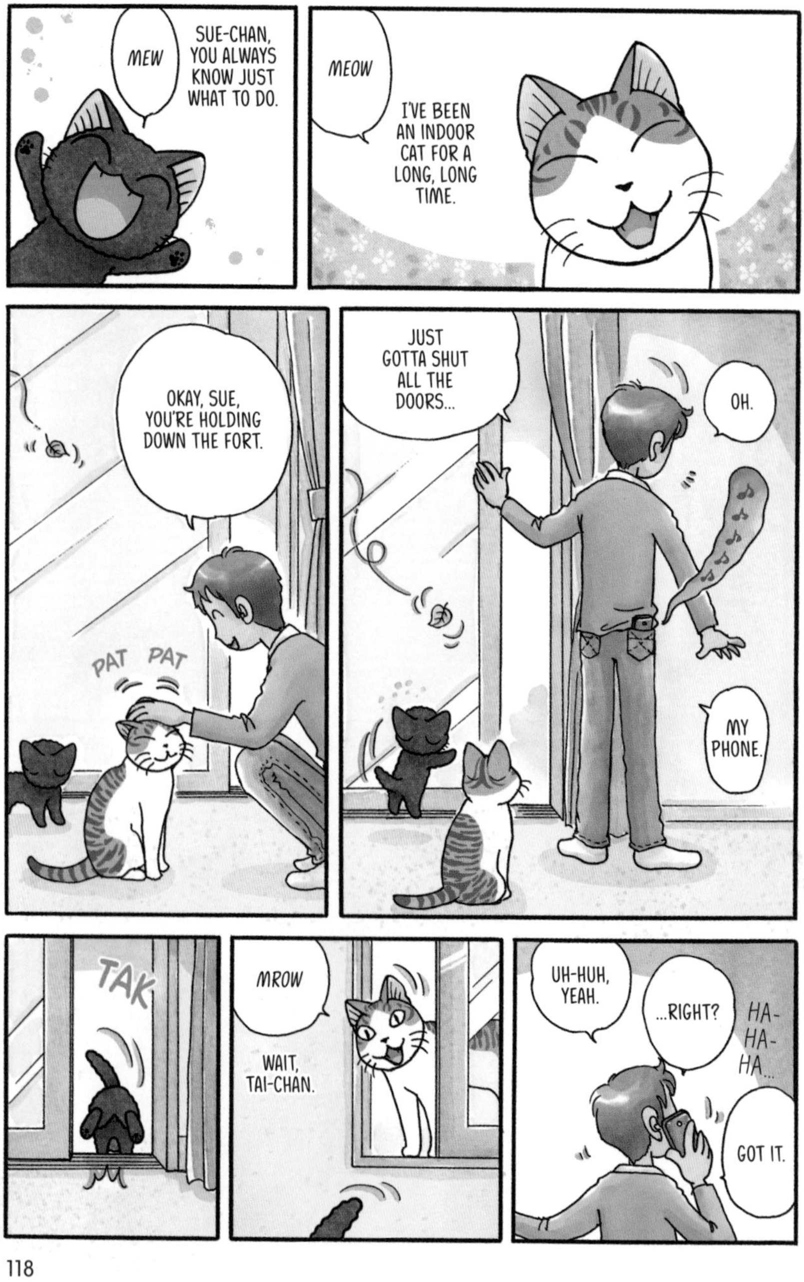
MEW
SUE-CHAN, YOU ALWAYS KNOW JUST WHAT TO DO.
MEOW
I'VE BEEN AN INDOOR CAT FOR A LONG, LONG TIME.
OKAY, SUE, YOU'RE HOLDING DOWN THE FORT.
PAT PAT
JUST GOTTA SHUT ALL THE DOORS...
OH.
MY PHONE.
TAK
MROW
WAIT, TAI-CHAN.
UH-HUH, YEAH.
...RIGHT?
HA-HA-HA...
GOT IT.

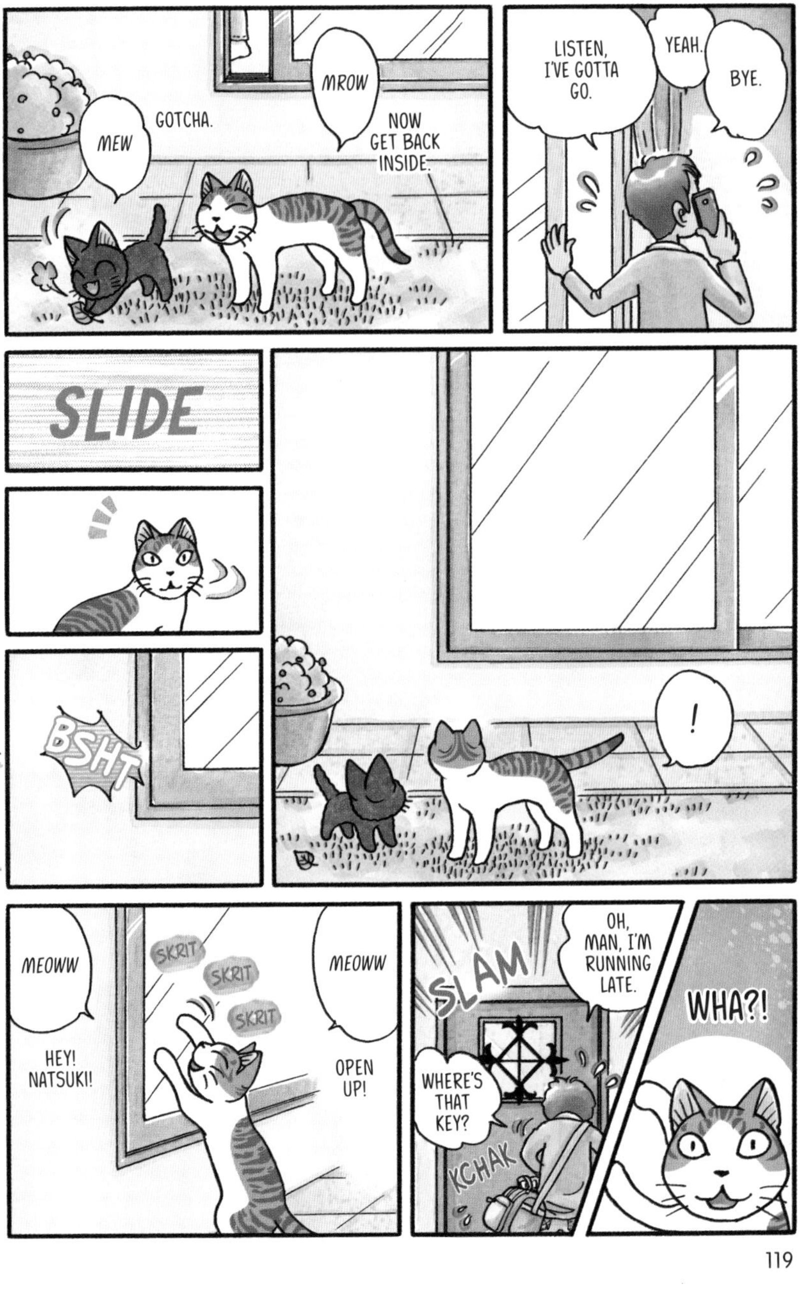
MEW
GOTCHA.
MROW
NOW GET BACK INSIDE.
LISTEN, I'VE GOTTA GO.
YEAH.
BYE.
SLIDE
BSHT
!
MEOWW
HEY! NATSUKI!
SKRIT
SKRIT
SKRIT
MEOWW
OPEN UP!
SLAM
OH, MAN, I'M RUNNING LATE.
WHERE'S THAT KEY?
KCHAK
WHA?!

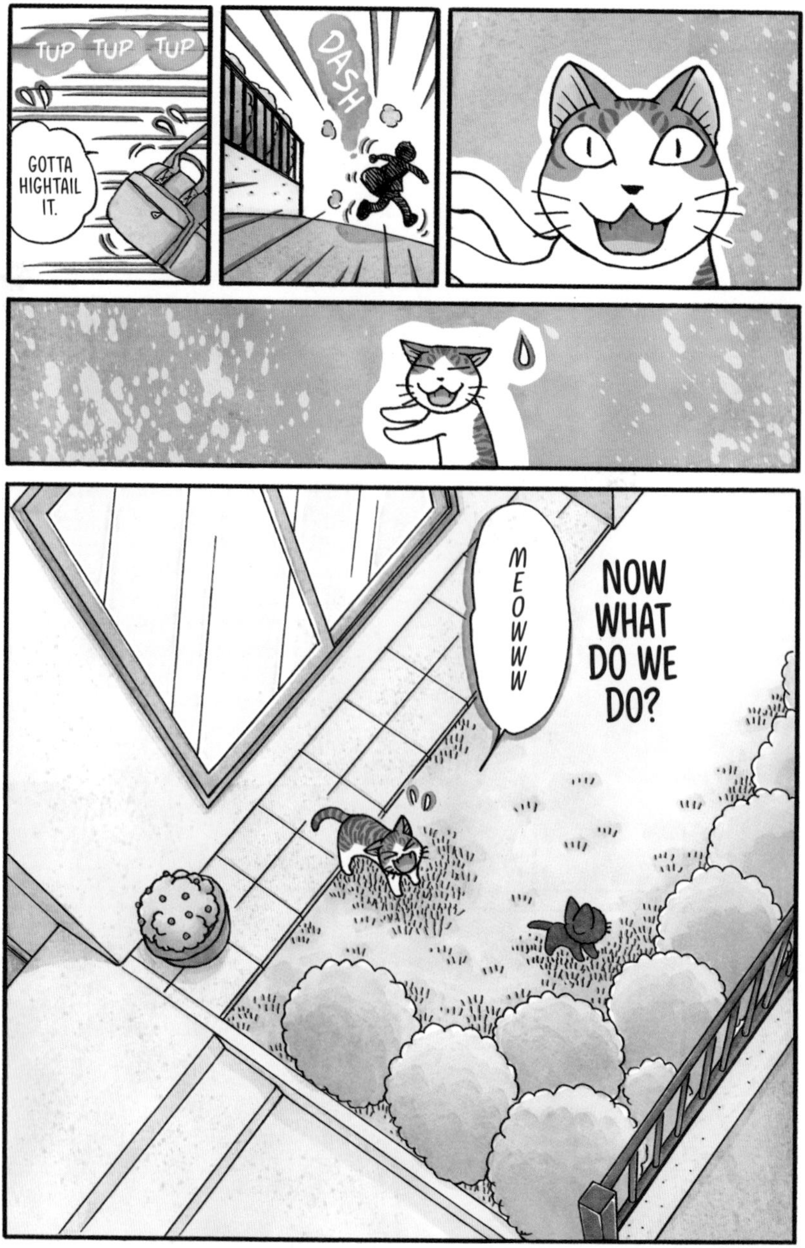
TUP TUP TUP
GOTTA HIGHTAIL IT.
DASH
MEOWWW
NOW WHAT DO WE DO?

TO BE CONTINUED IN *SUE & TAI-CHAN* 5!

KITTY TRIVIA

• Cat Rescue Edition •

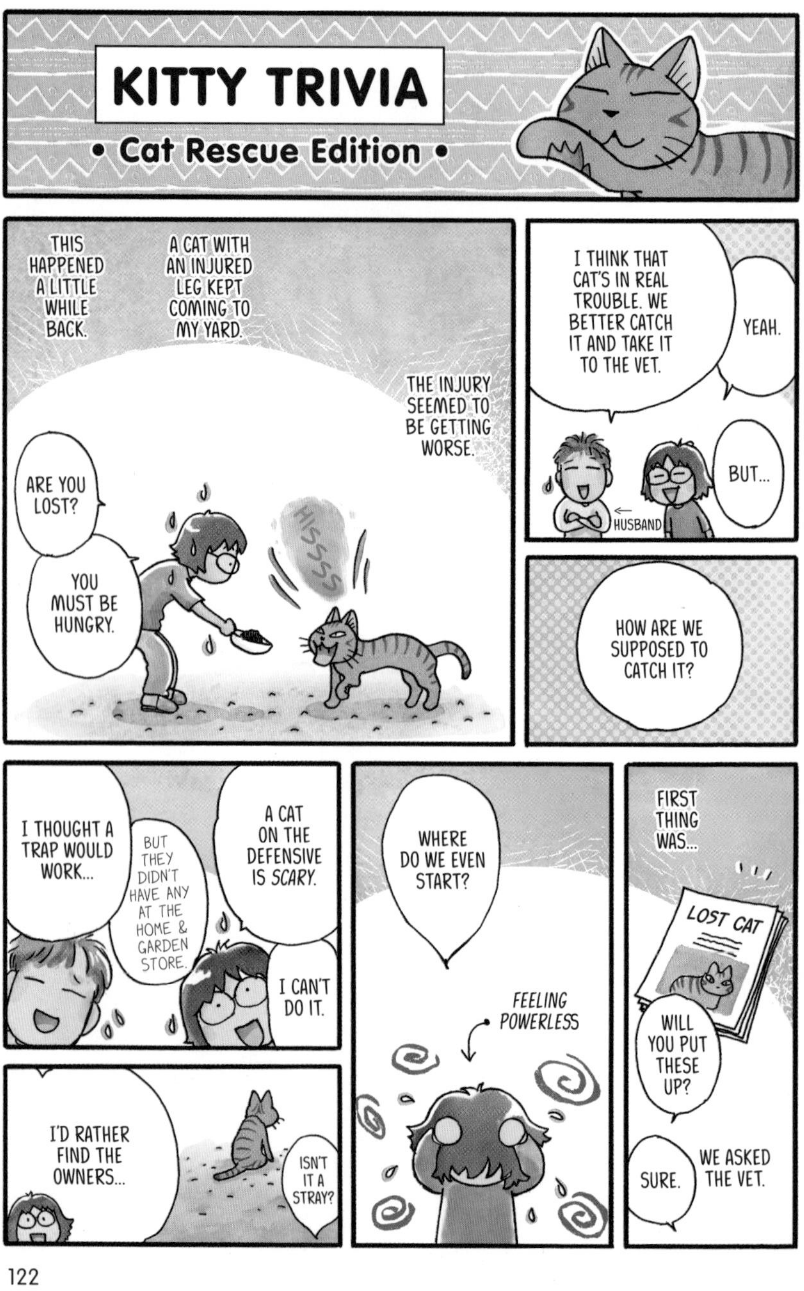
THIS HAPPENED A LITTLE WHILE BACK.
A CAT WITH AN INJURED LEG KEPT COMING TO MY YARD.
THE INJURY SEEMED TO BE GETTING WORSE.
ARE YOU LOST?
YOU MUST BE HUNGRY.
HISSSS
I THINK THAT CAT'S IN REAL TROUBLE. WE BETTER CATCH IT AND TAKE IT TO THE VET.
YEAH.
BUT...
← HUSBAND
HOW ARE WE SUPPOSED TO CATCH IT?
I THOUGHT A TRAP WOULD WORK...
BUT THEY DIDN'T HAVE ANY AT THE HOME & GARDEN STORE.
A CAT ON THE DEFENSIVE IS *SCARY*.
I CAN'T DO IT.
I'D RATHER FIND THE OWNERS...
ISN'T IT A STRAY?
WHERE DO WE EVEN START?
FEELING POWERLESS
FIRST THING WAS...
LOST CAT
WILL YOU PUT THESE UP?
SURE.
WE ASKED THE VET.

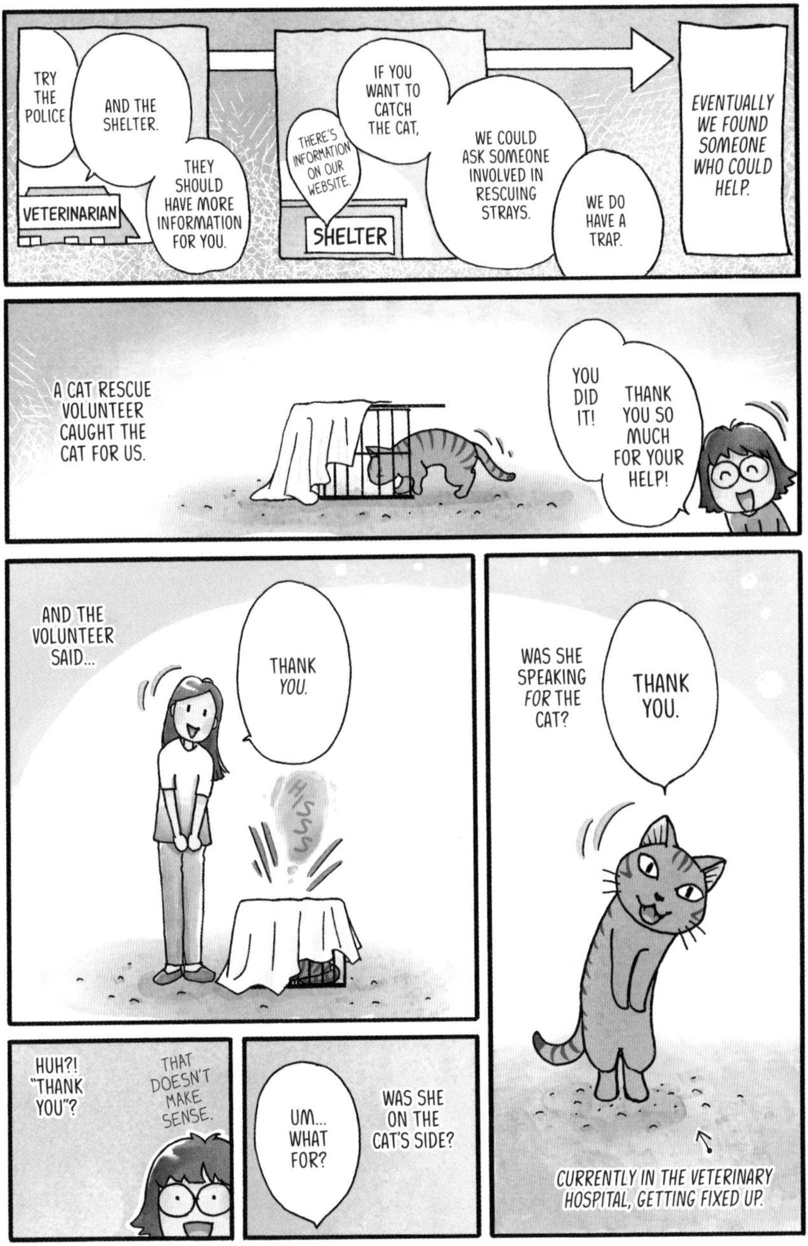
TRY THE POLICE
AND THE SHELTER.
THEY SHOULD HAVE MORE INFORMATION FOR YOU.
VETERINARIAN
THERE'S INFORMATION ON OUR WEBSITE.
IF YOU WANT TO CATCH THE CAT,
WE COULD ASK SOMEONE INVOLVED IN RESCUING STRAYS.
WE DO HAVE A TRAP.
SHELTER
EVENTUALLY WE FOUND SOMEONE WHO COULD HELP.
A CAT RESCUE VOLUNTEER CAUGHT THE CAT FOR US.
YOU DID IT!
THANK YOU SO MUCH FOR YOUR HELP!
AND THE VOLUNTEER SAID...
THANK *YOU.*
HISS
HUH?! "THANK YOU"?
THAT DOESN'T MAKE SENSE.
UM... WHAT FOR?
WAS SHE ON THE CAT'S SIDE?
WAS SHE SPEAKING *FOR* THE CAT?
THANK YOU.
CURRENTLY IN THE VETERINARY HOSPITAL, GETTING FIXED UP.

WHAT'S THAT?

PAGE 52

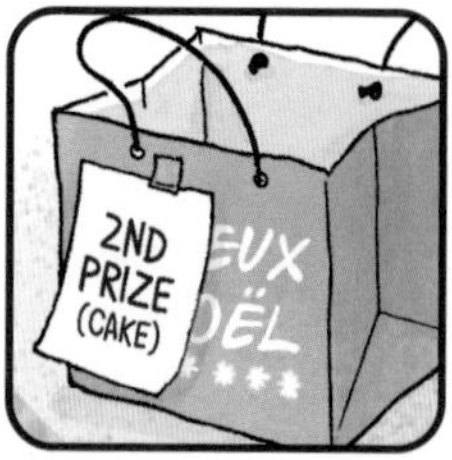
2ND PRIZE (CAKE)

Natsuki's won the lottery! On special occasions, small businesses in shopping centers may hold lotteries with special prizes. Natsuki won a Christmas cake, a traditional holiday treat in Japan.

PAGE 89

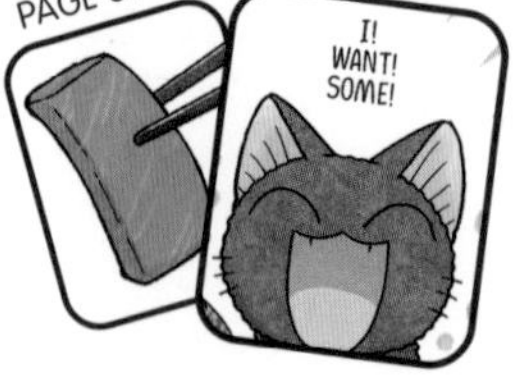
I! WANT! SOME!

Natsuki is enjoying some sashimi, or slices of raw fish. Because of the price, it's considered a premium treat for humans and *comic* kitties!

Honorifics Review

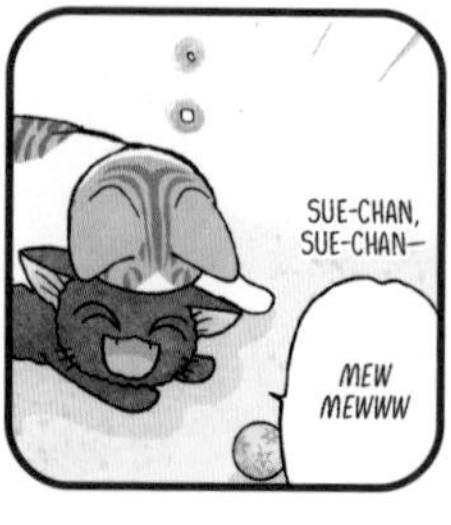
SUE-CHAN, SUE-CHAN—
MEW MEWWW

-chan is a cutesy honorific for showing affection, like saying "Little Tai."

-san is a polite honorific for showing respect, like "Mr.", "Ms.", or "Mx."

Not using an honorific means you must be *very* close to someone!

Sue & Tai-chan

FUKU FUKU

Kitten Tales

Konami Kanata

Craving More Cute Cat Comics?

Want to see more furry feline antics? A new series by Konami Kanata, author of the beloved *Chi's Sweet Home* series, tells the story of a tiny kitten named FukuFuku who lives with a kindly old lady. Each day brings something new to learn, the change of the seasons leads to exciting discoveries and even new objects to shred with freshly-grown claws.

Join FukuFuku and her charming owner on this quietly heartwarming journey of kittenhood.

Both Parts 1 and 2 On Sale Now!

Next Volume

Natsuki is away on a trip?!

They get some inside time...

MEOW
LICK
LICK

JUST

RELAXING

Or so they thought...

Instead...

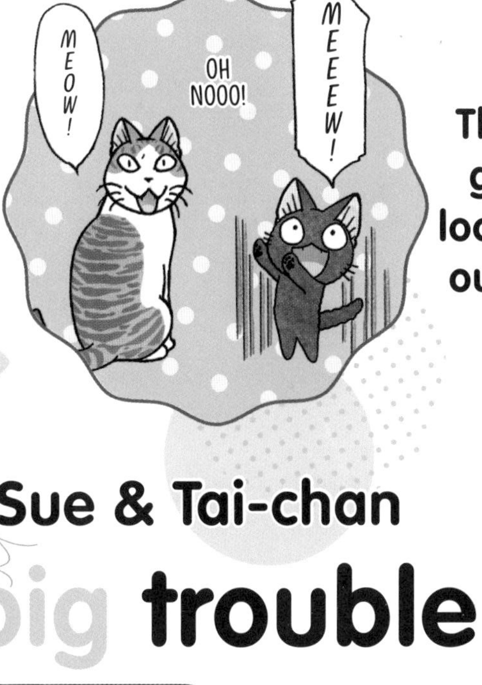
MEOW!
OH NOOO!
MEEEW!

They got locked out...!

Sue & Tai-chan in big trouble!!

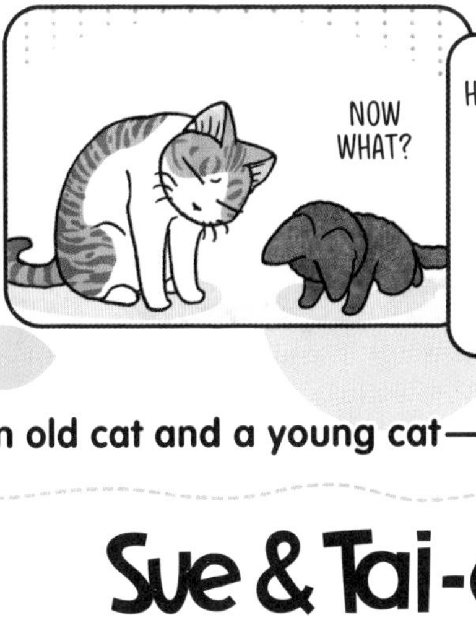
NOW WHAT?

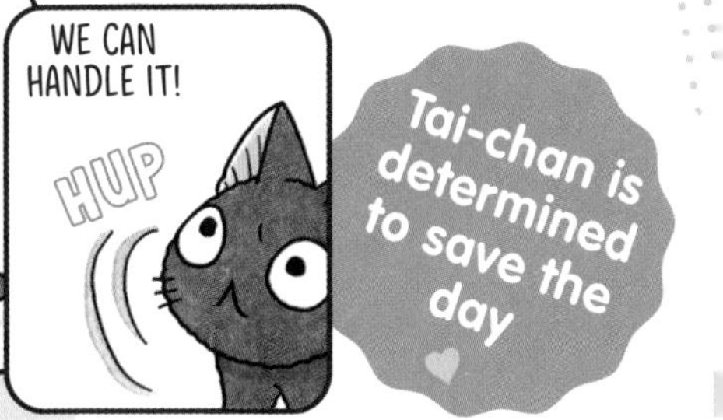
WE CAN HANDLE IT!
HUP

Tai-chan is determined to save the day

An old cat and a young cat—the oddest but cutest pair!

Sue & Tai-chan 5

A Kodansha Comics Trade Paperback Original
Sue & Tai-chan 4 copyright © 2020 Konami Kanata
English translation copyright © 2022 Konami Kanata

All rights reserved.

Published in the United States by Kodansha Comics, an imprint of Kodansha USA Publishing, LLC, New York.

Publication rights for this English edition arranged through Kodansha Ltd., Tokyo.

First published in Japan in 2020 by Kodansha Ltd., Tokyo.

ISBN 978-1-64651-165-5

Original cover design by Kohei Nawata Design Office

Printed in China.

www.kodansha.us

9 8 7 6 5 4 3 2 1
Translation: Melissa Tanaka
Lettering: Phil Christie
Editing: Vanessa Tenazas
Kodansha Comics edition cover design by Phil Balsman

Publisher: Kiichiro Sugawara

Director of publishing services: Ben Applegate
Associate director of operations: Stephen Pakula
Publishing services managing editors: Alanna Ruse, Madison Salters
Production managers: Emi Lotto, Angela Zurlo
Logo and character art ©Kodansha USA Publishing, LLC